The Political Geography
of the New World Order

THE POLITICAL GEOGRAPHY OF THE NEW WORLD ORDER

edited by
Colin H. Williams

Belhaven Press
London and New York

*Co-published in the Americas by Halsted Press,
an imprint of John Wiley & Sons, Inc.*

Belhaven Press
(a division of Pinter Publishers Ltd)
25 Floral Street, Covent Garden, London WC2E 9DS, United Kingdom

First published in Great Britain 1993

Copublished in the Americas by Halsted Press, an imprint of
John Wiley & Sons, Inc., 605 Third Avenue, New York, NY 10158–0012

British Library Cataloguing in Publication Data
A CIP catalogue record for this book is available from the British Library

ISBN 1 85293 276 7

Library of Congress Cataloging-in-Publication Data
The Political geography of the new world order / edited by Colin H. Williams
    p.   cm.
  Includes bibliographical references and index.
  ISBN 1–85293–276–7 (Belhaven Press). —ISBN 0–470–22019–8
(Halsted Press)
    1. Political geography.   2. International economic relations.
3. World politics—1989–   I. Williams, Colin H., 1950–
JC319.P584   1993
320.1′2—dc20   93–10054
                                        CIP

ISBN 0 470 22019 8 (in the Americas only)

Typeset by Florencetype Ltd, Kewstoke, Avon
Printed and bound in Great Britain by Biddles Ltd of Guildford and King's Lynn

Contents

List of contributors

John Agnew
Department of Geography, Syracuse University, 343 H.B. Crouse Hall, Syracuse, New York, USA 13244 1160.

Philip Cooke
Department of City and Regional Planning, University of Wales College of Cardiff, PO Box 906, Column Drive, Cardiff, UK CF1 3YN.

Jim MacLaughlin
Department of Geography, University College Cork, Donovans Road, Cork, Ireland.

John O'Loughlin
Department of Geography and Institute of Behavioural Science, University of Colorado, Boulder, Colorado, USA 80309 0487.

Gearóid Ó Tuathail
Department of Geography, Virginia Polytechnic Institute and State University, Blacksburg, VA, USA 24061.

Ronan Paddison
Department of Geography and Topographic Science, University of Glasgow, Glasgow G12, 8QQ UK.

Colin H Williams
Division of Geography, Staffordshire University, Leek Road, Stoke-on-Trent, ST4 2DF UK.

Stephen W Williams
Division of Geography, Staffordshire University, Leek Road, Stoke-on-Trent, ST4, 2DF UK.

Preface and acknowledgements

It is evident that we have entered a transitional period following the collapse of formal communism in Eastern Europe and the emergence of the United States of America as the hegemonic power of the world system. We are accosted on all sides by daily reminders of the world in transition, whether they be a renegotiation of the GATT treaty, confirmation of a revised Maastricht treaty, the spread of famine, pestilence and disease in too many developing societies, ecological disasters and energy crises. But what sort of transition is it? Does it lead to a new world order? If so, what are its structural characteristics? What are its implications for states, for multinational actors, for voluntary agencies, for threatened identities and warring passions, for you and for me? These were some of the questions which prompted me to invite specialist contributors to speculate upon the political geographic consequences of this transition period.

This volume of essays has its origins in the Political Geography Study Group session on 'Readjustment in Europe and America' as a contribution to the Institute of British Geographers Annual Conference, held at the University College of Wales, Swansea, 7–10 January 1992. Seven of the essays which follow are revised versions of papers delivered at the conference while chapters 1, 6, 7 and 11 have been written especially for this book. Although the title implies a catholic coverage of a new world order, it should be made clear that ours was essentially a European and American focus on world issues. The perspectives recorded herein are, I believe, representative of current geographic thinking about major political issues, although the perceptive reader may well discern a certain flavour to the volume as all the contributors are of Celtic origin. I am grateful to the contributors for their very fine essays, which I hope will prove stimulating interpretations of this process of readjustment to a new world order. I am also grateful to yet another Celtic geographer, Dr Iain Stevenson of Belhaven Press, for his encouragement and assistance. But, as we shall see, even drawing attention to the putative origin of these authors is not without its difficulty in the new world order, for questions of identity and representation are not necessarily fixed or capable of being used as a basis for any real generalization.

Thanks are due to Penguin books for their kind permission to reproduce three paragraphs from D. Healey's *When Shrimps Learn to Whistle* (Penguin, 1991: 270). Mrs Kerry Summerfield typed portions of the manuscript with her customary skill and patience, while the support of Professor George Kay, my former Head of Department, is also very much appreciated.

1

Towards a new world order: European and American perspectives

Colin H. Williams

Preliminary considerations of globalization

Since 1945 the world has witnessed successive periods of opening and closing. At present we are asked to believe that we are in an opening, transitional phase from a modern to a post-modern context. The phase would be characterized by a fluency of interaction, acute interdependence, routinization of international bureaucracies, a multi-level approach to problem solving and, above all, the conceptualization of a shrinking world as economically beneficial and politically rewarding. That there are contradictory tendencies and structural tensions within this new world order should come as no surprise because, clearly, the new order serves the interests of some actors at the expense of others. In this volume we shall be equally concerned with charting the new tendencies in, for example, inter-state relations at the world system level as we shall with the plight of, for example, beleaguered racial and ethnic minorities at a regional or local level. If the political geography of this new world order is to be effective it must seek to deal with the synchronization of separate but related processes at all levels in the territorial hierarchy. Yet the local–global nexus, or the recent concern with the rediscovery of place, and place-centred politics is far too crude and simplistic to be an effective basis for interpretation of a changing reality, even if it is a useful heuristic device in compensating for the over-concentration on the state as the most significant actor in world affairs.

The dominant process of this new order is, of course, globalization and its concomitant manifestations. Easy to appreciate yet hard to define, globalization has been the subject of a number of fresh initiatives within geography and the social sciences, ranging from the world systems perspective of Johnston and Taylor (1989), Chase-Dunn (1990) and more especially Wallerstein (1980) to a sociological theory of transnational practices outlined by Sklair (1991). In the current context, I wish to present strands of an argument developed with fellow members of the Research Committee for Social Ecology of the International Sociological Association and ably summarized by Zdravko Mlinar (1992). In an attempt to go beyond the merely illustrative, we have sought to provide an operational definition of globalization based upon the following five dimensions.

Firstly, globalization is conceived as an increased interdependence at world level. Consciousness of global repercussions of a specific action, whether it be a particular decision of the World Bank, a medical discovery or an intensification of ozone depletion or atmospheric pollution, leads to sensitivity to new differences which are emerging on the world scale. The closure of time and space implies that the traditional solution to many problems by relocating or spatially withdrawing from them no longer offers a guaranteed means of coping, either individually or collectively. In consequence, Mlinar argues that 'the higher the level of globalization *the narrower the scope for 'escape alternatives'*. In this sense globalization is also a kind of *totalitarianisation* of world space' (Mlinar, 1992: 20).

Secondly, globalization is the expansion of domination and dependence. World-system theorists have been particularly sensitive to the possibility that global interdependence can be a misnomer for a new form of neo-colonialism. Thus the North–South divide, however it is characterized, is usually conceived as a permanent feature of the new world order with the metropolitan cores exercising hegemonic control over the world's periphery in what Taylor (1989: 118) calls 'informal imperialism: dominance without empire'. Its principal structural mechanism is the process of unequal exchange which produces unequal development and, because it is so implicated in the history of imperialism and colonialism, it is tightly interwoven into the very fabric of world patterns of trade and labour remuneration. No wonder then that an intensification of such trends can produce a widening of the North–South differentials which seem inevitable and unchallengeable. For as Taylor forcefully reminds us:

Unequal exchange is an integrated mixture of inter-state and intra-state issues which conventional international politics cannot deal with. The world market appears to be based upon the impersonal forces of supply and demand which determine prices. . . . The fact that these terms do not reflect the hidden hand of the market but are defined by centuries of imperialism producing global differentials in labour costs is conveniently forgotten. This non-decision-making represents a major political achievement of the dominant interests of the modern world economy (Taylor, 1989: 125).

Thirdly, globalization may be seen as the homogenization of the world, an inexorable development of a global culture. Despite being subjected to intense scrutiny and associated with negative connotations, it is still not clear what a global culture would look like. Most often it is summarized in terms such as 'Westernization', 'Americanization' and manifested in the material spread of symbolic institutions such as Coca Cola, Sony Walkman, and the Benetton factor, or personified in famous actors or performers such as Madonna, Michael Jackson or Luciano Pavarotti. This form of globalization relies on a well developed infra-structure permitting social communication and physical communication to proceed relatively unhindered. Clearly modern technology, the spread of a world language such as English, and the ideological subtlety of television contribute to this link between globalization and post-modernity. However, it also has profound implications for the manner in which we organize our political space and the flows between political units. The tendency is towards the 'elimination of mutual exclusiveness which posed no problems as long as there were closed systems co-existing at the level of the nation–states' (Mlinar, 1992: 21). However, in a new world order characterized by the introduction of uniform standards and a global culture, the utility in the system of the nation-state must come under increasing threat. Bauman (1989: 152) offers a similar prognosis when he writes 'the models of postmodernity, unlike the models of modernity, cannot be grounded in the realities of the nation–state'. Thus the role and future of the nation–state constitute one of the prime questions to be analysed within the perspective of globalization.

Fourthly, globalization is not merely the sum of its parts, not just a mechanical aggregation of constituent units. It also has the reverse effect, of penetrating local spaces by global processes as part of the rhythm of opening up to new ideas and challenges. Thus we can speak of the simultanaeity inherent in globalism of both increased uniformity and increased diversity. New possibilities reawaken or give birth to alternative identities, practices and preferences. Nowhere is this trend more evident than in the cultural infrastructure of world cities where choice, specialist entertainment and exotica are the watchwords of a new consumerism. Nowhere is it more meaningful than in the myriad local responses to global environmental change, whether they be in protests about acid rain in Scotland, Chernobyl fallout in Rovaniemi, or Slovakia's diversion of the waters of the Danube and damage to water levels in Hungary and Romania. 'Think global, act local' presumes an empathy and a familiarity with the common plight of humanity and demands a place-specific response if it is to be effective. Globalization, thus conceived, is a constant, interactive process breaking down the unique, the particular and the traditional, and reconstructing it in the form of a local response to a general set of systematic stimuli.

However, this insistence on the interdependence of space and place through all levels of the spatial hierarchy from the local to the global also presumes a fifth characteristic of globalization, the overcoming of temporal discontinuities. Space and time are intrinsically linked in the new world order as in all previous forms. Globalization implies a new logic to make sense of formally discontinuous social processes and to connect the various asynchronous rhythms of activity such as financial transactions, 'real-time' ordering, live transmission of significant events to a world audience via television à la the Barcelona Olympics or major boxing matches.

The collapse of both space and time (Brunn and Leinbach, 1991) demand a fresh appreciation of the interdependence of all these aspects of global-ization. We are quick to characterize the elements of change inherent in this process and to point out very specific advantages and opportunities which accrue to well-placed individuals or societies. We are less careful to scrutinize the impact such a transition might have on human rights in an increasingly fluid, open political system; on religious beliefs in an increasingly secular and challenging social order; on the process of de-territorialization and its obligation to redefine spatial relationships; on the old certainties of the global, strategic power relations; on the nature of the state and its legitimizing philosophy of national self-interest enshrined in the sovereignty of the citizens; on the direction of world development and on our common hopes and fears as we face a succession of global environ-mental crises. New world order! What new world order?

These problems are beginning to sound like old problems dressed up in new clothes, in the new language of post-modernism. Is this merely playing the game of academic fashion-watching? Or has there truly been a structural change, for example, in the international economy? A recent survey of the globalized economy has identified five trends which serve as a context for the process of adjustments we are examining in this volume. Hirst and Thompson (1992) argue that the first of these trends is the increase in the share of world trade and investment accounted for by economic relations within the Organization of Economic Cooperation and Development (OECD). Thus in 1989 the Group of Five (G5) main economies accounted for 75 per cent of foreign direct investment and the primary producers of the Less Developed Countries (LDCs) and Newly Industrialized Countries (NICs) are still largely dependent upon the More Developed Countries (MDCs) for markets and investment.

Secondly, in contrast to the 1945–80 period, there has been a progressive internationalization of money and capital markets. Although many would claim that this makes it increasingly difficult for national governments to control capital flows, as illustrated by 'Black Wednesday' (1992), the real consequence of this trend is to demonstrate the variability of financial market behaviour from periods of routinization to intense volatility.

Thirdly, there has been an increasing volume of trade in semi-manufactured and manufactured goods between the industrialized econo-mies. This has led to a fourth trend, namely the progressive development of internationalized companies. But we should be careful not to exaggerate either the significance of Transactional Corporations (TNCs) as compared with Multinational Corporations (MNCs), or the role of foreign direct investment in influencing another economy. As we shall see in Chapter 3 by Cooke and Chapter 9 by Ó'Tuathail, the most successful industrial states, e.g., Germany and Japan, have shown a great reluctance to invest and develop core manufacturing abroad; the bulk of their value-adding capacity remains within the domestic economy. Hirst and Thompson (1992: 369) are acutely conscious of the political imperative to maintain this pattern for:

German and Japanese financial capital remains 'nationalistic', committed to its domestic manufacturing sector in a way Anglo-American capital is not. German and Japanese firms have a strong commitment to highly skilled and motivated labour forces, and a national 'deal' between labour and capital to sustain prosperity is a core-part of their post-1945 politico-economic settlements. In both countries there would be a massive political price to pay were a major part of manufacturing to be shipped abroad and the prosperity of recent decades to falter.

Doubtless the most profound change in the past two decades has been the formation of supra-national trading and economic blocs. The trilateral pattern of the North American Free Trade Area (US/NAFTA), an expanded European Community (EC), and Japanese-dominated Pacific Rim bloc structures the new world order. But will the liberal multilateralism of the post-1945 period be overtaken by 'globalization' in whatever form it evolves? Probably not, argue Hirst and Thompson (1992: 371) for the nation-state will still remain crucial as a political context for economic development and the three named trading blocs are unlikely to develop into super-states capable of exploiting the potential of a continental scale of organization. What then of 'globalization' as a dominant paradigm and organizing principle?

If the concept of 'globalization' has had any merit it is as a negative ideal-type that enables us to assess the shifting balance between international economic pressures and international governmental regulation and national and bloc level economic management. We do not have a fully globalized economy, we do have an inter-national economy and national policy responses to it (Hirst and Thompson, 1992: 394).

I agree with this conclusion and aver that too often in the past we have assumed that macro-economic changes would lead to appropriate political mechanisms being established to channel and promote socio-economic change. However, periodic conflict, economic collapse and a crisis of confidence can also follow structural economic change until our learning-curve adjusts to a new reality. The political and economic ramifications of the new world order may not be fully understood but certain of their chief characteristics are discernible and we seek to analyse them in the chapters which follow.

'Strangers in our midst'

The most visible aspect of the changing world order, in Europe at least, is the demographic character of our societies. Europe is a multi-cultural, multi-lingual mélange of peoples, as it has always been. What is striking today is the intensity with which defenders of European culture and society are monitoring the integrity of the old order in the face of a presumed racial threat by 'newcomers' and 'foreigners'. In the old order we were taught to draw physical and ideological lines demarcating the 'we' from the 'they', whether in the form of an 'Iron' or 'Bamboo' Curtain or in the form of 'Believers' or 'Infidels'. Increasingly, in this transition to a new world order, the fresh challenge is ambivalence and uncertainty as to what to believe. In the words of Zygmunt Bauman (1990: 143) 'There are friends and enemies. *And there are strangers'*. How are these 'strangers' treated within the European Community? What is the relationship between racism, immigration and unfree labour? Is there a political geography of race in the European Community? These were some of the questions which animated Jim MacLaughlin's analysis (Chapter 2) of European attempts to defend their racial frontiers while simultaneously opening their trade and political borders.

Race is a powerful weapon for the construction of political arguments and the conferment or denial of citizen rights. Too often in the past our attention has focused on the reprehensible tactics and propaganda of the ultra-right. The burden of Chapter 2 is that, in addition to extremist positions of either left or right, there are more pervasive, subtle and therefore pernicious institutionalized barriers to racial and ethnic harmony in the European Community. There are four strands to his argument. The first is that Western Europe has been transformed from a major exporter to a major importer of labour during the past century. The intricacies of capitalism necessitated that racism be used to structure free and unfree relations of production in post-World-War-II Europe. The size, scale and location of migrant communities justifies their description as pools of unfree labour. Following Miles (1982) the argument insists that the labour power of racial minorities was a 'hidden transfer of value', a 'form of development aid' whereby the poorer reaches of the world system subsidized the industrial core of Europe by its export of talent and labour skills.

Secondly, MacLaughlin posits that media coverage of race issues has contributed to a new 'racial siege mentality' in many places. By legitimizing the new racial hegemony as 'common sense', sections of the media have institutionalized certain racial positions and have rendered alternative multi-cultural perspectives as unthinkable options in advanced, democratic societies. The logic of national self-determination, of exclusionary nationalism, is turned against stigmatized aliens. If it is currently true of North Africans in France, or Roma in Romania, it is an abiding truth for Jews in most European societies. It is understandable that Jews fleeing from anti-Semitic hostility in Moscow, Kiev or Warsaw might feel apprehensive among Berlin's 9000-strong Jewish community and share such fears with fellow believers at the Jewish cultural centre in Monbijouplatz. But for German-born Jews this new wave of racial animosity is all the more intolerable. The sensitivity of German–Jewish relations is captured in an individual incident involving Mr Ignatz Bubis, the new Head of Germany's Jewish Council, as reported by Anna Tomforde in *The Guardian*:

Mr. Bubis, during a visit to riot-scarred Rostock, was implicitly told by a CDU local politician that, as a Jew, his homeland was Israel, not Germany. Polish-born Bubis, who lost both parents in the Holocaust held back tears when he replied: 'There was once a flourishing Jewish community in this country. It was wiped out by the Nazis . . . and questions like yours are partly responsible for the fact that it no longer exists. Do you want to marginalise a Jew as something alien?' (Tomforde, 1992).

On 6 October 1992 I celebrated Yom Kippur, ushering in the Jewish New Year at the Central Synagogue in Bucharest and understood well that

Romania's tiny Jewish community, officially estimated at only 9107 in 1992, is simultaneously more free in the post-Ceauşescu era and more guarded in its activities because the price of freedom is the resurgence of anti-Semitism. Having been forbidden to emigrate in the early post-World-War-II period, hundreds of thousands of Romanian Jews fled to Israel, Australia and the USA during periods of official relaxation of exit-visa controls. Those who remain face a double-edged sword. If they stay they may incur the full wrath of anti-Semitic violence; if they depart they deny their legitimate contribution to the multi-racial reality of Romanian society and yield to the logic of conservative nationalism's dictum of one people, one language, one nation, one state.

The Romanian cameo illustrates the third strand of MacLaughlin's argument, namely that there is no uniform response within Europe to the question of 'aliens', whether perceived as 'insiders' or 'outsiders' in society. Rather, there is a specific set of geographies of racism and we would do well to adopt a place-centered perspective so that we do not represent racism in Europe as a product of innate Xenophobia and a residual from our colonial past. To do so would be to accept racism as 'natural', 'endemic' and woven into the fabric of everyday life, from which there is no escape. By insisting on a contextual interpretation of racism, whereby it is constantly being challenged, interrupted and reconstructed, MacLaughlin takes us back to the basics of time and space. For to deny racism its history is to surrender to a kind of fatalism. 'To deny it its geography is to ignore the role of place as the structuring and strucutured context of racist attitudes in a wide variety of European settings' (MacLaughlin, 1993: 36).

These new racist attitudes are powerful instruments for legitimizing the relative power positions of groups in the new European order. It might have been assumed that in tandem with the ethnic revival of post-World-War-II Europe would have come a new tolerance of racial as well as of ethnic minorities. However, as MacLaughlin (Chapter 2), and Williams (Chapter 5) both demonstrate, ethnicity and race are being used in increasingly different ways to categorize groups and structure policies which 'defend' the integrity of Europeans, Thus 'ethnicity' is increasingly used to construct a positive, quasi-biological identity while 'race' is used as a classificatory category to reflect negative tendencies of dissociation and exclusion at national and community levels. The former concern with phenotypical discrimination has been strengthened by cultural and religious legitimations for racial inferiority. Thus 'race' has come 'to signify a set of imaginary properties of inheritance which fix and legitimate real positions of social domination or subordination in terms of cultural differences between native and foreigner in the European Community' (MacLaughlin, Chapter 2: 41). But for this crude division to be maintained in an increasingly multi-ethnic, multi-racial world Europe has to re-interpret its position, to defend its frontiers from incursion in the east, mass migration from the south and 'contamination' from the Balkan borders. What sort of society would a Fortress Europe thus conceived seek to construct? Surely such isolationism and 'racial cleansing' is an anathema to the European dream of free movement and open borders? Perhaps so, but to date there is enough evidence to argue that it is not an inevitable prospect. In times of economic difficulty race can once again be used as an exclusionary category in any of the European 'shatterbelts' and we should be careful not to let our liberal ideals cloud our judgement in respect of racial victimization, whether directed against Islamic fundamentalists or guestworkers. The watchwords of the open society are social justice and mutual tolerance but they are maintained only in strict proportion to the degree to which we are vigilant defenders of the basic rights of all constituent peoples in Europe.

Challenges to the established nation–states

Economically, the division of the world into sovereign nation–states, has long been called into question, even if we recognize that psychologically the local community and nation–state are still the most important levels of territorial attachment and identification. Operating according to 'national economies' in a globalized era is not only increasingly dysfunctional, it is also inherently unstable. Philip Cooke's contribution (Chapter 3) to this debate on challenges to the nation-state is to examine the potential of inter-regional cooperation within the European Community. Like other contributors, he recognizes two distinct sources of pressure on contemporary nation–states, namely the emergence of supranational state institutions with significant political power (the EC); and the weakening of supranational states, such as the former USSR and possibly Canada.

Within this new European order one may recognize two dynamic trends. The first is the weakening of national economic sovereignty by the transfer of key economic powers from state legislatures to the European Commission. Cooke cites the following as illustrative domains: competition policy; trade policy; monetary exchange rate policy; science and technology research policy; even to some extent aspects of foreign policy. Secondly, there has been the parallel tendency to encourage inter-regional, cross-boundary initiatives, not only within the European Community but also beyond (as witnessed by Baden-Württemberg's agreements with Ontario, Hungary and Kanagawa). The recent debate over the ratification of the Maastricht Treaty, and the implications for decision-making and power-sharing as regards the interpretation of the term 'subsidiarity' inserted into Article 3b of the Treaty of European Union, suggest how vital these dynamic trends are to state sovereignty and autarchy. The clearest example of regional-level cooperation to date has been the Four Motors agreement of 1988. Baden-Württemberg, Rhônes Alpes, Lombardy and Catalonia sought to mobilize their own resources and thereby to strengthen their position within the EC through multilateral cooperation. Cooke examines the performance of the Four Motors initiative in the context of globalization and strategic alliances and suggests several key implications which have ramifications for all the other themes discussed in this volume.

Firstly, several leading industrial conglomerates are seeking to construct a defensive alliance against 'foreign' multinationals by building a 'Fortress

Europe' against the USA and, more importantly, Japanese competitors. We have already seen the parallel thrust in terms of racial frontiers to 'Fortress Europe' discussed in Chapter 2. Chapters 7, 8 and 9 will each tackle a variant on the European, American and Japanese relationship in the world economy by examining their characteristics as trading blocs and strategic actors.

Secondly, the EC (and incidentally most other European agencies) is committed to encouraging trans-border cooperation with the effect that previously suspect or fragile strategic regions now become pivotal nodes in a new European network of communication and trade – thus emphasizing the manner in which geography and place become periodically reinterpreted and transformed. In consequence, the Friulian–Slovene corridor once again offers a strategic gateway to Central Europe, much as it did in the days of the Austro–Hungarian Empire; the Western Mediterranean ports-metropolises of Genoa and Barcelona are revitalized, and Berlin again becomes a focus not only for German unification but also for physical and social communication throughout Europe as a key intellectual and political cross-roads.

By emphasizing the internal diversity and comparative advantage of the Four Motors regions the EC hopes to build up a substantial network of Research and Development (R & D). However, this thrust can only be maintained because there is a political will to build upon the idea of innovative decentralism in a context of regional federation. In the current single market such initiatives will have profound implications in at least five areas, according to Cooke. First, state sovereignty will not be ceded willingly to the EC but will be eroded *en passant* by the single market legislation and by the Free Trade Agreements between Canada, the USA and Mexico. Secondly, some firms and regions have recognized that in order to maintain any locally-perceived economic advantage in a deregulated community they will have to intensify the scope of their partnership compacts – thereby overcoming some of the negative externalities of economic success. Thirdly, such trends are expressions for a redistribution of power at all levels in the political hierarchy to maximize the self-determination of the unit in question. Clearly not all levels can be mutually satisfied and new sources of tension and political competition are thus unleashed. Fourthly, we should recognize that the mechanisms which channel such dynamic tensions are inherently political rather than merely economic in nature. Finally, although such regionalist pressures may indeed transform elements within the international system, they do not, as some have argued, constitute a sea change of reform whereby they threaten to replace the modern nation–state as the key instrument for spatial economic development.

'New nationalism'

A further source of challenge to the state order is the abiding sub-state pressure of devolution of power to the constituent nations of Europe. The drift towards fragmentation has been captured in a wide variety of terms and concepts, *viz* autonomy, devolution, decentralization, independence, separatism, freedom, national liberation. The core of each concept may have different implications for ideology and actual real politics but at root we are discussing the transfer of tangible power from one unit to another in the political system. Old-style nationalism has spawned an extensive literature and an identifiable corpus of writing which we may describe as a Political Geography of Nationalism (Agnew, 1988; Johnston, Knight and Kofman, 1988; Williams and Kofman, 1989; Williams, 1982; Zelinsky, 1988). However, in Chapter 4 Ronan Paddison contends that a 'new nationalism' can be discerned in several European states and analyses the Scottish response to sub-state territorial demands for greater autonomy. The basis of this 'new nationalism' is a recognition that political sovereignty can only be exercized within the evolving context of a fluid, power-sharing hierarchy of political units. Sovereignty is no longer an absolute nor a feasible reality in an inter-dependent world. Although the Scottish case will still be mediated through a British political system, it has increasing ties to a European political order which acts both as a fillip and as a constraint upon the limits of political possibility. 'The nationalist party's new claim to independence represented an attempt to take advantage of the new opportunities created by the European dimension; new nationalism is expressed in terms of Euro-nationalism, in which membership of the supranational organisation is not only seen as a constraint on the sovereignty of the small nation-state, but also as a safeguard for it' (Paddison, Chapter 4: 60).

Dualism, embeddedness and opportunism characterize this 'new nationalism'. But is it really so different from the old? Did not the earlier generations of Scottish and Welsh nationalists appeal to the European-wide values of Christendom and the League of Nations to distance themselves from British imperialism and to join common cause with the newly-independent nations carved out of the Austro–Hungarian Empire? Certainly Saunders Lewis, the first President of Plaid Cymru (1926–39) turned away from the classic British insistence on a mission–destiny view of white supremacy in establishing a new, imperial order. Equally, while many nationalist writers at that time turned to the Celtic realm for moral inspiration and contemporary models for imitation in the national struggle, Lewis sought this authenticity in the Catholic, Latin civilization of Europe. He argued that mediaeval Europe possessed a unity of spirit and of law which nurtured minority cultures because diversity could be accommodated within a universal European civilization. He sought to re-orientate Welsh politics by counterposing the relative merits of the twin external forces acting on contemporary Wales, the British Empire and the League of Nations. He urged his fellow nationalists to shun the imperial dream and work to reconstruct a Europe of the nations in which Wales, along with the other nations of the United Kingdom, would be represented as a free democratic country and be 'Europe's interpreter in Britain' (Williams, 1991: 8–12).

The claim to 'newness' rests less on such pan-European appeals than on the specifics of the Scottish experience and a new reality which nationalists must face – a reality which runs counter to the general trends of European politics. Contrary to most other states, who when faced by an ethno-regional challenge sought to decentralize power, the British state did not accommodate the demands for greater power-sharing from the Celtic periphery and English regions. Rather, it became emphatically more centralized under Mrs Thatcher's leadership. This led to a suppressed separate Scottish identity and an increased anglicizing influence, whereby the historical multi-national character of the UK state was formalized into a tripartite division of a local, regional and national British government. The alienation of the Scottish electorate throughout the 1980s resulted in a reactive assertion of a new Scottish identity, founded on a reconstructed basis of popular sovereignty and accompanied by the strengthening of Scottish civil society.

If true, why did the Scottish National Party (SNP) not fare better in the general election of 1992 and why did the Conservative Party increase its share of the popular vote in Scotland? In Chapter 4, Paddison argues that at the heart of the Scottish situation there lies an inherent paradox. On the one hand the dualistic nature of political identity, both Scottish and British, meant that many voters were cautious of the perceived national benefits which would accrue if an autonomous Scotland in Europe became a possibility. Sceptical of British performance in a renegotiated, post-Maastricht Community, they were even more sceptical of a Scottish performance. On the other hand, the twin assaults on the sovereignty of the state, from European Federalism at one level and British Federalism at another, weakened the capacity of the central state to promise a bright future for all British regions, irrespective of their location and political persuasion. With its greater emphasis on 'negotiated sovereignty', the new nationalism offered a more flexible model within which the global–local forces could be mediated but it could guarantee neither a more promising material future nor a larger slice of the European cake than good old Albion United!

Minority rights

Earlier in this chapter consideration was given to the role which race and racist attitudes played in the construction of a new European order. A distinction was made between ethnic minorities and racial groups suggesting that over the past 30 years the concept of 'ethnicity' was increasingly used to construct a positive identity while 'race' continued to reflect negative tendencies of discrimination and exclusion, despite comprehensive programmes for legislating in favour of racial equality in many societies. Part of this trend is attributable to the so-called ethnic revival and the remarkable turn about in the formal public fortunes of selected minorities.

In Chapter 5, I survey the development of autochtonous minority rights in Western Europe, paying particular attention to the recent specification of such rights in European law and within pan-European agencies. I then suggest that several of these post-World-War-II experiences are applicable to the protection and development of minority rights in Central and Eastern Europe. But I warn that unless the state is prepared to construct an appropriate cultural infra-structure in domains such as formal education and the mass media then the recognition of minority rights at the state level is a sham. In an increasingly multi-ethnic continent, European states must recognize the legitimacy of establishing conditions where such rights may be exercized as a normal function of daily life. Attention is given to the role of formal language-planning in devizing and implementing strategies for cultural reproduction and language survival. Although I recognize that language-planning is a necessary element in the satisfaction of minority rights, I also raise several questions which I believe are urgent if we are to avoid the more harrowing consequences of denying minorities their right to flourish in a Europe of the Peoples.

Signs of such tensions abound in most European states, none more so than in Germany and the Czech lands which are struggling with problems of mass migration, refugee absorption, and asylum seekers. The old Iron Curtain, it is said, sought to keep Eastern Europeans in their societies, the new Iron Curtain seeks to keep Eastern Europeans out of the European Community. Minority tensions will be exacerbated by such mass movements along the borders of the EC and unless long term structural relief is instituted so as to improve the socio-economic development of former communist states then such tensions will grow and could turn into a fresh wave of violent conflict between East and West, based not upon ideological differences but on relative deprivation.

What price peace?

The frightening stability which Europe enjoyed during the Cold-War era was predicated upon the massing of nuclear and conventional weaponry which sustained two spheres of influence and a developing *détente* between the superpowers. Having realized the limits of their power, they initiated a series of Strategic Arms Limitation Talks in 1972. Following the 1975 Helsinki Accord, great strides were made in constructing a gradual but effective security architecture for a post-Cold-War Europe. In Chapter 6 S.W. Williams and I examine the issue of peace and security in transitional Europe. The new 'Euro-Atlantic security architecture' is scrutinized, as is the role of the The Conference for Security and Cooperation in Europe (CSCE) process in institution building. Several of the challenges which threaten European security have yet to run their course, but we can discern the most salient. They include the long-term effects of the collapse of the Soviet empire, resurgence of chauvinistic nationalism and persecution of minorities, economic and environmental consequences of totalitarian state management, disputed territories and boundary conflicts. Measures to promote a general security are examined and particular attention is paid to experimentation in trans-frontier cooperation. We conclude our overview with a consideration of several lessons to be learned from the conflict in former Yugoslavia.

An American trilogy: whither God's own country?

No country has done more to establish the parameters of the new world order than the United States of America. With the end of the Cold War and the retreat from the Reagan–Bush version of macro-economic theory under the new Democratic leadership of Bill Clinton, what now for the home of the brave and the land of the free? Does its future lie in a period of domestic entrenchment, isolation and protectionism or in a renewed set of alliances with European or Asiatic partners? We started this volume with the observation that world order oscillated between periods of opening and closing and that globalization suggested the growth of new geographies and new linkages. In Europe such linkages serve to threaten the functional capacity of the state to protect its citizens from war, to satisfy their democratic thirst for representative government and accountable politicians and to challenge the legitimacy of state sovereignty both from above and below. What of the US state, and its response to the myriad global and domestic challenges? How has it fared in this process of adjustment? Does it face the same set of challenges as European states?

In a trenchant and yet truly humane analysis of the nation–state experience of the USA, Wilbur Zelinsky (1988) strikes a realistic chord on the persistence of statism, despite all its shortcomings:

In the United States and other postindustrial lands, statism may well be enjoying a (pen)ultimate (?) flush of glory, and for the same reason that ethnicity, regionalism, fundamentalism, piety, greed and nostalgia in all their variations have staged comebacks. First, there is the distressing realization that the future that once beckoned so alluringly has become a dark, forbidding place that obviously frightens us; the womblike certitudes of the past have considerably greater appeal. Secondly, none of the available substitutes for the nation-state are as yet practically or emotionally acceptable. A truly welcome alternative is not yet on the horizon. (Zelinsky, 1988: 253).

Is the American state ideal so tenacious because of the special character of its people or because it bolsters US hegemony within the world economy? Or is it simply that it has not yet run its course? Unlike its northern neighbour, the USA does not face a significant ethno-territorial challenge from a domestic, constituent region but it does face a challenge to its role as world leader. Recently, it has become fashionable to argue that the USA is beginning to lose its global hegemonic position. Japan and eventually China and Brazil are set fair to challenge the economic and geographical dominance of the USA. By assuming the role of global policeman and peacemaker, the USA has over-burdened its economy and strategic commitments and will, in time, pay for its supremacy.

Paul Kennedy (1987) has popularized the conviction that military spending at the expense of economic investment eventually undermines global power status. The word is out that the USA is on the slide. Some slide! To test this assumption, the final three contributors offer differing perspectives on the US role in the world order. In Chapter 7, John Agnew reconstructs the post-World-War-II transition to American hegemony within the world economy. John O'Loughlin (Chapter 8) examines the evidence for the thesis of the relative decline of the USA between 1966–91. In Chapter 9, Gearóid Ó'Tuathail scrutinizes the contemporary geo-economic discourses on the US–Japan relationship.

John Agnew argues that unlike previous transitions of hegemonic succession, notably that from Spain to the Netherlands to Britain, the US accession to world dominance was achieved with both a lack of conflict and with an inevitable accommodation and equanimity by Britain. The key to this smooth transfer was the 'special relationship' between the UK and the USA and the recognition that the USA would continue the British policies of reducing barriers to trade, encouraging currency convertability, stimulating international investment and opposing regional trading blocs. Though never equal, the 'special relationship' nevertheless contained a high degree of mutual conviviality and cultural empathy. For their part British politicians could continue to exercize a significant influence on world politics while the Americans nurtured a dependable European ally and a senior if less virile partner in global policing.

However, Britain's full participation in a reformed and expanded European Community has placed structural strains on the 'special relationship', particularly because of Britain's insistence on upholding the principles of the 'free world' economy rather than community-orientated protectionist measures. This has resulted in accusations that Britain is either the 'Trojan Horse' of the USA in Europe or less charitably her 'pet poodle'. The severe difficulty in the recent GATT talks and eventual threat to French agricultural imports led to sharp recriminations as to whether, under Britain's presidency, the EC was following its own trade and tariff agenda or that of an Atlantacist alliance. Britain's credentials as a European partner are open to question because it is simultaneously attempting to keep all its options open, a throwback to the days when it was truly an international leader. Does the current desire of the UK to maintain the 'special relationship' create more advantages than drawbacks *vis à vis* its role in world affairs?

In the triangular economic relationship between Europe, Japan and the USA, Britain is simultaneously essential and somehow tangential to all three in a manner in which France, for example, clearly is not. Professor Agnew argues that this awkward partnership is likely to continue for at least four reasons.

First, Britain acts as a bridgehead into Europe for many non-EC member states, particularly the USA and Japan. Secondly, Britain's financial frontiers are worldwide and favour an open world economy whereby its position as a financial capital may be secured. Thirdly, ideological opposition to European monetary and political union guarantees that Britain will continue to optimize its membership of a number of overlapping associations, even if the EC becomes the dominant political identification. Finally, an historical predisposition towards liberal internationalism favours a continuing cultural-economic justification for the 'special relationship'.

Having thus ensured a stable pattern of European alliances via Britain, and more recently Germany, American hegemony is surely unchallenged elsewhere in the world. What is the strength of this global giant? Is it in the ascendant now that it is no longer challenged by a Soviet equal or does the new world order presage a decline in American power?

No longer saviours: not even priests

It is now commonplace within both international relations theory and political geography generally to observe that the controlling functions which the superpowers used to exercize in world politics from 1945 had begun to lose their immediacy by the early 1980s. Both superpowers had experienced a considerable loss of authority as their military, economic and ideological structures began to falter. American experience in Vietnam and Soviet experience in Afghanistan had demonstrated that a formidable military capacity alone could not dictate the outcome of events in war-torn situations. For the USA in particular the Vietnam débacle has sparked off a political controversy as to whether it is in relative decline *vis à vis* other world powers, repeating the mistakes of earlier global leaders by engaging in 'imperial overstretch'.

One cannot over-emphasize the effect of the Vietnamese War on the subsequent course of American foreign policy or indeed on the American collective psyche. Savigear has summarized the American dilemma thus:

The experience of a war in which the USA was not only defeated for the first time and obliged to withdraw its forces and allow South Vietnam to be absorbed by the Communist North, but also which divided the American people as no previous war had done, was a turning-point in the foreign policy of the United States. That war was tremendously expensive in material and lives and emotional disruption. It lasted from 1961 until 1975. At its height there were more than 500,000 Americans in South Vietnam, and every act was photographed and reported in such an open and public manner that the world's attention and finally its disapproval fell upon the USA. They were no longer saviours as they had been in the First and Second World Wars, nor champions of democracy, but ineffective and cruel and themselves the victims of war, unable to control events and policies (Savigear, 1992: 340).

Subsequent difficulties, such as the failure to dislodge the Sandinistas in Nicaragua, the 'Irangate' episode, the invasion of Grenada, and the relative lack of US involvement in the radical affairs of Europe during 1989–92, all conspired to indicate that the USA was in relative decline. This is a contentious issue as her victory in the Iraq-Kuwait conflict, her continued economic power and her growing cultural imperialism seem to suggest the very opposite, namely the emergence of the USA as the undisputed world leader.

Evolving world-systems theory, as illustrated in Wallerstein's work (1991) would interpret the US military actions of the past decade, its disproportionate military spending (20 times that spent on aid) and its threatening trade postures (as witnessed in the breakdown of the GATT talks, November 1992), as the actions of a post-hegemonic state. Kennedy (1987) and Wallerstein (1991) both agree that the USA cannot regain through military might what it has lost through the processes of capitalist shifts in the world-system during the past 25 years. But how may we evaluate this presumed process of decline? What are its manifestations and consequences? In Chapter 8, John O'Loughlin seeks to advance the debate on the 'decline thesis' by measuring the evidence of 14 indicators chosen on the basis of world-system principles to reflect the anatomy of the comparative strength of the USA.

These indicators are in turn factor-analysed, with 4 resultant factors accounting for 85 per cent of the variance. The first component, accounting for nearly half of the total variance, supports the decline thesis by demonstrating that in terms of foreign aid, global trade, terms of trade, the great power Gross National Product (GNP) ratio, and military spending ratio the USA has experienced a falling-away in certain key areas. Successive components support the decline thesis on the basis of the temporal and spatial trends of the indicators selected. O'Loughlin advises that without a major national policy shift these declines can be expected to continue. In the debate between Wallerstein (1991) and Madelski (1987) on the rate of decline, O'Loughlin's analysis offers greater support to Wallerstein's interpretation that, having lost production and commercial leadership while retaining its financial leadership, the USA is already in the process of deep decline.

Such a prognosis offers little comfort to either world-system or long-cycle theorists. In the absence of an unchallenged leader, competing core powers will seek to usurp part or all of the US hegemony. Faced with such challenges, O'Loughlin warns that the USA may be tempted to use its military power to keep economic, cultural and political challengers in check. Pre-eminent amongst such challengers at present are Japan and a united Europe, both core capitalist regions; both capable of generating conflict within the global capitalist economy. We are reminded that the global wars of this century were fought precisely between powers that shared a similar economic ideology. Thus, although we may be tempted to aver that an invigorated China or an expanded Brazil would pose a regional or eventually global challenge to the USA, it is more probable that Japan or a United Europe will compete more successfully in the race for resources and markets and perhaps overtake the American giant.

So far we have traced the American position in the New World Order as one which has gravitated away from the Atlanticist perspective of the East Coast establishment based upon a continuing, if less significant, 'special relationship' with the UK, and by extension, with Europe, America's spiritual and ideological homeland. Does it necessarily follow that during a transition period of relative decline the USA will look for revival and salvation in the Pacific? To see the Pacific as the 21st century's replay of the current Atlantic century is to impose a Euro-centric nation on world order, a fact poignantly noted in a recent essay by Gerald Segal who argues that:

If 'thinking Pacific' means thinking of the geographic region as a coherent, cultural, political, military or economic bloc, then 'thinking Pacific' is obsolete. The true importance of the changes taking place in the Pacific, concerns the new trends in ideology, military security, and economic relations, none of which depends on there being some coherence to the region commonly known as the Pacific (Segal, 1992: 406).

Segal's implication is clear. East Asia is contributing to the growth of a world economy, not a regional economy based upon trans-Pacific relations. As Japan comes to replace the USA as a major trading partner in the Pacific Basin, so it also comes to play a greater role than the USA in Europe;. Japanese investment in and trade with Europe is growing faster than its equivalents with the USA. Similar trends are already becoming evident for South Korea and the NICs, and Japan may well find the lure of the New Europe more appealing than the difficulties of dealing with a grumpy United States (Segal, 1992: 416).

Why is the USA described in these terms? Is Japan a real threat to its hegemony or merely an over-eager junior partner? In Chapter 9, Gearóid Ó'Tuathail seeks to assess the current US-Japanese relationship. Starting from the same assumptions as O'Loughlin, Ó'Tuathail reaches quite different conclusions. He argues that geo-economic discourses explicitly locate US decline in the context of the rising power of Japan, foreseeing a Pax Nipponica in the early part of the next century and a bankrupt USA forced to acknowledge that the imperial mantle has been transferred from Washington's to Tokyo's shoulders. The USA needs to awaken to the Japanese strategy of linking economic penetration to questions of national security, whereas America's own performance has been hampered by a yawning chasm between 'traders' and 'warriors', between trade negotiators and geostrategists, each pursuing different and conflicting goals and thereby damaging national interests. Should the USA continue to police the Pacific Rim? Or should it seek to share this responsibility more equitably with Asian partners?

Prestowitz (1989) confirms the ultimate irony of the Japanese colonization of America when he remarks that the current USA–Japan relationship is 'surely the first time in history that a territory in the process of being colonized has actually paid for the right to defend the colonizer'. Others urge that the USA should no longer pay for the defence of Japan, but should imitate Japan in harmonizing its economic and security needs and adopt a far more instrumental or self-interested strategic policy. Faced with these interpretations, many outside the USA will be astonished by such claims as it has long been thought that the interests of the American state and of its multinational corporations have always determined US foreign policy and shaped the contours of its geo-strategy!

Be that as it may, Ó'Tuathail claims that those critics who view the American decline as a direct response to a Japanese challenge misconceive the changed nature of the world economy in the 1980s. Rather than typify the relationship as a zero-sum conflict, one should appreciate the weak nature of the state in both Japan and the USA and awaken to the threat posed by unregulated transnational corporate capitalism to the 'subaltern classes' in these states. Indeed, Ó'Tuathail's analysis goes further to offer a sympathetic account of the new Orientalism, warts and all. He is at pains to expose the inadequacies of those analysts who presume a subordinated East Asia, and argue that élites within the Asian Rim speak to each other through the mediation of Washington.

The USA may be dominant in the absence of a mythic, regional collective consciousness, but it is not all dominant. Both geo-economic theorists and transnational liberals are alert to the fact that a new geography of trade and security is being constructed in the Pacific Rim, but it is being constructed as part of a global, not just a regional, transition. The growth rates of both Western Europe and parts of East Asia have outpaced those in the USA and are likely to continue to do so. Furthermore, neither East Asians nor Europeans need American military security as much as they did in the old world order, thereby diminishing the hegemony of the USA (Segal, 1992: 417). However, global interdependence presumes the continued cooperation of these three trade blocs in the global market economy and presumes the continued existence of the USA as the global lynchpin of the world system. To argue otherwise is to dismiss the pivotal role of US-based financial, resource, intellectual and manufacturing interests in the world economy.

The general implications to be derived from American readjustment to the new world order have more to do with the operation of transnational capital, the construction of new relationships and the immediacy of globalization in structuring our everyday lives and activities than with the more focused discourse on the USA–Japan debate. The real crisis facing the USA today is a crisis of confidence, of authority and of identity. The USA no longer claims to be the saviour of the oppressed, but neither does it slip comfortably into the lesser role of priest pointing the way to the saviour, or administering the sacraments of democracy and free trade. American ideals and actions are increasingly divorced from one another and the evidence for spiritual depression is that the gods seem to be favouring other ways of organizing society, space and souls. Thus, the mirror of Japanese success held up to American eyes is an uncomfortable reflection that the mission–destiny view of US history no longer guarantees primacy, let alone prosperity, for all her citizens.

References

Agnew, J. (1988), *Place and politics*, London, Allen and Unwin.

Bauman, Z. (1989), 'Sociological responses to postmodernity', in C. Mongardini and M.L. Maniscalco (eds), *Modernismo & postmodernismo*, Rome, Bulzoni Editore.

Bauman, Z (1990), Modernity and Ambivalence', in Featherstone, M. (ed.), *Global Culture*, London, Sage, pp. 143–69.

Bayliss, J. and Rengger, N.J. (eds), (1992), *Dilemmas of World Politics*, Oxford, Clarendon Press.

Brunn, S. and Leinbach, T.R. (1991), *Collapsing space and time*, London, Harper Collins Academic.

Chase-Dunn, C. (1990), 'World-state formation', *Political Geography Quarterly*, **9**, No. 2, 108–31.

Featherstone, M. (ed.), (1990), *Global culture*, London, Sage.

Gellner, E. (1992), *Postmodernism, reason and religion*, London, Routledge.

Healey, D. (1991), *When shrimps learn to whistle*, London, Penguin.

Hirst, P. and Thompson, G. (1992), 'The problem of "globalization": international economic relations, national economic management and the formation of trading blocs', *Economy and Society*, **21**, No. 4, 357–96.

James, H. (1989), *A German identity, 1770–1990*, London, Weidenfeld and Nicolson.

Johnston, R.J., Knight, D. and Kofman, E. (eds), (1988), *Nationalism, self-determination and political geography*, London, Croom Helm.

Johnson, R.J. and Taylor, P.J. (eds), (1989), *A World in Crisis?*, Oxford, Blackwell.

Kennedy, P. (1987), *The rise and fall of the Great Powers*, New York, Random House.

Lich, G.E. (ed.), (1992), *Regional studies: the interplay of land and people*. College Station, Texas A. and M. U.P.

Madelski, G. (1987), *Long cycles in world politics*, Seattle, University of Washington Press.

Miles, R. (1982), Racism and Migrant Labour, London, Routledge and Kegan Paul.

Mlinar, Z. (ed.) (1992), *Globalization, and territorial identities*, Aldershot, Avebury Press.

Newhouse, J. (1989), *The nuclear age*, London, Michael Joseph.

Palmer, A. (1992), *The decline and fall of the Ottoman Empire*, London, John Murray.

Prestowitz, C. (1989), *Trading places: how we are giving our future to Japan and how to reclaim it*, New York, Basic Books.

Prestowitz, C. (1992), 'Beyond laissez faire', *Foreign Policy*, **87**: 67–87.

Savigear, P. (1992), 'The United States: superpower in decline?', in Bayliss, J. and Rengger, N.J., *Dilemmas of world politics*, Oxford, Clarendon Press.

Segal, G. (1992), 'A Pacific century?' in Bayliss, J. and Rengger, N.J., *Dilemmas of world politics*, Oxford, Clarendon Press. 406–18.

Sklair, L. (1991), Sociology of the Global System, London, Harvester Wheatsheaf.

Taylor, P.J. (1989), *Political geography*, London, Longman.

Tomforde, A. (1992), 'When the old hatred awakes', *The Guardian*, 6.11.92.

Wallerstein, I. (1991), Geopolitics and Geoculture, New York, Cambridge University Press.

Walzer, M. (1989), *The company of critics*, London, Peter Halban.

Williams, C.H. (ed.), (1982), *National separatism*, Cardiff, University of Wales Press.

Williams, C.H. (1991), 'Language, nation and territory', in P. Meara and A. Ryan (eds), *Language and nation*, London, B.A.A.L. and C.I.L.T: 7–27.

Williams, C.H. (ed.), (1991) *Linguistic minorities, society and territory*, Clevedon, Avon, Multilingual Matters.

Williams, C.H. and Kofman, E. (eds), (1989), *Community conflict, partition and nationalism*, London, Routledge.

Zelinsky, W. (1988), *Nation into state*, Chapel Hill, University of North Carolina Press.

2
Defending the frontiers: the political geography of race and racism in the European Community

Jim MacLaughlin

This chapter suggests that popular perceptions of race, migrant labour and immigration are fuelling racism by constructing racial meanings for social and political developments in the European Community (EC). The idea of race is also increasingly used to define minority populations, to explain their social behaviour and to 'fundamentalize' their cultural practices. This is especially noticeable in the case of Islamic minorities but it is also true of other 'unmeltable' ethnics in the European Community. Unlike media coverage of indigenous minorities in the EC, media treatment of exogenous minorities is contributing to their racialization and exaggerating their threat to the socio-economic and cultural fabric of the Community. Thus the popular press has regularly carried reports of 'hordes' of immigrants 'clamouring' at Europe's doors and portrayed foreign minorities in the EC as welfare 'spongers' and perpetrators of inner-city revolts.

This chapter also suggests that the media exaggerate the political threat of the ultra-right while ignoring other more subtle structural and institutionalized barriers to racial and ethnic harmony in the European Community. It also suggests that a differential neo-racism has emerged since the 1970s which advocates the protection of European culture and the 'European way of life' against the Third World and the process of Islamization. The chapter is divided into four sections: section one traces the growth of Western Europe's 'foreign population' in the post-World-War-II period and analyses the functions of migrant labour in the core areas of European capitalism between the 1950s and the mid-1970s, section two suggests that media coverage of such issues as immigration, migrant workers and asylum seekers is simultaneously aggravating 'common sense' racism while 'racializing' solutions to certain social and economic problems in the EC; section three calls for a 'place-centered' approach to race and racism to counteract aspatial and ahistorical reifications of European racism.

The chapter concludes with a discussion on distinctions between race and ethnicity and the social and geographical implications of racial thinking in the European Community, suggesting that 'ethnicity' is used increasingly to construct a positive, quasi-biological European identity while 'race' is used as a classificatory category to reflect negative tendencies of dissociation and exclusion at national and Community levels. It also suggests that the racialization of state policies, and statistics relating to migrant workers, since World War II reflects widespread assumptions that foreign workers and racial and ethnic minorities should be accorded separate treatment and that their growth, regional distribution and social status should be carefully monitored.

Racial minorities and migrant workers in post-World-War-II Europe

Although it is widely recognized that Western Europe was transformed from a major exporter to a major importer of labour between the mid-19th and mid-20th century, the size of Europe's foreign population has generally only been emphasized at times of social or economic crisis. Since the 1950s, Western Europe has acquired a non-indigenous population proportionate in size to the Latino population of the United States of America. In Belgium, France, Germany and the UK the minority populations are proportionately similar to America's Black minority. An approximately estimated 30 million people entered Western Europe between 1945 and 1975 –, one of the largest migratory movements in modern history (Castles, 1984: 1). There are an estimated 13 million legally settled non-Europeans and perhaps as many as 2 million 'illegals' in the twelve EC countries (Nanton, 1991: 191). Just under two thirds of non-Europeans living in France and 70 per cent of those in Germany and the Netherlands are citizens of countries outside the European Community. The foreign population of the European Community is comprised of a predominance of North Africans in France, Turks in Germany, Turks and Moroccans in the Netherlands and Moroccans in Belgium. The population of New Commonwealth and Pakistan origin in Britain has been estimated at 2.43 million, or 4.5 per cent of the total population.

The social composition of post-World-War-II immigration has been well documented elsewhere. Most analysts have emphasized its racial, ethnic and geographical diversity. It included political refugees from Eastern Europe, Black workers from Europe's ex-colonies, and 'guest' and migrant workers from Spain, Portugal, Greece and Turkey. In Switzerland most migrant workers were from peripheral areas within Europe, particularly from Italy and Spain. In the Netherlands they tended to be drawn from Turkey, Morocco and Spain. Significant numbers were also recruited from the former colonies of Surinam, Indonesia and the Dutch Antillies. In

Belgium post-War minority populations were largely of Turkish and Moroccan origin. In France post-War immigration was a mixture of colonial and post-colonial migrant workers, supplemented by significant influxes of workers from neighbouring states. In the former Federal Republic of Germany migrant workers were initially drawn from Italy, Yugoslavia, Spain and Greece and were subsequently drawn from Turkey. Turks now constitute the largest foreign minority in the country. Post-War immigration to Britain was significantly different from that of other West European countries in that 'foreign' workers constituted a relatively small proportion of total labour force. The ready availability of Irish immigrants reduced but did not eliminate dependence on former colonies such as India, Pakistan and the Caribbean (Layton-Henry, 1990; MacLaughlin, 1991).

Castles identifies three phases in post-War migration to Western Europe. These in turn broadly coincide with distinctive phases in the process of ethnogenesis and the formation of new racial and ethnic minorities (Castles, 1984: 11–15). In phase one, which lasted from approximately 1945 to 1974, Western Europe absorbed a mass immigration of mostly male workers from the peripheries of Europe and the Third World. When capital was hegemonic at the start of this phase employers regarded migrant labour as indispensable to the expansion of post-War capitalism. Thus, for example, in France it was widely claimed that a minimum 5,290,000 permanent immigrants were needed to renew the labour force, stabilize the country's skewed demographic structure after World War II and reinforce French claims to Great Power status (Freeman, 1979: 69). In Britain prominent members of the Labour Party ignored the potentially xenophobic reactions of their constituents and advocated the widespread utilization of 'foreign' labour in the re-industrialization of the post-War economy. A constitutional provision allowed for millions of East Germans to enter West Germany after World War II. These expellees from the former territories of the Third Reich, together with demobolized soldiers and 'guestworkers' from Italy, Yugoslavia, Turkey and Greece, provided the basis for capitalist expansion in post-War West Germany.

However, when organized labour became hegemonic in the 1960s and 1970s, and when recession hit in the 1980s, a virulent indigenous working-class xenophobia later contributed to stricter immigration controls and the victimization of guestworkers in the Community (Cohen, 1991: 153; Castles, 1984: 25). This showed that the interests of 'rational' capital often conflicted with those of organized labour and could contribute to the revival of grassroots working-class nationalist movements throughout Western Europe. It also revealed that state policies on immigration and employer-access to migrant labour had to consider the countervailing and racist sentiments of the indigenous working class. Finally, it rendered hopelessly idealistic the left wing belief that patterns of international class solidarity could obviate ethnic allegiances and transcend racial divisions in multi-ethnic Western Europe. Thus in the 1970s protectionist trade unionists in the automobile and engineering industries in Britain used 'closed shop' and demarcation agreements to exclude migrant workers from indigenous working-class spheres of interest (Duffield, 1988: 67–73). In France a municipal Communist Party ordered the demolition of hostels erected for migrant workers (Cohen, 1991: 152–161). In Switzerland anti-immigrant agitation resulted in referenda on the issue of the size of the migrant population and the forced expulsion of migrant workers in the 1960s (Miles, 1987: 166). In the Netherlands the government considered a reintroduction of the rotation principle in 1974 to allow migrant workers only two years' residence (Entzinger, 1985; 66–7). In West Germany legislation introduced in 1983 offered migrant workers who returned 'home' a payment of DM10,000 and additional sums for dependents (Miles, 1987: 166).

Victimization and 'scapegoating' of migrant workers continued throughout the second phase of the migratory process when migrant workers insisted that family members should be allowed to settle in Western Europe. Family reunification contradicted an important principle of the guestworker system which was designed to rotate workers between home and host country and thereby *deter* settlement and reduce the social costs of migrant labour. It also made migrant labour less mobile and more difficult to repatriate in the event of recession. Finally, it aggravated tensions between the indigenous working class and new racial and ethnic minorities in the inner-city areas and contributed to the racialization of working-class conflict within Europe. Inter-racial conflict was aggravated by the lack of social investment in inner-city areas where the new ethnic and racial minorities were concentrated (O'Loughlin, 1980: 257–9). Moreover the 'clustering' of immigrants in inner city and suburban areas was not simply reflective of immigrant desires to stay apart from indigenous populations but was strongly influenced by the socio-economic status of immigrants and their life-cycle characteristics. As migration streams matured during the phase of family reunification, racial and ethnic communities were formed which were dominated by family groups.

As we have already seen, single males were dominant in the initial phase of the migration process. White's analysis of the urban geography of racial minorities in Western Europe in the early 1980s emphasized differences in the occupational status and demographic structure between resident foreigners of different nationalities and concluded that it is more accurate to speak of a variety of migrant groups rather than of labour migrants as a single unitary entity in any one city. As White states:

Recently-arrived single migrants are concentrated in inner-city areas, just as other single people (such as students and the old) are similarly concentrated. Family groups are more noticeable in more peripheral housing areas, just as is the case for the indigenous populations, although it would also be true to say that the speed of movement out from central areas has been relatively slow. This is because foreign migrants are under-represented in areas of public-sector housing so that they are confined, to a great extent, to the cheapest levels of the privately-rented sector and such property is most concentrated in and around older inner-city areas (White, 1984: 132).

Despite the clear need for housing and other social amenities to meet the needs of the indigenous working-class and racial and ethnic minorities in inner-city areas, most governments failed to make the necessary social investment to reduce or defuse racial tensions. Tensions were aggravated by state policies that permitted family re-unification despite the existence of discriminatory regulations to prevent it and by growing working-class opposition to 'foreign' immigrants. By the mid-1970s the post-War migratory process reached a new phase with the permanent settlement and development of new racial and ethnic minorities in Western Europe.

Racism, immigration and unfree labour

While Cohen and Castles provide a detailed account of the links between migration and the development of Western Europe's new racial and ethnic communities in the post-War period, they tend to view racism as a problem of poor race relations aggravated by immigration. They also suggest that racial intolerance in post-War Europe was an historical anachronism and a product of historical racism revived by influxes of foreign workers. They assume that migration simply refers to changes in the spatial mobility of workers and that the significance of migration lies in spatial mobility *per se* rather than in social class relations before and after migration. This assumption also underpins other geographical perspectives on the relationship between race and migration in post-War Europe (Johnson and Salt, 1990; Salt and Clout, 1976; Kayser, 1977; King, 1993; Knox, 1984).

There are a number of problems with these geographical accounts of the connections between race and immigration. Firstly, contrary to the dominant anti-immigration discourse, immigration did not 'cause' racism in Western Europe, although it did give post-War racism a new focus and created new targets for racial victimization and 'scapegoating'. Secondly, by no means all migrations to post-War Britain, France and Germany were determined by the demand for wage labour. Especially in Germany and France, they reflected the demand for unfree labour which could only be satisfied by hiring 'foreign' workers. Thirdly, geographical explanations which link racism to immigration often ignore the racial reasons for the widespread use of unfree labour. Missing from these accounts is any perception of racism caused by anything other than the immigration of 'foreign' workers into Western Europe since 1945. Missing also is any perception of migration as movements of people to different class situations and different relations of production in Western Europe. To transcend the race relations problematic at the centre of this mode of theorizing we should focus less on the effect of capitalist development upon 'race relations' and more upon the cultural and ideological content of specific instances of capitalist development (Miles, 1987: 7). This compels us to ask why in certain historical and geographical contexts were the ideology of 'race' and 'race relations' central to class formation and the development of capitalism in Western Europe. It also traces racism and racial intolerance to the 'unfreedoms' of racial and other ethnic minorities and to the widespread use of unfree migrant labour in Western Europe.

Miles has argued that the social and economic inferiority of large numbers of migrant workers in post-war Europe justifies their classification as unfree labour. He suggests that they legally were:

citizens of proximate social formations, and therefore 'aliens' as far as the state of the social formation where they sold their labour was concerned. The state in the social formation of recruitment therefore had to devise a legal and administrative mechanism which would allow the entry and residence of persons defined as 'foreigners' and which would regulate their activities once having emigrated. By entering spatially the Western Europe social formations contract migrants entered simultaneously a web of state-defined and regulated rights and restrictions which affected their right to remain and reproduce themselves and their families (Miles, 1987: 160).

He also suggests that the scale of labour migration and the size of the 'foreign' working–class population suggest that unfree labour cannot be regarded as peripheral to the expansion and reproduction of post-War capitalism in Western Europe (Miles, 1987: 166). Racism not only provided the ideological justification for the political unfreedoms of migrant workers in the social democracies of Western Europe; it also gave states power to deny 'foreign' immigrants and their children permission to remain in countries where their labour power was commodified; restrictions on the commodification of the labour power of racial minorities were rationalized. Thus, the formation of interest groups to negotiate for social and political rights of racial and ethnic minorities was obstructed, preventing full participation in Europe's increasingly multi-ethnic and multi-racial societies.

The result was that racism became an important element in the formation and reproduction of free and unfree relations of production in post-War Europe and was responsible for the production and reproduction of particular cultural forms, social classes and class factions. Indeed, just as ethnic minorities contributed to core-formation and the expansion of capitalism in the 19th century, the labour power of racial minorities was 'a hidden transfer of value' and form of 'development aid' from the ex-colonial world and the peripheries of Europe to the industrial centres of Europe in the post-War period (Miles, 1987: 165). This was reflected in the settlement patterns of migrant workers, most of whom were located in low-amenity urban areas and in expanding conurbations where the labour market was already ethnically stratified and where opportunities for social advancement were few.

Britain's Black communities were established in London, the West Midlands and the industrialized North of England. In Belgium foreign workers were mainly concentrated in the Walloon industrial belt and in mining centres in the south of the country. Foreign workers in France were concentrated in and around Paris, and in Marseilles and Lyons. In Germany they were concentrated in the industrial-growth areas of the Ruhr, Frankfurt, Stuttgart, Mannheim, southern Bavaria and the Rhine-Main industrial spine. Foreign workers have also accounted for a considerable proportion of the population of urban areas in West Germany since the 1970s (O'Loughlin, 1980). They were an estimated 24 per cent of the population in Frankfurt, 18 per cent in Stuttgart, 17 per cent in Munich, 15 per cent in Cologne, Mannheim and Düsseldorf and 13 per cent in West Berlin (Booth, 1986). In 1970, foreign residents made up 34 per cent of the population of greater Geneva and 20 per cent of the population of Switzerland's four largest conurbations were foreigners (White, 1984: 103).

While each country that imported labour is a special case deserving detailed analysis of the regional distribution and socio-economic functions of migrant labour, it is no coincidence that most industrial economies in Western Europe resorted to the widespread utilization of migrant labour between the mid-1950s and the early 1970s. Thus the need for migrant labour in post-War Europe was the result of important qualitative and quantitative developments in European capitalism. The form of these developments was such that it led to increased reliance on methods of mass-production and conveyor-line production, including shiftwork and piece-work (Castles, 1984: 36). As Braverman has shown, this in turn contributed to the de-skilling of large sections of the industrial labour force of Western Europe and the creation of new jobs that often were dirty, monotonous, poorly paid, insecure and unhealthy (Braverman, 1974: 70–83). Prevailing attitudes towards race and the ex-colonies suggested that migrant workers and racial minorities were best suited to the type of work practices and occupations that post-War economic expansion required. Thus, while the stage of capitalist development made it necessary to transcend the boundaries of national labour markets, the nature of that development, and the prevalence of racial attitudes in Western Europe suggested that Third World workers (including those from internal 'Third Worlds' in the peripheries of Europe) were best suited for these jobs. Migrant workers from the Third World were not only proletarianized into the European labour market but also accepted conditions and occupied positions deemed by the indigenous working class to be below them or against their interests. However, while a generation of Third World immigrants were 'habituated' to work in a capitalist mode of production in post-War Germany, Britain, France and Switzerland, many migrant workers have since been barred from 'the organisational traditions of the indigenous proletariat by means of racism and legal restrictions on their employment, residence and familial rights' (Cohen and Henderson, 1991: 50).

Castles traces racism in contemporary Western Europe to qualitative changes in European capitalism after World War II (Castles, 1984: 23–36). However core-periphery and race relations in Western Europe also entered a new stage during this period. Large numbers of migrant workers were drawn from former ex-colonial territories and were so exploited here that the history of their presence in metropolitan Europe rightly belongs with the history of colonialism and neo-colonialism (Berger and Mohr, 1975: 8).

Certainly the differential incorporation of migrants and foreign minorities into capitalist relations of production facilitated the capitalist monopoly of the means of production and recreated racism in Western Europe. That said, it is important to emphasize that racism in post-war Europe is historically and geographically contingent. Contrary to a dominant anti-racist discourse, the socio-economic and political subordination of racial minorities in Western Europe did not reflect the racist 'essense' of the 'European Tribe' (Phillips, 1987: 178). Neither did it represent a 'deviation' from non-racial patterns of capitalist development or a 'revival' of 19th century colonialism. Rather, racism was central to the expansion of capitalism and the articulation of social class relations in a wide variety of regional contexts in the nation–states of Western Europe after World War II.

Thus Third World countries and peripheral areas in Europe became 'emigrant nurseries' which supplied cheap labour to the core areas of the European economy. Similarly, after World War II European colonial powers did not dispense with empire and revive capitalism from within Europe. They relied on labour supplies from former colonies and from Europe's internal Third World. The historic relationship between colonizer and colonized gave way to new relationships between ex-colonial subjects and European employers within Europe. Ethnic minorities from the Mediterranean and South Eastern Europe were also transplanted to the core areas of European capitalism. This exodus from the peripheries to the redeveloping core areas of the European economy was a consequence and a cause of the peripheralization of peripheral areas in Europe. However, while the influx of 'foreign' workers meant that the underdevelopment of ex-colonies and the European periphery was often linked to core-formation in Western Europe, at other times it may have contributed to their development. For example, in Turkey and in other underdeveloped countries the export of surplus workers and the inflow of emigrant remittances were strategies for regional development (Paine, 1974: 143). In the case of Turkey at least governments seemed to have been mainly concerned with exporting as many surplus workers as possible and did not consider the negative impact of emigration on emigrants (Adler, 1982, p. 82). Similarly in Spain, Portugal, Greece and Ireland it was also argued that the more migrant workers could 'hone' their skills and develop a work ethic in countries like Germany, France or Britain the better they could contribute to the development of the home country when they returned (MacLaughlin, 1991: 319). However it remains to be seen to what extent peripheral economies in Europe and the Third World actively promoted emigration to attract emigrant remittances from abroad and to alleviate poverty at home (Aral, 1990; Brandes, 1975; Pennix, 1982).

Racialization of core-periphery relationships

While migration from the colonial to the metropolitan world clearly involved a change in the location of colonizer and colonized relationship, it could be argued that it did not involve any fundamental change in the nature of that relationship. Racial and other 'unmeltable ethnics', many of them from Third World countries engaged in the process of nation-building, were expected to subordinate their identities to that of their host society. Just as nationalism was the prerogative of industrial capitalist expansionist White societies in the 19th century, ethno-nationalism in post-

War Europe was tolerated only if it derived from Europe's *indigenous* minorities, not from foreign minorities.

The revival of post-War racism has commonly been attributed to the unpreparedness of both political regimes and the public in Western Europe for the scale and diversity of immigration. This was particularly true during the 1960s when immigration from traditional labour surplus areas on the peripheries of Western Europe was supplemented by influxes of workers from Third World countries, from Turkey and from Greece. As we have already seen, migrant labour was perceived initially as a temporary expedient and the entire system of recruitment depended on the rotation of workers, which in turn was designed to deter settlement and reduce the social costs of migrant labour in Western Europe. It was also assumed that those who decided to stay would, like previous migrants, assimilate into European society on the host society's terms. However many more were caught in 'emigrant traps' and were either unable to save enough to return home or unwilling to do so because of the deterioration of political and economic circumstances. Berger and Mohr categorize the latter as people who had 'changed faster than their country' (Berger and Mohr, 1975: 213).

However, the relegation of racial and ethnic minorities to the margins of European society is not explainable simply in terms of the 'unpreparedness' of European nation–states for influxes of foreign workers. The 'guestworker system' in Germany and the social and economic status of Asian, Turkish, African and Caribbean minorities elsewhere in Europe reflected racist attitudes towards ex-colonial and minority populations. It was not just that many accepted the legitimacy of labelling the latter as 'foreigners' – they frequently also legitimized their social inferiority in racial terms. Castles has argued that the imposition of the citizenship of the colonizer on the colonized was an ideological instrument of domination in the age of empire. He also suggests that European states were unwilling to abandon citizenship legislation in the post-War period because this would have been 'tantamount to accepting the breakdown of colonialism, which they were still trying to resist' (Castles, 1984: 92).

What made post-War racism all the more significant was the fact that revolutionary developments in the organization and functioning of communications in the post-War period linked the peripheries of Europe and ex-colonial societies with the core areas of the world-system. This transformed the world economy from a functioning geographic unit composed of separate but interdependent economies into a space of 'unified and monopolized communications in which, potentially at least, all populations were somehow immediately visible to, and in contact with, one another' (Balibar, 1991: 14). Racial tensions in Western Europe were exacerbated and racially and ethnically mixed inner-city areas were transformed into contested domains where 'foreigners' and 'unmeltable ethnics' were seen to have no legitimate claim to rights of citizenship, including rights to welfare payments and state recognition of their social and cultural aspirations. Thus it is not enough to argue that 'race' is simply a psychological 'memory' or a relic from the Nazi past. As Balibar argues, we must also explain why racist ideology has remained one of the most persistent and virulent forms of European historical consciousness and account for the fact that racism still affects the imaginary fusion of past and present for many Europeans (Balibar, 1991: 45). We should certainly avoid writing the story of neo-racism in Europe as though it began after 1945. The destruction of racist complexes in post-colonial Europe was predicated on the demise of racist attitudes and the decomposition of racist communities. This did not occur in 1945. Neither did it follow the retreat from empire in the 1950s and 1960s. Post-war racism is a continuation of a 19th century racial tradition of grouping people by an affinity that mythically predates the current economic and political scene. As Wallerstein suggests, it is also 'a claim to a solidarity overriding those defined in class or ideological terms' (Wallerstein, 1991: 193). Then as now its central function was to permit people to organize into social, cultural or geopolitical entities and to compete with others for goods and services essential for social and political survival (Skinner, 1965: 173).

In the 19th century European imperialism created racial stratifications in colonial societies and rendered Europeans 'tribe-like' by making them members of a special global status group with claims to preferential power and allocation of goods and services. Stavenhagen argues that the stratifications arising from such status groupings were 'social fixations' that were created by juridical means and maintained by specific social relations of production and social class relationships (Stavenhagen, 1962: 99). As he also points out:

Into these social fixations intrude other secondary, accessory factors (for example, religious, ethnic) which reinforce the stratification and which have, at the same time, the function of 'liberating it of its economic base changes. Consequently, stratifications can be thought of as justifications or rationalizations of the established economic system, that is to say, as ideologies. Like all phenomena of the social superstructure, stratification has a quality of inertia which maintains it even when the conditions which gave it birth have changed. As the relations between classes are modified . . . stratifications turn themselves into *fossils* of the class relations on which they were originally based (Stavenhagen, 1962: 101).

In the 19th century these racial stratifications arose out of the need to maintain core-periphery antimony. While nationalism divides core and periphery intrazonally, national categorizations in the world system reflect competition between states in a hierarchically-structured international order. Race and racism 'unify intrazonally the core zones and the peripheral zones in their battles with each other' (Wallerstein, 1991: 82). One aspect of this conflict is the gradual abandonment of the principle of *jus soli* in favour of the principle of *jus sanguinis* and the movement away from inclusive to exclusive definitions of citizenships in the European community. The binding guarantees of citizenship rights for colonial subjects that were formulated in the twilight of European imperialism have since been ignored or circumvented by subsequent legislation. Similarly, while technical innovations in communication transformed the functioning of the world economy and relationships between Europe and the Third World in the post-colonial era, they did not transform attitudes to racial minorities in

Europe or alter significantly racial attitudes towards Third World societies. They may in fact have hardened them. Indeed, Balibar traces the structural roots of neo-racism in 'Fortress Europe' to the changing relationships between the old colonial powers and the Third World and the fact that:

the '*two humanities*' which have been culturally and socially separated by capitalist development – opposites figuring in racist ideology as 'sub men' and 'supermen', 'underdeveloped' and 'overdeveloped' – do not remain external to each other, kept apart by long distances and related only 'at the margins'. On the contrary, they interpenetrate more and more within the same space of communications, representations and life. Exclusion takes the form of *internal exclusion at world level*: precisely the configuration which, since the beginnings of the modern era, has fuelled not only xenophobia or fear of foreigners, but also racism as fear and hatred of *neighbours* who are near and different at the same time. (Balibar, 1991: 14).

As the pace of decolonization increased after World War II, a new multi-ethnic and multi-racial space emerged in the world economy. This was not merely a space where geopolitical strategies were formed and where capital, technology and information circulated. It was also a space wherein populations were subjected to the laws of supply and demand and often came into physical and symbolic contact with each other for the first time. Thus the 'equivocal interiority – exteriority configuration' which formed one of the structuring dimensions of modern racism was now reproduced, expanded and re-actived in post-War Europe. Balibar also suggests that it is a commonplace to remark upon this in regard to those 'Third world within' effects which are produced by immigration from the former colonies into capitalist 'centres'. He goes on to argue that:

this form of *interiorization of the exterior* which marks out the horizon against which the representations of 'race' and 'ethnicity' are played out cannot be separated, other than abstractly, from apparently antithetical forms of *exteriorization of the interior*. And in particular it cannot be separated from those which result from the formation – after the more or less complete departure of the colonizers – of states which claim to be national (but only become so very unequally) throughout the immense periphery of the planet, with their explosive antagonisms between capitalist bourgeoisies or 'Westernized' state bourgeoisies and wretched masses, thrown back by this very fact upon 'traditionalism' (Balibar, 1991: 43–44).

While post-War immigration rendered Third World labour as flexible as European capital, this development was not without problems. First there were quite substantial differences in the work-cultures of some immigrant groups in Europe. Like 'unmeltable ethnics' in the USA, they often have different attitudes towards work, play, time and community from those habituated to industrial production for generations. In Europe, as in the USA, cultural differences and different attitudes towards work and play heighten the visibility of racial and ethnic minorities and contribute to anti-immigrant racism (Berger and Mohr, 1975; Powles, 1965; Horton, 1970). As a result racial and ethnic minorities act as scapegoats for those who insist that 'foreigners' are not just different but are lazy and dirty and 'welfare spongers' (Blauner, 1972; Gambino, 1970; Henderson, 1976). It could be argued that the problem of racism in the EC is less the attitude of the ultra-right than the fact that racial explanations of social problems are gaining currency and acceptability, and that large sections of the population are passively and uncritically prepared to accept separate treatment for non-indigenous workers and their descendants. It could also be argued that the different treatment of racial and ethnic minorities for purposes of data collection reflects a need to monitor the foreign population, to accord 'foreigners' separate treatment and to control their regional distribution within the EC. Ohri has argued that the racialization of statistics in Great Britain not only recorded the Black population as 'different' but also had a direct impact on the conditions which confronted Black workers and their families from their point of entry to their subsequent treatment by employers, trade unions, housing and educational authorities and the welfare state (Ohri, 1988: 13).

'Common sense' racism and the mass media

The popular media in the European Community are also alerting member states to the dangers of Third World immigration, particularly from the Maghreb, and elevating the issue of race to an increasingly prominent position in the agenda of issues which they consider important both at national and Community level (Wilson and Gutierrez, 1985: 147). They are communicating messages and symbols and selectively inculcating groups and individuals with the values, beliefs and codes of behaviour which integrate them into the institutional structures of European society while simultaneously portraying migrant workers and their descendants as 'foreigners' who do not belong in the EC. While the mass media constitute a vital component enabling social systems to function, it is important to emphasize that they also influence the way societies function by articulating their ideological and national interests.

Chomsky has argued that monopolistic control over the media in countries where the levers of power are in the hands of state bureaucracy makes it clear that the media serve the ends of a dominant élite (Chomsky, 1988: 1). It is much more difficult to see a propaganda system at work where the media are privately owned and where formal censorship is absent. In these societies élite domination of the media and the marginalization of critical discussion occurs so naturally that those engaged in the media, frequently operating with complete integrity and goodwill, are able to convince themselves that they choose and disseminate information 'objectively' and on the basis of professional values' (Chomsky, 1988: 2). In such circumstances news is not only filtered through ethnic and racial lenses but filtering constraints are often so powerful and such an integral part of the media system that alternative ways of looking at social and political issues are hardly imaginable. This is particularly noticeable in class-structured and in racially-mixed societies. In the latter, racial and ethnic minorities often begin their experience of dominant cultures as outsiders who are excluded from mainstream news-gathering and reporting and are subjected to media victimization, 'scapegoating' and misrepresentation. The media information which concerns them is filtered almost entirely through the institutions of the dominant population by members of the social majority. 'Race-thinking' as a mode for 'conceptualizing and organizing social worlds composed of persons whose differences allow for arranging them into groups that come to be labelled 'races' is clearly influencing perceptions of immigration and non-indigenous minorities in the European Community (Outlaw, 1990: 61). Thus while race has been recognized as a constitutive element in 19th century European thought and a taken-for-granted valid reference schema in the USA, it is now re-entering and being re-interpreted in European political discourse. It is no coincidence that this is happening at a time when the European Community is struggling to construct a new supra-national sense of place and sense of identity, modifying its structural dependence on Third World labour and confronting the issue of multi-culturalism and racial diversity.

'Race-thinking' is also becoming increasingly hegemonic at both national and Community level. Gramsci used this term to describe the process of structural and cultural negotiation whereby one class establishes ideological leadership over the society in general, in such a way that its ideology comes to be accepted as 'common sense' (Gramsci, 1971: 261). Hegemony clearly also describes the processes of negotiation whereby national societies defend their material and cultural interests. It could be argued that the hegemonic mass media are currently winning the consent of the majority to racial solutions for social and economic problems in contemporary Europe. They are achieving this by remaining within the framework of representative democracy and by making alternative ideas and policies favourable to multi-culturalism and racial diversity appear 'unthinkable' or unacceptable. Moreover, the consolidation of national hegemony is not the sole prerogative of the ruling class. In multi-racial and multi-ethnic Europe, racial and ethnic discourses are also mobilized to defend national boundaries, promote national moral standards and to defend national culture from internal and external 'enemies'. Cohen has shown that institutionalized racism is the product of a social class and ethnic hegemony that is so co-ordinated and sustained that the racism of one class, not necessarily the dominant class, may become the dominant or common-sense racism of society as a whole (Cohen, 1988: 26). Thus common-sense racism is an arena of intense political and ideological struggle between state racism and the practices of popular prejudice.

Recent press reports on immigration and racial tension in the European Community have done much to inform readers on the revival of the ultra-right and racism in Europe. They are also responsible for exaggerating the organized strength of ultra-right racism and ignoring other subtler forms of institutionalized racism. Certainly the tabloid press has fuelled 'common-sense' racism by encouraging a 'racial siege mentality' in the European Community. It has also contributed to the racialization of socio-political issues by extending racial meanings to new areas of social relationships in the European Community. This is particularly true of their treatment of issues such as unemployment, housing and immigration policy. 'The Liars' was the front-page headline in one tabloid newspaper when Bangladesh immigrants joined their families in Britain prior to the introduction of immigration restrictions in 1986. The so-called '1001 lies' allegedly told to *Sun* journalists were spread across the same page and, along with words like 'flood', 'hordes' and 'swamped', they recalled the anti-immigration xenophobic rhetoric of Enoch Powell in the early 1970s (Searle, 1987: 61). Similarly, press coverage of the 'race riots' in Brixton and Tottenham in 1985 suggested that racism should be redefined as something that Black aggressors practised against their White victims. Referring to 'Black rioters', one press report stated:

Either they forego the anarchic luxury of these orgies of arson, looting and murderous assaults on men and women whose task it is to uphold the laws of this land or they will provoke a paramilitary reaction unknown to mainland Britain (*Daily Mail*, 5 October 1985).

Reports like this suggested that a French-style riot control force to protect property and responsible citizens from the chronically lawless was the only solution to 'inner city revolts' in Britain and elswhere in the Community. They also placed racial minorities beyond the pale of assimilation and view these marginalized communities as the problem and reinforced the imagery that tough, rough people required a tough, rough police response. It has been argued that such aggressive attitudes towards migrant workers and their descendants are so deeply institutionalized within the EC that they underpin differential policies and strategies for dealing with racial minorities and link the political–economic processes of marginalization to the process of criminalization (Scraton, 1989: 15).

French columnists have also accused Black and Muslim minorities of refusing 'to become assimilated by a French society whose values they do not acknowledge and whose rules they refuse to respect' (*Le Figaro*, 13 June 1991). A cover story under the title of 'Get Out of Here' in a recent issue of *Time* magazine stated:

Already the face of Europe has changed. In Germany the Muslim faithful are called to worship at more than 1,000 mosques. In Italy, transitory camps for destitute migrants have sprung up around major cities. Elsewhere Filipino housemaids dust and clean in Spanish, French and Italian homes; Brazilian transvestite prostitutes work the streets of Rome. In Burgundy and the Rhone Valley region Poles and other East Europeans swell the ranks of the 62,000 seasonal workers who flock to the French vineyard and farms each year. Meanwhile, illegal immigrants from all over the former East bloc have turned the German border with Poland into a European parallel of the so-called cactus curtain along the Rio Grande which separates the U.S. from Mexico (*Time*, 26 August 1991).

The liberal press has also reported on the increasing international linkages of Europe's ultra-right who have capitalized on the threat of 'foreign invasion' and the need to 'get tough' with racial minorities in the European Community. A recent report in *The Independent* argued that British right-wing extremists were forging close ties with a German neo-Nazi organization, running paramilitary training camps and orchestrating much of the racist violence that has swept through Eastern Germany since unification (*The Independent*, 21 November 1991).

Political geography of race in the European Community

The idea of race is not a universal ideal but emerges from specific social, regional and historical circumstances where race is introduced to define and explain particular populations, not least their social behaviour and cultural practices. History and historical geography suggest that the 'idea' of race has rarely remained at the level of pure theory or 'ideology' either in the 19th century or in contemporary Europe. Although we have become accustomed to making fastidious distinctions between the ideology and social practice of racism, we should be more accurate historically if we did not do this glibly in the case of 19th century European imperialism which provided racial justifications for the annexation of colonial territory and the appropriation of most of the world's population. Said suggests that:

the distinction between an idea that one *feels* to be one's own and a piece of land that one claims by right to be one's own is really non-existent, at least in the world of nineteenth century culture out of which imperialism developed. Laying claim to an idea and laying claim to a territory were considered to be different sides of the same, essentially constitutive activity, which had the force, the prestige, and the authority of *science* (Said, 1979: 89).

It could similarly be argued that the closure of the gap between metropolitan cores and ex-colonial peripheries of the world economy and the arrival of new racial minorities in Britain, France, Germany and other European countries after World War II brought the issue of race back home to Europe. It certainly eliminated distinctions between the idea of race as an increasingly unpopular scientific category and the renewed practice of treating racial minorities as socially inferior. It was not just that the growing numbers of 'foreign' workers in France, Britain and Germany added a racial dimension to the labour forces of these countries. In an era dedicated to the elimination of anti-Semitism this gave race-thinking new political significance and created new subjects for racial victimization within Europe. This was especially obvious with the emergence of anti-immigrant racism against Asian and Black workers in Britain and France. It has also been evident in the racial victimization of Muslim communities and in criticism of *Gastarbeiter* system operating in West Germany, France, Belgium, Switzerland and the Netherlands since the 1960s. Because we still know relatively little about the geographical contexts of racism in Europe most writers prefer to talk of European racism as though it were a monolithic inheritance from the colonial past. This presumes a uniformity in responses to immigrants and their descendants from one European country to another, rather than a diversity of regional and national situations in which connections between racism and the new immigrants and their descendants were unevenly imposed (Balibar, 1991). However it is clearly possible to develop a geography of racism not just because of the diversity of social attitudes to 'foreigners', including those from Eastern Europe, but also because of the regional diversity of European racism and the intrinsic geographic nature of racism.

To understand racism in post-War Europe we should adopt the place-centered perspective applied to the geographical study of nationalism in multi-ethnic states. Such an approach would emphasize the local and communal roots of political action and examine the social psychology of intergroup and inter-racial relations from a regional perspective (Billig, 1976). Only then can we abandon the dominant perspective which regards racism in Europe as a product of innate xenophobia and a residual from our colonial past. In his criticism of European racism Phillips argues that:

Europe, at this late hour, is trying to forge a new unity through trade, despite the divisions at the heart of European consciousness, as squabbling tribes stare at each other across national boundaries. She still looks askance at 'strangers' as they alone reinforce a sense of self. Ultimately, the one certainty for Europe is that she knows a 'nigger' when she sees one: she should – they were a figment of her imagination, a product of her creative mind (Phillips, 1987: 121).

This argument reifies European racism and fails to explain its political geography and historical varieties. It is also fundamentally racist because it suggests that colour prejudice is an innate characteristic of the European psyche for which there is no remedy. Racism is treated as a quasi-universal norm; social psychological models applied not just to individuals or social groups but to national societies in Europe provide the best frameworks for analysing race and racism in the European Community. As Cohen suggests, the problem with this form of psychologism is that it promotes but does not explain notions of racism (Cohen, 1988: 97). At best it sees racism as a matter of 'false consciousness'. At worst it sees it as part of the 'natural' psychopathology of everyday life in multi-racial capitalist societies in Europe (Poliakov, 1974; Curtis, 1984).

In the 19th century, environmentalists thought that race was a quasi-ideological category for explaining global patterns of development and underdevelopment in terms of cultural differentiation which created a hierarchy of civilizations based on phenotypical characteristics of social groups. However, in contemporary Europe skin colour and phenotypical characteristics are less the distinguishing features of common-sense racism. Cultural norms, particularly those deemed traditional and 'fundamentalist' by Europeans, are increasingly used to categorize racial and non-indigenous minorities as socially inferior and consequently deserving less rights than EC citizens. The cultural and religious practices of these minorities are similarly categorized as retrogressive and taken as evidence that, despite efforts to assimilate them, the EC's 'unmeltable ethnics' and racial minorities have spurned opportunities for advancement and irrationally refused to enter the Community's progressive, open society. This idealist perspective perceives race in cultural terms and regards the cultural baggage of racial and non-indigenous minorities as barriers to assimilation. In so doing it ignores the importance of context and conjuncture to the origins of racism and abandons any pretence at historical and geographical analyses.

The concentration of racial minorities in particular regions in post-War Europe, their socio-spatial relegation to particular neighbourhoods in

European cities and their subsequent treatment in a wide variety of regional and national contexts was a conjunctural effect of specific social relations existing within Europe and between core areas of European capitalism and its European and ex-colonial peripheries. The socio-economic relegation of racial minorities to the margins of European society does not mean that they constitute a special 'people class' or 'underclass' for all times and all places. We have already suggested that this was determined by a variety of factors, including the differences in recruitment policies of European countries, their labour and industrial requirements and their settlement provisions for foreign workers. Reifications of minority social inferiority are to be resisted both because they provide positive reading of negative stereotypes of immigrant communities and because they simplify complex racial realities and falsify the historical processes responsible for their production in post-War Europe. To insist that racism is an inherent aspect or innate disposition of certain national societies in the European Community is to fail to see that even in its most entrenched and institutionalized forms it is continually being challenged, interrupted and reconstructed. As Cohen suggests, to deny racism its history is to surrender to a kind of fatalism (Cohen, 1988: 25). To deny it its geography is to ignore the role of place as the structuring and structured context of racist attitudes in a wide variety of European settings.

Frontiers, racism and grassroots nationalism

We have already suggested that the significance of racism lies in the socio-spatial extent of anti-immigrant feeling and the degree of opposition to multiculturalism in contemporary Europe. Ultra-right voting patterns in contemporary Europe are also class specific and place specific. Although we need much more detailed analysis to establish the political geography of the ultra-right in the European Community, ultra-right wing voting appears to be strongest in places that neighbour large immigrant communities rather than in racially-mixed communities. Support for the ultra right is also significant in the 'slow lane' of the 'two speed' economy, particularly in urban areas marked by industrial decline where the break up of the working class leads to the erosion of communal identities. It is precisely in such environments that foreign immigrants and their descendants often settle. Having settled, they either join a confused and apolitical underclass or, by working to preserve their own identity, feed the type of racism that sustains the ultra right. The situation is not confined to urban areas of Britain and Germany. It is also penetrating Copenhagen's Blaagaard district and extending to Nice, Lyons and the Côte d'Azur where working-class supporters of M. Le Pen resolve their 'identity crises' by opposing immigration and 'scapegoating' on migrant workers and their descendants.

The focus of modern anti-immigrant racism in these areas is only partly explainable in terms of the perceived threat of immigration, particularly of 'illegals' and asylum seekers whose numbers are quite small (*see* Figure 2.1). It is also a product of a post-Cold-War agrophobia and the feeling that the European Community is now open to an unprecedented invasion from both East and South; with the collapse of political barriers ethnic barriers must be constructed to keep out the foreigner.

Anti-immigrant voting sentiment may also be attributed to a decade or more of neo-conservative rule under right- and left-wing European governments. By abandoning the full employment and welfare policies of their predecessors and embracing an unprecedented degree of deregulation, right-wing government has created 'damaged classes' and extended 'damaged areas' throughout urban Europe. In so doing they have created conditions where racist and right-wing sentiment find expression. Thus where neo-conservative and Keynesian agendas attract little popular support, traditional ideas of race and nationality and traditional myths of 'blood and soil' have acquired new meaning and renewed significance in more and more areas in contemporary Europe. This has been aggravated by the fact that it was precisely 'community' and 'nation' that many European governments forgot when they discarded full employment and the full-scale welfare state and began to make decisions on the basis of economic advantage (Woollacott, 1991). As immigrant communities spilled across the boundaries separating them from host societies, and particularly when they asserted claims to social justice, a more aggressive form of racism emerged based on the rationale of relative deprivation. Cohen calls this a racism of 'radical disavowal' because racial minorities are attacked for seeking to acquire properties and espouse social values which European workers felt were their prerogative (Cohen, 1984: 35). This genre of grassroots racism is often indistinguishable from grassroots nationalism and can also spark off racial nationalism in minority populations as they perceive the European Community and its member states as hostile monolithic blocs. Racial integration is made more difficult as a swing away from cultural pluralism towards racism is encouraged on both sides of the racial divide. This does not mean that working-class communities are innately more racist than other social groups. However they often 'go racist' whenever and wherever the presence of racial or ethnic minorities threatens to expose the ideological structures which they construct to protect themselves from recognizing their own subordinate position.

We have already seen that a virulent, indigenous working-class xenophobia was one of the key variables in opposition to importation of migrant workers into core areas of the EC from the Third World and peripheral areas in Europe from the early 1970s. Most analysts of labour relations ignored this factor in the 1950s and 1960s and assumed the hegemony of 'rational' capital over labour. On the other hand, most governments assumed that their hegemonic control over working-class communities was beyond question and underestimated the latters' ability to oppose official immigration policy on racial and nationalist terms (Cohen, 1991: 153). Moreover, it is not because immigrants or their descendants have actually been undermining the standard of living of the indigenous working class and causing racism. It is because the crossing of the local labour and housing market brings home to indigenous classes the fact that they do not control either their jobs or their neighbourhoods; this renders the

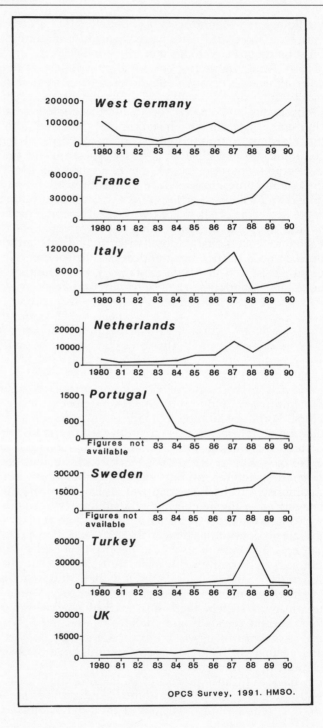

Figure 2.1
Number of people seeking asylum in selected European countries, 1980–90

immigrant presence a threat (Cohen, 1988: 34). This is why political destinies in Europe are increasingly discussed in terms of origins and the consanguinity of 'kith and kin'. In this discourse 'they', the 'foreigners', neither 'fit in' nor belong here. It also underlies similar concern to control and own one's territory, defend one's birthplace and mobilize racial/ethnic crusades to exclude 'others' from 'our' territory.

These racial and ethnic crusades are seen as frontline defences of homeland and neighbourhood in terrains contested by foreigner and native in the European Community. They seek to prevent minority populations from breaking out of racial or ethnic enclaves and call for stricter control over immigration policy. Thus ethnic crusading and the victimization of immigrant communities operates at both local and national levels. At the local level, the quasi-biological construct of community as 'kith and kin' and the proprietorial pride of working-class communities constructs places as sites of control and ownership and involves strategies of social closure. Balibar attributes this to population movements and the internationalization of social relations in the post-colonial period. He also suggests that these will lead to a rethinking of the notion of frontier and a redistribution of its mode of application. The frontier will be accorded:

a function of social propohylaxis and tie it in to more individualized statutes, while technological transformations will assign educational inequalities and intellectual hierarchies an increasingly important role in the class struggle within the perspective of a generalized techno-political selection of individuals (Balibar, 1991: 26–27).

Viewed thus, racism combined with nationalism protects the racial purity of homelands by controlling population movements between the Third World and Western Europe and creates a European political community which transcends class divisions but transverses racial divisions. The dominant themes of this genre of race thinking are not biological differences or heredity but the dangers of open frontiers, the insurmountability of cultural differences and the incompatibility of 'foreign' life-styles and traditions with the European way of life. Through the medium of 'social imagery' a distinctive body politic is being constructed which allows the working class and other subordinate groups to exercize certain forms of jurisdiction over and against each other and to invent themselves as a local 'ruling class' without either adopting ruling-class values or challenging ruling-class hegemony' (Cohen and Bains, 1988; Balibar, 1991). What Adorno termed 'identitarian thought' here develops from national crises of identity and neurosis about invasion and contributes to racism. This is being aggravated by the over-centralized decision-making at Community level and the devaluation of nationalism as a philosophy informing social and economic policy within European nation–states. Indeed, some have argued that we are not so much witnessing the construction of a 'super-state' as the passing of the traditional state in the European Community – if by state we mean a power-centralizing institution with responsibility for policy which exercizes 'public' mediation between social interests (Balibar, 1991: 7). Popular grassroots nationalism which call for a reinstatement of nationalism as the proper basis for political and economic decision-making are political strategies for filling political vacuums. The futility of this type of nationalist attitude is revealed in efforts to 'rekindle' traditional values and return to the *status quo* before the 'foreign invasion' at a time when dominant social classes in the European Community seek to transcend nationalism. Said suggests that the strengthening of ethno-nationalisms in contemporary Europe may be the result of contests and tensions between stable identities that have been cultivated, on the one hand by affirmative agencies such as nationality, education, tradition, language and religion and on the other by all sorts of marginal, alienated or, anti-systemic forces:

As one side gathers more dominance and centrality, the other is pushed further from the centre, towards either violence or new forms of authenticity like funda-mentalist religion. In any event the tension produces a frightening consolidation of patriotism, assertions of cultural superiority, mechanism of control, whose power and ineluctability reinforce the logic of identity (Said, 1988: 55–6).

Balibar insists that this situation will prevail until we know just what constitutes 'the people' in Europe and how popular sovereignty is con-ceived and organized in the European Community. He also suggests that it is necessary to 'turn away from the formula 'We are a people' or 'We are peoples' and revert to 'We are the People' and to the question: '*Was ist daas*, "*das Volk*", *in Europa?*' (Balibar, 1991: 19).

Race and ethnicity in the European Community

Although there are important distinctions between race and ethnicity that merit discussion in their own right, they are also important because new quasi-biological, ethnic constructs of what it means to be European are now being developed which are in danger of excluding racial minorities and non-indigenous, 'unmeltable' ethnics from the European Community. The question of an endogenous, self-referring definition of 'Europeans' has emerged relatively recently. With the downfall of Soviet satellites in Eastern Europe and the Balkanization of the USSR, it is clear that answers to this question are by no means settled. Prior to the mid-20th century the term ethnic European was often used exogenously to refer to groups of colonizers in the European colonial world.

Cashmore has argued that ethnicity in its contemporary form describes 'a group possessing some degree of coherence and solidarity composed of people who are, at least latently, aware of having common origins and interests' (Cashmore, 1984: 97). This suggests that an ethnic group is less a social aggregate or group-in-itself than a self-conscious social bloc or group for itself. Unlike race in contemporary Europe, ethnicity is less a 'classifi-catory category' or 'structural construct', than a 'historical happening' (Thompson, 1961: 9). It implies a process of historical individuation in that ethnic groups choose their own linguistic and cultural markers and create their own sense of identity and ethnic 'roots'. Ethnicity is not only trans-mitted from one generation to the next but changes in the process by adapting to new social and political circumstances. Race, on the other hand, particularly when used as a denigratory or pejorative term, is less a social category than an ideological construct. In contemporary Europe it tends to reflect the negative tendencies of dissociation and exclusion. Ethnicity on the other hand, especially since the post-War revival of indigenous ethnic groups, tends to reflect the positive tendencies of rootedness, identification and inclusion (Smith, 1981; Williams, 1984). Moreover, whereas in ethnic discourse 'ethnicity' is acquired and culti- vated, in contemporary European racist discourse race has all the characteristics of a pejorative category. We have already seen that it is also a denigratory category imposed on minorities to legitimize their socio- spatial exclusion from mainstream European society.

Where 'race' is still used in a 19th-century sense in extreme racist discourse to categorize minority populations in phenotypical terms, it is now more common to find cultural and religious legitimations for racial inferiority in the European Community. Thus 'race' today increasingly signifies a set of imaginary properties of inheritance which fix and legitim- ate real positions of social domination or subordination in terms of cultural differences between native and foreigner in the European Community. Similarly, while connotations of innate superiority distinguished ethnicity from race, connotations of ethnic superiority have also been associated with ethno-nationalisms such as Basque nationalism and Ulster Unionism. Ulster Unionists and the Basque people were self-categorized as both racially and ethnically superior to Spaniards or Irish people (Heiberg, 1989, 1990; MacLaughlin, 1986). However, the two terms are generally treated as essentially asymmetrical and should not be used interchangeably. When conflated with race, ethnicity tends to be reified into a set of essential defining traits – Jewishness, 'Germanness', Irishness and Blackness, for example – and ceases to be part of concrete historical processes. Instead it becomes an abstract expression of an eternal trans-historical and supra- national identity (Cohen, 1988).

In this reified form ethnicity can be exploited to create new 'imagined communities' and 'unmeltable ethnics' in the European Community (Anderson, 1983). This is particularly noticeable in the characterization of racial and non-indigenous ethnic minorities as so tradition-bound that they are incapable of coping with modernity and threaten national cultures in the European Community. Williams has shown that in the past the treat- ment of tradition and modernity as mutually exclusive and assymetrical categories led to a pejorativization of Europe's indigenous minority cul- tures and placed them at 'the wrong end of the tradition–modernity continuum' (Williams, 1980). Political geographers have clearly shown that ethno-nationalist and separatist movements in Europe have successfully challenged the inevitability of cultural assimilation by establishing formal and informal organizations of self-government in their refusal to follow the logic of modernization theory to cultural assimilation and ethnocide. Capitalizing upon linguistic and cultural characteristics to mobilize support for separatist objectives, indigenous minorities throughout the European Community have escaped pejorativization and shifted minority cultures to their proper place on the tradition–modernity continuum. Non-indigenous ethnic and racial minorities are being placed increasingly at the hostile end of the tradition–modernity continuum in contemporary Europe. Moreover, often they do not have the option of challenging assimilation and are generally in a worse position than the ethnic minorities of 19th-century Europe's age of 'big nation' nationalism (MacLaughlin, 1986a). At best they are expected to accept social inferiority and follow the logic, despite the obstacles to assimilation. At worst they are expected to repatriate back home where they belong. This is particularly true of Algerian and other Muslim minorities in France, Germany, Spain and the Netherlands. Discussing the integration problems confronted by these groups in French society, one Moroccan-born writer argued that some French people demand that young Arabs must 'make amends' and distance themselves from the Islamic values of their parents in order to be accepted into French society (Ben Jelloun, 1991). He also pointed out that successful integration was not a question of renouncing the whole fabric of social being of Islamic minorities, sweeping away the past and denying cultural origins. Such demands not only provoke annoyance among minority populations but can also rebound back on those who make them. This genre of race–thinking not only creates boundaries, between insider and outsider in contemporary Europe but suggests that the political boundaries of the European Community must be policed if they are to be maintained.

References

Adler, S. (1982), *A Turkish Conundrum: Emigration, Politics and Development*, Geneva, ILO.

Adorno, T.W. (1950), *The Authoritarian Personality*, New York, Harper.

Agnew, J.A. (1987), *Place and Politics*, London, Allen and Unwin.

Agnew, J.A. (1989), 'The Devaluation of Place in Social Science', in J.A. Agnew and J. Duncan (eds), *The Power of Place*, Boston, Unwin Hyman.

Anderson, B. (1983), *Imagined Communities: Reflections on the Origin and Spread of Nationalism*, London, Verso Press.

Appiah, K.A. (1990), 'Racisms', in D.T. Goldberg, (ed.), *Anatomy of Racism*, Minnesota, University of Minnesota Press.

Aral, B. (1990), 'Free Movement of Workers between Turkey and the European Economic Community', University of Kent, Unpublished MPhil thesis.

Balibar, E. (1991), '*Es gibt keinen staat in Europa*': 'Racism and politics in Europe today', *New Left Review*, **186**: 5–19.

Banton, M. (1982), *The Idea of Race*, London, Tavistock.

Begag, A. (1991), 'French-born Youths Originating in North African Immigration', *International Migration*, **XXVIII**, No. 3, 81–8.

Ben Jelloun, T. (1991), 'France and its New Impressionists', *The Guardian*, 12 June.

Berger, J. and Mohr, J. (1975), *A Seventh Man*, Harmondsworth, Pelican.

Bhat, A., Carr-Hill, R. and Ohri, S. (eds), (1988), *Britain's Black Population*, Aldershot, Gower.

Billig, M. (1976), *Social Psychology of Intergroup Relations*, Academic Press, New York.

Blauner, R. (1967), *Alienation and Freedom: The Factory Worker*, Chicago, University of Chicago Press.

Booth, Heather (1982), 'On the role of demography in the study of post-war migration to Western Europe', *European Demographic Information Bulletin*, vol. 13, no. 4.

Braverman, H. (1974), 'Labour and Monopoly Capital', *Monthly Review Press*, New York.

Cashmore, E.E. (1984), *Dictionary of Race and Ethnic Relations*, London, Routledge.

Castles, S. and Kosack, G. (1973), *Immigrant Workers and Class Structure in Western Europe*, London, Oxford University Press.

Castles, S., Booth, H. and Wallace, T. (1984), *Here for Good: Western Europe's New Ethnic Minorities*, London, Pluto Press.

Chomsky, N. (1988), *Culture of Terrorism*, London, Pluto Press.

Chua-Eoan, H. (1991), 'Get out of Here!', *Time Magazine*, 26 August.

Cohen, D.R. and Henderson, J.B. (1991), *Health, Prevention and Economics*, Oxford, Oxford University Press.

Cohen, P. and Bains, H.S. (1988), *Multi-racist Britain*, London, The Macmillan Press Ltd.

Cohen, R. (1991), *Contested Domains*, London, Zed Books.

Cohen, R. and Henderson, J. (1991), 'Debates in International Labour Studies', in Cohen, R. (ed.), *Contested Domains*, London, Zed Books.

Curtis, L.P. (1984), *Nothing But the Same Old Story*, London, The Macmillan Press Ltd.

Duffield, Mark (1988), 'Research Unit on Ethnic Relations, Birmingham', quoted in Castles, S. (1984), *Here for Good: Western Europe's New Ethnic Minorities*, p. 92.

Feldstein, S. (1972), *The Poisoned Tongue*, New York, William Morrow.

Fisher, P.L. and Lowenstein, R. (1968), *Race and the News Media*, New York, Praeger.

Freeman, G. (1979), *Immigrant Labour and Racial Conflict in Industrial Societies*, Princeton, Princeton University Press.

Gooch, A. (1991), 'Fascist Youth Pine for Franco', *The Independent* (18 November).

Goldberg, D.T. (ed.), (1990), *Anatomy of Racism*, Minnesota, University of Minnesota Press.

Gow, D. (1991), 'Racist Attacks Mar Unity Celebration', *The Guardian*, 4 October.

Graham, G. (1991), 'Newcomers Hit by Left, Right and Centre', *Financial Times*, 8 August.

Gramsci, A. (1971), *Selections From the Prison Notebooks*, London, Lawrence and Wishart.

Harrison, D. (1991), 'Family Hounded After "Racist" Homes Story', *The Observer*, 7 July.

Heiberg, M. (1989) *The Making of the Basque Nation*, Cambridge, Cambridge University Press.

Heiberg, M. (1990), *The Basques*, London, Routledge.

Herman, E. and Chomsky, N. (1988), *Manufacturing Consent: The Political Economy of the Mass Media*, New York, Pantheon Press.

Ignatieff, M. (1991), 'France's Born-again Fascist', *The Observer*, 8 November.

Ignatieff, M. (1991), 'The tricolor Seen in Whiter Shades of Pale', *The Observer*, 21 July.

Johnson, J.H. and Salt, J. (1990), *Labour Migration and the Internal Geographical Mobility of Labour in the Developed World*, London, David Fulton.

Kayers, B. (1977), 'The Effects of International Migration on the Geographical Distribution of Population in Europe', *Population Studies 2*, Strasbourg, Council of Europe.

Kelsey, T. and Bridge, A. (1991), 'Secret Network of Activists who Seek a Fourth Reich', *The Independent*, 21 October.

King, R. (1990), 'The social and economic geography of labour migration: from guestworkers to immigrants', in Pinder, D. (ed.), *Western Europe: Challenge and*

Change, London, Belhaven Press, pp. 162–78.

King, R. (ed.), (1993) *Mass Migrations in Europe*, London, Belhaven Press.

Knox, P. (1984) *The Geography of Western Europe: a socio-economic survey*, London, Croom Helm.

Layton, Henry, Z. (ed.), (1990), *The Political Rights of Migrant Workers in Western Europe*, London, Sage.

MacLaughlin, J. (1986a), 'The Political Geography of Nation-building and Nationalism in the Social Sciences: Structural Versus Dialectical Accounts', *Political Geography Quarterly*, **3**, No. 49, 299–329.

MacLaughlin, J. (1986b), 'State-centered Social Science and the Anarchist Critique', *Antipode*, **18**, No. 39, 11–38.

MacLaughlin, J. (1991), 'The Social Characteristic and Destinations of Recent Emigrants from Selected Regions in the West of Ireland', *Geoforum*, **22**, No. 3, 319–31.

Miles, R. (1987), *Racism and Migrant Labour*, London, Routledge and Kegan Paul.

Miles, R. and Phizaclea, A. (1987), *Labour and Racism*, London, The Macmillan Press Ltd.

Miles, R. (1987), *Capitalism and Unfree Labour*, Tavistock.

Murray, N. (1986), 'Anti-racists and Other Demons: The Press and Ideology in Thatcher's Britain', *Race and Class*, **XXVII**, No. 3, 1–19.

Nanton, P. (1991), 'National Frameworks and the Implementation of Local Policies: Is a European Model of Integration Identifiable?', *Policy and Politics*, **19**, No. 3, 191–7.

Ohri, S. (1988), 'The Politics of Racism: Statistics and Equal Opportunity', in A. Bhat, (ed.), *Britain's Black Black Population*, Aldershot, Gower.

O'Loughlin, J. (1980), 'Distribution and migration of foreigners in German cities', *Geographical Review*, **70**, 253–75.

Outlaw, L. (1990), 'Towards a critical theory of "race" ', in D.T. Goldberg (ed.), *Anatomy of Racism*, Minnesota, University of Minnesota Press.

Paine, S. (1979), 'Replacement of the West European migrant labour system by investment in the European periphery', in Seers, D., Schafer, B. and Kiljunen, M. (eds), *Underdeveloped Europe*, Hassocks, Harvester Press, pp. 89–96.

Pennix, R. (1982), 'A Critical Review of Theory and Practice: The Case of Turkey', *International Migration Review*, vol. 16, no. 4, pp. 781–815.

Phillips, C. (1987), *The European Tribe*, London, Faber.

Poliakov, L. (1980), *Casualité diabolique*, Paris, Marschsal.

Said, E.W. (1988), 'Identity, Negation and Violence', *New Left Review*, **171**: 46–60.

Said, E.W. (1990), 'Zionism From the Standpoint of its Victims', in D.T. Goldberg (ed.), *Anatomy of Racism*, Minnesota, University of Minnesota Press.

Salt, J. and Clout, H. (eds.), (1976), *Migration in Post-war Europe: geographical essays*, London, Oxford University Press.

Scott, J. and Clout, H. (1976), *Migration in Post-War Europe*, Oxford University Press, Oxford.

Scraton, P. (1989), 'The Law Unto Themselves', *The New Statesman and Society*, 28 July.

Searle, C. (1987), 'Your Daily Dose: Racism and the Sun', *Race and Class*, **XXIX**, No. 1, 55–71.

Skinner, B.F. (1965), *Science and Human Behaviour*, Glencoe, Free Press.

Smith, A.D. (1981), *The Ethnic Revival*, London, Cambridge University Press.

Stavenhagen, R. (1962 and 1970), *Agrarian Problems and Peasant Movements in Latin America*, Boston, Doubleday.

Thompson, E.P. (1963), *The Making of the English Working Class*, Harmondsworth, Pelican.

Wallerstein, I. (1991), *Geopolitics and Geoculture: Essays on the changing world-system*, Cambridge, Cambridge University Press.

White, P.E. (1984), *The West European City*, London, Longman.

Williams, C.H. (1984), 'Ideology and the Interpretation of Minority Cultures', *Political Geography Quarterly*, **3**, No. 2, 105–125.

Williams, C.H. (ed.), (1982), *National Separatism*, Cardiff, University of Wales Press.

Williams, G. (1980), 'Review of E. Allardt's *'Implications of the Ethnic Revival in Modern Industrial Society'*, *Journal of Multilingual and Multicultural Development*, **1**: 363–70.

Wilson, C.C. and Gutierrez, C. (1985), *Minorities and Media*, New York, Sage.

Woollacott, M. (1991), 'Race and Nationality Within Fat City's Gates', *The Guardian*, 16 November.

Woollacott, M. (1991), 'Cry of a Lost Community', *The Guardian*, 15 November.

3
Globalization of economic organization and the emergence of regional interstate partnerships

Philip Cooke

Introduction

Starting from the viewpoint that national movements are political rather than primarily economic expressions of the desire for autonomy means drawing attention to the questions of power and powerlessness, rule and regulation at the heart of the national question.

Power in this respect differentiates into qualities of exclusion and inclusion. Nations are objects of struggle which are created and recreated as power-bases by processes of exclusion. Modern nation formation initially excluded the popular masses, but included educated elites who defined citizenship as an exclusive property of the included. Inclusion occurs as dominant groups exert power or regulate subordinate groups' self-identification. Normally, this sense of identity is 'manufactured' in opposition to a dominant 'otherness'.

The form of inclusion in the modern nation–state can be one in which the state defines the acceptable limits of particular national identities. Often those limits include the cultural dimension but to varying degrees exclude the political and, particularly, economic dimensions. The successful modern nation–state normally, though not inevitably, became coterminous with the modern 'national economy'. The latter though, in the period of imperialism, extended to the global scale for the most successful imperializers. The designation of a common territory, language and educational/cultural base is thus a pre-condition for the successful pursuit of economic expansion. The modern nation–state is, of course, the key regulator of this process.

Hence the modern era of nation–states produces (contra pre-modern conditions) the segmented, parcelled, territorialized form of space. Expansion and inclusion also threaten oblivion to submerged nations within the modern nation–state. This may, under appropriate conditions, provoke new rounds of attempted state formation by the submerged nationalities. The modern nation–state as a regulatory form is thus inherently unstable, threatened both by external and competing successful nation–states and by internal putative neo-nation states. (For further discussion see Poulantzas, 1978; Jessop, 1982; Cooke 1989.)

Threats to the modern nation-state

During the last decades of the 20th century when modern institutions (those established or consolidated during the 15th and early 20th-century era of modern nation–state building) have been experiencing significant challenge and, in some cases, transformation, two major pressures inherent in nation–state instabilitity have come to the forefront:

(i)   the emergence of supranational state institutions with significant political power, notably the European Community (EC);
(ii) the weakening of supranational states, most obvious in the case of the submerged nations within the former Soviet multinational state (possibly also Canada).

The focus of this chapter will be on the EC, the first of these points, though the analysis also has relevance for the second point.

The dynamic in the EC is two-pronged. First, there is a weakening of national economic sovereignty by the accretion of powers hitherto located in national parliaments to the European Commission (e.g. competition policy; trade policy; monetary exchange rate policy, science, technology and research policy; even, to some extent, foreign policy). The second and, from a regionalist viewpoint, somewhat unexpected dynamic is the rapid move by some regional (i.e. sub-national) economic powers within the nation–states comprising the EC to form inter-regional, cross-boundary political alliances or agreements, primarily of an economic nature but also social and cultural within and beyond the EC. The clearest example of this is the 'Four Motors' agreement of 1988 between Baden-Württemberg, Rhône-Alpes, Lombardy and Catalonia. Key features of the 'Four Motors' regions are that:

(i)   each has a democratically elected regional governmental structure;
(ii) each is an economically dynamic non-capital-city region in its respective nation-state.

Interestingly, this combination of features is seen as providing key advantages in the Open Market of Europe. A *Financial Times* report on Rhône-Alpes states that it exemplifies the view that:

the European single market will only work on the back of cooperation between regions, irrespective of what passes between national capitals. Ironically, the creation of a single market is encouraging the region, like many of its European neighbours, to try to pull more decision-making power from a central government which it has always felt has interfered too much in local affairs (Dawkins, 1990).

Hence, deregulation of, amongst other things, national controls on foreign investment, means that regions can increasingly negotiate directly with foreign companies. The latter, of course, frequently have their own inter-firm alliances. Supranational deregulatory impulses enable regional states to regulate their own economic trajectories with more ease.

Importantly, regional governments may find themselves pushing up against nation-state constitutional constraints. In the Rhône-Alpes case, the 1982 French devolution was criticised for not going far enough. Thus regional and local politicians have been enlarging powers piecemeal. In the case of Baden-Württemberg, there has been criticism of the mercantilism and 'expansionism' of the approach of former CDU Minister President Lothar Späth in establishing something resembling a mini nation-state in its dealings with foreign governments and firms over trade, research, technology and investment decisions. Baden-Württemberg leads this new wave of politically strong regions, forming alliances not only with those already mentioned, but also with (amongst others): Portugal, Wales, Ontario, Hungary, Sachsen-Anhalt (former East Germany) and Kanagawa (Japan). See Figure 3.1.

Recent research into the Baden-Württemberg link shows:

(i)   UK growth-regions such as East Anglia or the South East of England were not selected as partners because they had no formal, regional governmental structure;
(ii) links with less-favoured regions are, in part, stimulated by overheating within Baden Württemberg's economy;
(iii) agreement covers the following: economic cooperation; technology transfer; design promotion; research; education and advanced training; youth exchanges; urban development; environmental improvements; and culture (Cooke and Morgan, 1990).

It is perhaps worth adding that this 'new politics' is not confined to Europe. A *Guardian* article (Walker, 1990) notes how the business class of Quebec has become vocal in calling for political independence within a Canadian economic union transformed by the Free Trade Treaty with the USA.

The second form of modern nation-state instability, as seen in the break-up of the Soviet-controlled buffer states of Eastern Europe and nationalist pressures from the submerged nations of the former USSR, is clearly different. In the first case, the East European nation-states deploy their political integrity as a basis for the marketization of their economies. This includes the option of joining the supranational EC union. In the case of German reunification, the former East Germany has become six new Länder (including Berlin) in the greater Germany, which is making efforts to present itself as a strongly-EC Germany.

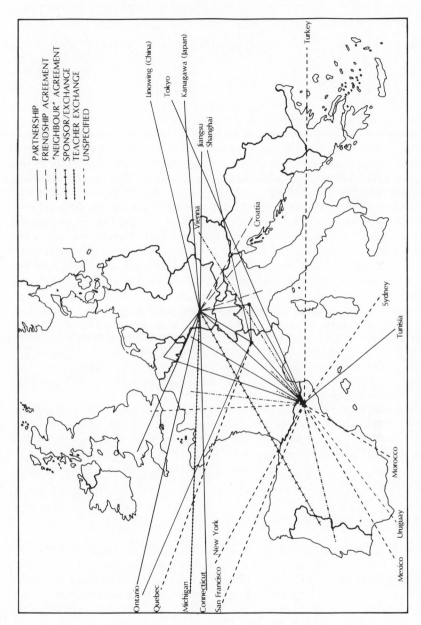

Figure 3.1 4 motors for Europe regional cooperation (including external relations)

For the former Soviet nations, the independence movements, particularly in the Baltic states, were fundamentally politico-cultural. The Baltics were economically better off than the rest of the former USSR. Their claims were to overturn what they perceived as an illegal military, thereafter political, occupation and to prevent the dilution of cultural identity by the larger Russian neighbour. This issue still rumbles on both in the Baltic and in many non-Baltic states of the new Commonwealth of Independent States, notably Moldavia.

Globalization and strategic alliances

Alliance building has by no means been confined to politically submerged nations or regions during the 1980s and 1990s. There is now a growing literature on the formation of global partnerships or alliances by business corporations (Chesnais, 1988; Mowery, 1988; Mytelka and Delapierre, 1987). Deregulation, technological convergence, and heightened competition have led to the emergence of networks of strategic alliances centred upon major corporations. To exemplify, the discussion which follows centres upon the two major American information technology (IT) corporations AT&T and IBM. Developments in Europe will be given consideration later in this chapter. Figures 3.2 and 3.3 focus upon the two US giants. It is clear that AT&T has been seeking major European partners either (as in the case of Philips and Telefonica) to 'hollow-out' these companies by getting them to market AT&T equipment in Europe, or (in the failed case of Olivetti), to acquire a product in which it is not expert, personal computers, to market in the USA. The latter argument also explains AT&T's link-ups with specialist computing companies. The partner companies also have their own alliances, often to acquire specialist electronic components.

The case of IBM is a mirror image in that it needs communications expertise, particularly to penetrate further into the European market. The failure of IBM's first efforts to become a communications and computing company are shown by its acquisition and then sale of three specialist communication firms. In future, IBM will rely on its alliance with Siemens to fill this gap.

The European dimension

Europe is a clear target for both AT&T and IBM as Japanese IT firms continue to make inroads into the American market. However, it is also clear from Figures 3.2 and 3.3 that European firms are significant nodes in alliance networks of their own. This is particularly true of Siemens and Philips. Apart from the close link between the German and Dutch companies, there is scarcely any overlap between the two US alliance networks, suggesting strongly that they are seeking to build up distinct corporate blocs of economic power within their chosen market areas (Teece, 1986). While their different strategic technological competences currently keep

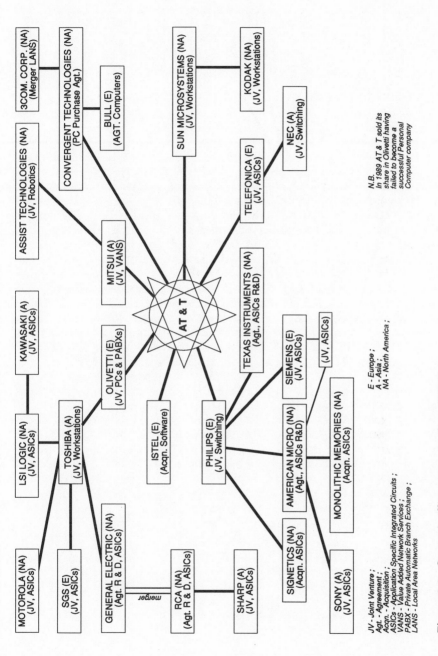

MOTOROLA (NA)
(JV, ASICs)

SGS (E)
(JV, ASICs)

GENERAL ELECTRIC (NA)
(Agt. R & D, ASICs)

RCA (NA)
(Agt. R & D, ASICs)

merger

SHARP (A)
(JV, ASICs)

LSI LOGIC (NA)
(JV, ASICs)

TOSHIBA (A)
(JV, Workstations)

OLIVETTI (E)
(JV, PCs & PABXs)

ISTEL (E)
(Acqn. Software)

PHILIPS (E)
(JV, Switching)

SIGNETICS (NA)
(Acqn. ASICs)

SONY (A)
(JV, ASICs)

MONOLITHIC MEMORIES (NA)
(Acqn. ASICs)

AMERICAN MICRO (NA)
(Agt., ASICs R&D)

SIEMENS (E)
(JV, ASICs)

(JV, ASICs)

TEXAS INSTRUMENTS (NA)
(Agt., ASICs R&D)

KAWASAKI (A)
(JV, ASICs)

ASSIST TECHNOLOGIES (NA)
(JV, Robotics)

MITSUI (A)
(JV, VANS)

AT & T

3COM. CORP. (NA)
(Merger LANs)

CONVERGENT TECHNOLOGIES (NA)
(PC Purchase Agt.)

BULL (E)
(AGT. Computers)

SUN MICROSYSTEMS (NA)
(JV, Workstations)

KODAK (NA)
(JV, Workstations)

TELEFONICA (E)
(JV, ASICs)

NEC (A)
(JV, Switching)

JV - Joint Venture ;
Agt. - Agreement ;
Acqn. - Acquisition ;
ASICs - Application Specific Integrated Circuits ;
VANS - Value Added Network Services ;
PABX - Private Automatic Branch Exchange ;
LANS - Local Area Networks

E - Europe ;
A - Asia ;
NA - North America ;

N.B.
In 1989 AT & T sold its
share in Olivetti having
failed to become a
successful Personal
Computer company

Figure 3.2   Strategic alliances centred on AT&T

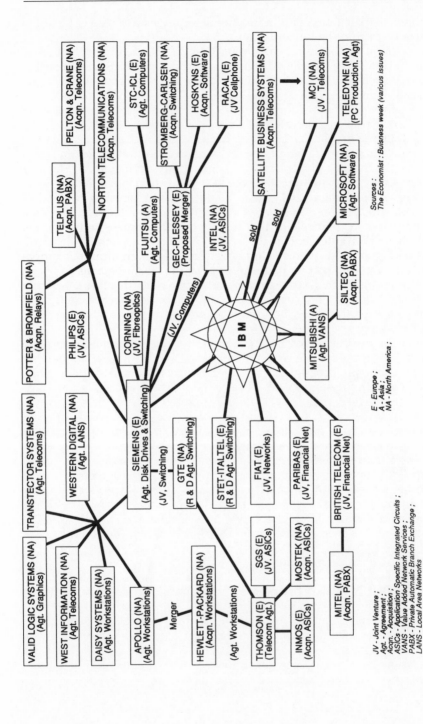

Figure 3.3 Strategic alliances centred on IBM

JV - Joint Venture ;
Agt. - Agreement ;
Acqn. - Acquisition ;
ASICs - Application Specific Integrated Circuits ;
VANS - Value Added Network Services ;
PABX - Private Automatic Branch Exchange ;
LANS - Local Area Networks

E - Europe ;
A - Asia ;
NA - North America ;

Sources :
The Economist : Buisness week (various issues)

their direct market areas apart in functional terms, each perceives the other as a major threat in the longer term.

The position of the European prime movers, Siemens and Philips, is different. They have developed tightly-linked partnerships, pulling other sub-nodes such as that of the Franco–Italian alliance Thomson–SGS and the British pair of 'hostile brothers' GEC and Plessey (now merged with Siemens) towards them (Morgan et al, 1989). This is unquestionably an effort to construct a defensive alliance against both AT&T and IBM's attempts at domination by building 'Fortress Europe' against American and, more importantly, Japanese competitors. The mixed geographical origin of the European partners' alliances is testimony to the historic development of their attempts to come to terms with relative technological backwardness in certain key IT areas. Thus most of Philips' early alliances were with American semiconductor companies in an attempt to upgrade the company's expertise in that competence. Siemens entered the American market enter but in the mid-1980s made a plethora of acquisitions and agreements with smaller American telecommunications companies as a base for marketing its technology in the USA. Siemens has been quite successful in that strategy, selling switches to the Bell Operating Companies (Soete & Von Tunzelmann, 1987). However, while continuing to pursue US market share, both have begun to turn their attention more towards Europe.

One of the devices which has facilitated intra-European IT cooperation has been EC support of pre-competitive research collaboration through the European Strategic Programme for Research in Information Technology (ESPRIT) and the Research and Development in Advanced Communications Technologies in Europe (RACE) programmes. At their inception these programmes were seen as rather weak reeds upon which to build competitive strength but, they have assisted the development of a European counter-thrust to American and Japanese hegemony. A recent study (Mytelka and Delapierre, 1987) shows that, from limited beginnings, the top 12 European C&C companies now have 71 R&D agreements with each other and 41 with other EC companies. These alliances easily outweigh in number those with American and Japanese firms. The Single European Market should both strengthen these links and, possibly, tilt the balance of dependence on IBM and AT&T in a different direction.

The 'Four Motors' programme

In the context of global partnering by business corporations, a recent political initiative marking a breakthrough in regional development thinking has been the EC 'Four Motors for Europe' programme. Under the heading 'Science, Technology and Social and Economic Cohesion in the European Community', DG XII–H–3 and DGXVI–A–1 of the European Commission have been cooperating with: Conseil Régional de la Région Rhône-Alpes; Generalitat de Catalunya; Giunta Regionale, Regione Lombardia; and Ministerium für Wirtschaft, Mittlestand und Technologie Baden-Wurttemberg under the Forecasting and Assessment in Science and

Technology (FAST) programme to assess the prospects for greater inter-regional cooperation in the spheres of technology transfer, science and technology policy, research and development. It is important to recognize that this is the EC's part of the process of inter-regional partnering. The regions themselves have their own separate agendas which are much broader than the narrow technical remit of the FAST programme.

The background to 'Four Motors' is the perception of new economic conditions such as heightened international competition, global partnering by multinational capital, scarcities of resources, lower economic growth rates, structural economic change and unemployment which pose new challenges and opportunities for the economic and social development of industrial societies. Part of this complex of changes impinges significantly upon regional and urban inequalities. Advanced technological activity tends to concentrate in leading regions, leaving other regions in a more dependent, relatively less-developed condition. The EC is constitutionally committed to minimizing economic and social imbalances and is seeking new ways of achieving this as part of the aims of the integrated internal market. So trans-border cooperation, especially in the technological field of development, is being sought.

This approach marks a new direction in EC regional policy thinking for the 1990s and can be compared with the idea of 'mobilising indigenous development potential' which was a strong theme of EC regional policy in the 1980s. This in turn, was a response to and perhaps a reaction against the policy of encouraging inward investment of a rather undifferentiated kind, characteristic of the 1970s, once international capital mobility entered decline after the oil shocks and consequent early 1980s recession. A key feature of the new thinking is the statement that 'European diversity is represented by territories and regions and not merely by individuals as is the case in a melting-pot society such as the USA'. Furthermore, '. . . by cooperation with partners representing different modes of using and diffusing new technology and new knowledge, the EC would be able to increase the social and economic cohesion of the Community, and give new impulse to European innovation and development trends in territories and regions' (Hingel, 1990).

Thus the key to EC thinking as is reflected in the Four Motors pro-gramme is that interregional technological and industrial cooperation will not reduce the diversity of the involved regions but will use and enhance it. Regions will not be encouraged towards uniformity, rather they will be helped to maximise comparative advantage. The initial Four Motors study has two key functions:

(i)   to test the hypothesis that interregional cooperation can improve cohe-sion, innovation potential and competitiveness while enhancing diversity;
(ii) to recommend appropriate approaches, measures and recipients of promotional instruments;

This builds on the fact that European (and non-European) regions have already embarked on interregional cooperation, most notably Baden-Württemberg. Among the aims of existing partnerships are:

(i)   the strengthening of scientific transfer and cooperation between appropriate individual research institutes in partner regions;
(ii) the promotion of transborder cooperation between industry and science in general;
(iii) the establishment of new international technology contacts to learn from partners and, by using local assets, to further the different potentialities of partner regions.

The Four Motors for Europe initiative began in 1987, building upon the idea of innovative decentralism in a context of regional federation. The predominant aim has been to build up an R&D network subnationally. This network includes suppliers, customers, export-brokers, universities, polytechnics and consultants. The strongest links so far are those developed between Baden-Württemberg and Rhône-Alpes. The danger of the Four Motors becoming a 'club for the rich' is recognized. Hence, the present phase of the programme includes non-motor regions such as Crete, Apulia and Wales (who in July 1990 received observer status in the FAST-Four Motors programme).

Research is now under way in the FAST Four Motors programme to establish the following aspects of a co-operative performance:

1. The development and significance of partnering measured by existing cooperative projects.
2. The methods, motivations and obstacles in cooperative ventures.
3. The expertise of the different partnering regions.
4. Conditions for success of diverse cooperations.
5. Assessment of the role of diversity in successful cooperation projects.
6. The long-term effects of cooperation on existing regional diversity in economic and technological development.
7. The prospects for building on such forms of partnership in future.
8. Suggestions for future possible developmental profiles of existing regional networks.

The results of the first empirical exercize on existing cooperative scientific and technological projects between the Four Motor regions are presented in Table 3.1.

It is clear that the level of cooperation between the regions is not great at present though links are developing, most notably between universities on research projects, some of which do not involve the region which took most of the early initiatives – BadenWürttemberg.

In parallel with the 'Four Motors' programme, the related European and non-European regional cooperation arrangements continue to develop. This was expressed at the meeting in Dresden in July 1990 of all the regions involved in links with Baden-Württemberg. An indication of the range of such links (as well as those of the 'Four Motors' regions) is given in Figure

Table 3.1   Four Motors for Europe Cooperations 1990

Subject of cooperation	Participants				Status	Institute involved
	Govt	R&D Inst.	Industry	Other		
4 Motors 'Expo'	BW, Cat. L, RA	BW, Cat. L, RA			Government-promoted	IReR, ISI, CERAT, UAB
Fibre Optics + Optronics	BW RA	BW RA	BW RA		Government-promoted	ISI, CERAT
Science & Technology Policy Workshop	BW, Cat. L, RA				Government-promoted	IReR, ISI, CERAT, UAB
Cooperation of CESTEC and Steinbeis Fndn.			BW L	BW L	Technology-transfer agencies	ISI, IReR
Karlsruhe Univ. + Univs. of RA	BW RA	BW RA			Universities + Fraunhofer Inst.	ISI, CERAT
Anti-Doping Tests	Cat. RA	Cat. RA			Universities	UAB, CERAT
Computer Services	Cat. RA	Cat. RA			Universities	UAB, CERAT

Note: Instituto Regionale di Ricerca, Milan (IReR); Centre de Recherche sur le Politique, L'Administration et le Territoire (CERAT); Universidade Autonomia de Barcelona (UAB); Fraunholer Institute for Systems and Innovation Research, Karlsruhe (ISI).
Source: ISI (1990)

3.1. page 52 or above. A key element of the European part of this network is the European High Technology Confederation, entered by Wales upon signature of its partnership agreement with Baden-Württemberg in March 1990. Potentially, Wales becomes a 'Fifth Motor' since the Confederation is centred upon the existing partnership arrangements of the Four Motors programme. The broad aims of the Confederation are to assist firms in the partner regions who are seeking locations or joint ventures in other parts of Europe. Such firms can expect to receive appropriate information about sites, possible inter-firm supplier links and other development resources available in the partner regions. It is plain that inter-regional cooperation will remain high on the policy agenda of these regions during the 1990s. The task ahead for regional governmental and private-sector agencies and institutions is to take advantage of the new environment to forge active links to their mutual benefit in the European Single Market.

Conclusions

What to make of these changes?

1. It is clear that the modern nation–states in the familiar forms of the 19th

and 20th centuries are not about to disappear. The UK government's discovery in 1992 of 'subsidiarity' as a defence of the *status quo* testifies to this, despite the illogicality of using the concept both to limit centralism from Brussels and to enhance it for London! No nation–state will give up political sovereignty, though some economic powers normally assigned to nation–states have been eroded, especially by the Free Trade Act between Canada and the USA and, in the EC, by the Single Market 1992 legislation.

2. Deregulation – the removal or relaxation of politically-imposed controls on economic functions – has created uncertainties which led firms and later regions to form partnerships with selected others as a partial means of re-regulating their developmental trajectories (Cooke, 1988). In this case, the regulation can be seen as an attempt to retain and develop particular, locally-perceived economic advantage, and to help overcome some of the negative externalities of economic success.

3. Such expressions of the desire for an increased level of self-determination are clearly power struggles either with exclusionary intent (closing part of the space of an overpowerful, centralized nation–state) or inclusionary intent (aiming to be part of a 'growth-region in-crowd').

4. As such, the appropriate mechanisms through which change is sought or effected are political rather than fundamentally economic (e.g. the firm). This is shown by the necessary condition of relative political autonomy conditioning the Four Motors example. Economic interest is a powerful but by no means exclusive motive for the changes being pursued.

5. Because they are so recent, it is too early to say how important these regionalist tendencies are with respect to the weakening of the nation–state. Unless the supranational state overrides the nation–state to grant the regional state apparata greater powers than the nation–states are willing to do, it seems likely that regionalist power struggles will produce piecemeal and uneven forms of spatial economic development. Nevertheless, it is also clear that some regions see inter-regional cooperation as an important method of bypassing some central state powers while accruing or assuming others to their own sub-national states. Despite the fact that these are turbulent times, rumours of the demise of the modern nation–state may turn out to have been greatly exaggerated.

References

Chesnais, F. (1988), 'Technical Cooperation Agreements Between Firms' *STI Review* **9**: 52–115.

Cooke, P. (1988), 'Flexible Integration, Scope Economies and Strategic Alliances', *Society & Space*, **6**: 281–300.

Cooke, P. (1989), 'Nation, Space, Modernity,' in R. Peet and N. Thrift (eds), *New Models in Geography*, London, Unwin Hyman.

Cooke, P. & Morgan K. (1990), 'Learning Through Networking: Regional Innovation and the Lessons of Baden-Württemberg', *RIR Report No. 5*, Cardiff, UWCC.

Dawkins, W. (1990), 'Rhône–Alpes: a Spirit of Independence, *Financial Times*, (27 March).

Hingel, A. (1990), 'Diversity, Equality and Community Cohesion', *FAST Working Paper PD 1/01*, Brussels.

Jessop, B. (1982), *The Capitalist State*, Oxford, Martin Robertson.

Morgan, K., Harbor, B., Hobday, M., Von Tunzelmann, N. and Walker, W. (1989), 'The GEC–Siemens Bid for Plessey: the Wider European Issues', *Centre for Information and Communication Technologies Working Paper 2*, Sussex, University of Sussex Science Policy Research Unit.

Mowery, D. (ed.), (1988), *International Collaborative Ventures in US Manufacturing*, Cambridge, Ballinger.

Mytelka, L. & Delapierre, M. (1987), 'The Alliance Strategies of European Firms in the Information Technology Industry and the Role of ESPRIT', *Journal of Common Market Studies*, **26**: 231–53.

Poulantzas, N. (1978), *State, Power, Socialism*, London, New Left Books.

Soete, L. & Von Tunzelmann, N. (1987), 'Diffusion and Market Structure with Converging Technologies', (mimeo) Sussex, University of Sussex Science Policy Research Unit.

Teece, D. (1986), 'Profiting from Technological Innovation: Implications for Integration, Collaboration, Licensing and Public Policy', *Research Policy*, **15**: 285–305.

Walker, M. (1990), 'Business Confidence Boosts Campaign for Free Quebec', *The Guardian* (27 March).

4
'New nationalism' in an old state: Scotland and the UK in the 1980s

Ronan Paddison

In what is widely accepted to be an increasingly interdependent global capitalist economy, the resurgence of nationalism poses an apparent contradiction. With its emphasis on social and cultural exclusion and its ambition of delimiting the territorial and sovereign limits of political authority, nationalism and, indeed, the nation–state would seem dysfunctional to the needs of international capital. While within earlier phases of capitalist development nationalism (as a socially binding ideology), and the nation–state (as the territorial arena within which political control and regulation could be organized), functioned as effective and necessary supports for accumulation their continued role in an increasingly internationalized economy has become questioned, not least by the rise of new power centres, supranational governmental organizations and transnational corporations (Hobsbawm, 1975).

Such a contradiction may be more apparent than real for several reasons. As much as the long-term effects of capitalism have unified economic space, its unfolding has had politically divisive effects on the world map. The impress of colonialism in the 19th century and its aftermath in decolonization, and the spread of nationalist agitation founded on uneven development are among a number of historical processes linking the development of capitalism to the subdivision of the world map and the proliferation of states. Once the social construct of ethnicity was allied to the demands of nationalism, beginning effectively in the latter half of the 19th century, the probability of further fragmentation of the world map was greatly enhanced. Nor was the spread of modernity to reduce the salience of ethnicity, as social theorists were to assume (Lipset and Rokkan, 1967: 1–64; Birch, 1989). Rather, the effects of modernization were to modernize ethnic difference renewing the demands for national self-determination in 'old' states and to increase the prospects of further fragmentation.

While the predictions of the left of the end of nationalism and of the nation–state would appear to be premature, the nature of both has shifted under the influence of growing forces of internationalization (Held, 1988). Perhaps the most obvious of these has been the undermining of the sovereignty of the state – the monopoly right of the state to secure legal and military control within the national territory. Equally, such a term as 'national economy' has lost some of its currency with the development of international organizations and globalizing networks of economic transactions, many of which function beyond the limits of state control. Care needs to be taken not to over-exaggerate such arguments – the nation–state remains a key political site and has retained much of its national sovereignty. Rather, as Jessop (1992) has suggested, the key shift lies in the more limited abilities of the state to project its power even within its own national boundaries.

'New nationalism' will need to take account of the shifts in sovereignty. Thus, while 'old' nationalism was linked fundamentally to the sovereignty of the state, in the contemporary world such a claim is more difficult to sustain, an argument which understandably has increasing currency as the number of states increases. Hobsbawm's argument that in a 'Europe of nations' determined along Wilsonian lines 'the first thing most such hypothetical new European states would do is . . . apply for admission to the EC, which would once again limit their sovereign rights' (Hobsbawn, 1990: 177) was to be reflected exactly by the slogan of the Scottish Nationalist Party in the late 1980s 'Scotland's Future: Independence in Europe'. Yet Hobsbawm misses the point in suggesting that such a settlement is hardly likely to be 'lasting' or that it compromises the claim to sovereignty. As a measure of the new realism with which small nations (and many of their larger counterparts) need to come to terms, such an association was broached 'voluntarily' by the nationalist party. Implicit within the nationalist slogan is a growing recognition of the dynamic, complex restructuring of powers taking place within contemporary Europe, upwards to supranational institutions, downwards to the locality, and horizontally between localities and regions in new trans-border fora which bypass the state, each of which is represented in the developing labyrinth of EC organizations. The nationalist party's new claim to independence represented an attempt to take advantage of the new opportunities created by the European dimension; new nationalism is expressed in terms of Euro-nationalism, in which membership of the supranational organization is seen not only as a constraint on the sovereignty of the small nation-state but also as a safeguard.

Predictably, the changes implicit in these processes become the contested ground for the nation–state, as the post-Maastricht debates were to illustrate. Partly because of its continued role as the institutional site within which political conflicts are centred, but more because such a restructuring of powers threatens to erode further its capacity to govern, the discourse has focused around the sovereignty of the nation–state. Among the EC member states, with their different political traditions, the articulation of such a discourse has differed: in France through nationalism; in the UK through the sovereignty of parliament. For sub-state nationalism and regionalism the implications are twofold – as much as its development is being (and will be) influenced by supranational institutions as well as its own ability to mobilize local support, the disposition of the nation–state will be decisive. Second, because of the differing political trajectories of the nation–states, themselves varying within volatile international and domestic environments, responses to sub-state territorial demands for greater autonomy will vary. This is already apparent from the differing nature of regional government and administration in Europe (Keating, 1988).

Within such a complex and dynamic framework predicting likely outcomes of how the political map may develop is hazardous. This is not to deny the place of normative analysis. Rather it is to emphasize that such constructs as the 'Europe des régions', still more that of regionalism as developed by its proponents (de Rougemont, 1984), remain visionary and polemic statements which fail to show how such a destination will be reached. What is obvious is that a regionalizing Europe represents a further threat to the power base of the state, precisely the reason why the extrapolation of such a process is uncertain.

While the emergence of the European dimension has presented an opportunity, if somewhat ill-defined, for the construction by Scottish nationalists of 'new nationalism', the contest for independence remains firmly rooted within the state. Within Scotland, following a decade in which apparent mounting disaffection with the central state was matched by demands for political autonomy, and, for some, outright secession, the paradox is that both had become a more rather than a less remote possibility after the 1992 election. Critical here is the electoral hegemony of the Conservative Party and its ideological commitment to the Unionist cause.

More fundamentally, however, it is to be linked to the particular nature of Scottish nationalism and its limited, if recently growing, support for the nationalist cause. (The nationalist party attracted 21 per cent of the popular vote in the 1992 General Election compared to 14 per cent in 1987.) This, in turn, can be traced to the 'flawed' national identity of the Scots, whose dual nationalism undermines the ability of nationalist elites to mobilize mass support, even during a period in which the union of Scotland within the British state is being increasingly questioned. Before examining more closely the reasoning behind this argument it will be useful to look at the wider contexts in which secession has arisen within the evolving state system.

The limits to secession

Historically, the long-term trend has been one of the growth in the number of independent states, the process unfolding in a cyclical fashion in which a period of relatively rapid state creation has been followed by a longer phase in which the new (and pre-existing) states have sought to consolidate their position. The collapse of communism and the ending of the Cold-War stalemate ushered in the 'fourth phase' of modern state creation, a sequence which had begun in Latin America in the 19th century, continued in the aftermath of World War I with the application of Wilsonian self-determination to the nations of Eastern Europe, an ideal which was subsequently to be extended to the newest nation-states of Africa, Asia, the Caribbean and the Pacific in the post-War decades. What is apparent from this history is that each burst of state creation has accompanied the dismantling of empire, the most recent phase differing by virtue of the speed by which the reterritorialization of political space took place following the collapse of the Soviet hegemony in Eastern Europe and the failed coup in Moscow of August 1991. This most recent phase·had further established the durability of ethnic identity and its translation to the nationalist cause; communist regimes had suppressed ethnic differences but had failed to supersede them.

Much of the appeal of nationalism is rooted in the argument of political legitimacy, the promise it holds for the nationalist of capturing political control and the benefits, material and otherwise, which this harbours. Yet as much as national self-determination in the wake of the dismantling of empire has corrected the most obvious violation of the nationalist principle, how this has unfolded in each of the phases of modern state creation (with the possible exception of the earliest in Latin America) has fallen far short of creating nation-states *sensu stricto*. Typically, this is because of the minorities problem (Cobban, 1945) where, as in Europe, national groups had become scrambled or, as in the case of Africa, colonialism had acted not only to foster ethnic differences but had resulted in multi-ethnic states. As the process of state creation could never be conducted under the conditions of a *tabula rosa* there was little possibility of drawing boundaries congruent with the aspirations of the separate nationalist groups or without incorporating within the new states minority populations. Ironically, the ideal of national self-determination, the matching of libertarian ideals with political reality, harboured the danger of tyranny and the continued violation of the very principle which it sought to redress.

Each phase of modern state creation, and nowhere more so than in the most recent case, has been accompanied by an upsurge in political conflict, where rival nationalist groups compete for territorial space and advantage or where incorporated minorities within the new states strive for secession. Given the powerful demonstration effects of nationalism and the zero-sum nature of the outcome it could hardly be otherwise. Yet following the creation of new states the tendency is for boundaries to harden and for subsequent secession movements to fail, at least by the route of non-violence. Recent events in World War II have exaggerated the potential for secession in other geopolitical regions. Within the modern state system it is limited (Mayall, 1990). Certainly the conditions underlying its success within the break-up of the Soviet Empire are not likely to be replicated elsewhere. Yet the 'fourth wave' has had powerful demonstration effects, not only within the developing world but also amongst nationalist movements in the older states of the First World. That in the Baltic the Estonians and others have won their own nation–states, and have done so with international approval, suggests at the least that smallness is not necessarily an obstacle to gaining statehood.

Within Western Europe the 'failure' of secession is a lesson which has already been learned. In spite of the resurgence of peripheral nationalism in a number of the old multi-nation states of Western Europe, in each case secession has been successfully resisted. The pattern confirms a longer term historical trend. Thus, in the period between 1875 and 1945, 15 new states were added to the European political map, though only 2 were in Western Europe (Norway and Ireland), the rest being in Eastern Europe and established following the break-up of empire. Similarly, in the 40 years after 1945 8 new states have been established through secession, though most are small island states and/or former colonies at the geographical margins of the continent.

Several factors can be used to help explain the paradox: the ability of the central state to 'buy off' peripheral demands, or, if it is seen as necessary, to suppress them; the inability of nationalist élites and political parties to mobilize ethnic protest successfully; the failure to attract international support for the cause of peripheral separatism; the blurring and possible weakening of national identities through the accentuation of alternative territorial identities; internal splits between nationalists in terms of their political objectives, some seeking outright secession while others seek local autonomy within continued membership of the over-arching state. Each can be evidenced in particular cases ,though more usually it is a combination of such factors that helps to explain the failure of secessionist nationalism. Here, 'failure' is a term which needs to be qualified, not least because it is precisely these nationalist (and regionalist) demands which help to explain why in much of Western Europe within the last two decades there has been an underlying trend towards political decentralization, developments which have been broadly encouraged by supra-national (European) agencies. The extent to which such regional reforms have radically restructured the territorial state is more debatable. Yet even where they have, as in Belgium, the federalizing of the state has effectively countered its political break-up.

Such regional decentralization measures represent new positive-sum solutions to the continuing problem of centre-periphery relations, a response to peripheral demands while maintaining the territorial integrity of the state. In effect, regional government has become the means by which the centralized state–nations of Western Europe have been able to counter secessionist movements.

The alienating of Scotland

The UK state is the major exception to these trends. Unlike the other major West European states in the 1980s, and indeed most of the economically advanced nations, the UK state bucked the trend towards regional decentralization by becoming emphatically more centralized. As two political scientists were colourfully to suggest barely half-way through the Thatcher decade 'Britain stands within sight of a form of government which is more highly centralized than anything this side of East Germany' (Newton and Karran, 1985: 129). Predictably, it was a trend which sparked territorial protest, from the English regions as well as the peripheral nations, though this had little effect in halting the process of state centralism, which in turn compounded territorial disaffection with the central state.

The political alienation of periphery from core in Thatcher's Britain became most salient in Scotland. Several factors help to explain here. In a centralizing UK state, it could be argued that Scotland had more to 'lose' potentially than the other British 'regions' both because of its greater sense of individuality and because of the erosive effects centralization would have on its established measure of administrative devolution which had been used to maintain and foster its territorial distinctiveness. Added to this was the perception in Scotland that because a Tory British state had achieved electoral hegemony over an anti-Tory Scotland – the Doomsday scenario, as the nationalists labelled it in the lead up to the 1987 election – Thatcherism lacked an electoral mandate within Scotland.

The roots of the conflict stem from the particular nature of the multi-nation British state and of the changing relationships of Scotland within it. Historically, demographically and politically the British state has been dominated by England. As recently argued (Taylor, 1993), it is a particular part of England, the 'Crown Heartland', which was to establish its hegemony over the British state which is of less immediate concern to Scotland than it is to England *per se*. The contradiction of the British multi-nation state is that the English conflate England with Britain. Thus, unlike the dual identities of the Scots and the Welsh, the English are 'Anglo-British', a fused identity 'in which there is little sense of Britishness being a natural, additional dimension beyond Englishness' (Osmond, 1988:36). Even then, within the dominantly English Charter 88, a Bill of Rights, there was no specific acknowledgement of the UK being a multi-nation state, while the territorial division of powers was talked of loosely in terms of establishing 'an equitable distribution . . . between local, regional and national government'.

Added to this is the position of Scotland within the UK. As argued by Midwinter *et al* (1991), acceptance of the Union (which completed the establishment of the British state in 1707) has never been an absolute. Rather, it has been contingent of the changing relationships Scotland has had as a member of the British state. It is a relationship whose progress has fluctuated. During the middle of the 19th century, at a time of rapid industrialization, it is salutary to recall that it was from Scotland that the term 'North Briton' was coined to describe the Scots. Later, periodic outbursts of nationalist agitation were to seek concessions from the British state which would help to ensure its political and cultural identity. In the 1880s, 1920s, 1940s and, most recently, 1970s a limited autonomy has been successively added to through the establishment of administrative insti-tutions and their subsequent strengthening so that (with few exceptions) all domestic affairs are administered through the Scottish Office. Such developments were the result of bargaining and compromise between unequal partners (Paterson, 1992: 104–122). Their result was to contribute to the maintenance of a separate Scottish identity and, consequently, to counter its anglicization.

Within Scotland it was the apparent 'suppression' of the separate Scottish identity during the Thatcher decade, and the increasing influence of anglicization, that contributed to the development of nationalist feeling. For its proponents Thatcherism was conceived in British terms; for its opponents in the Scottish anti-Tory periphery it was an English 'solution'. Precisely because of the fused identity of the English the programme of reform was being presented as a British solution, compromising the separateness of Scotland. As Nicholas Ridley, one of the more outspoken of Thatcher's ministers, was to put it:

The Scots have fastened on their separate identity as a nation to try and establish that somehow all this (the Thatcherite reforms) does not apply to them, whereas the northern English – who are not perhaps so well off as the Scots – have accepted that they are part of England. . . . I hope that the Scots will join them because it will be to the benefit of the Scots. I don't think they can go on having a different political philosophy and at the same time expect to benefit economically like the rest of us. You cannot have it both ways . . . (*The Scotsman*, 2 May 1988; in Nairn, 1989: 245)

In other words, the Scots should become English.

In Scotland the Thatcherite project of shrinking the role of the state, reducing public expenditure, extending marketization and privatization and reducing the power of intermediate institutions, particularly local government, was to be even more contentious than elsewhere in Britain. In part, this can be traced to the problems predicted by the Doomsday effect, the claim that a Conservative-led British administration lacked legitimacy in Scotland where fewer than a quarter of the electorate had voted Conservative (as in 1987) and where an even smaller proportion of the country's MPs belonged to the ruling party.

It was more the detail of what Thatcherism aimed to achieve as well as its centralizing effects that was to be opposed by a substantial section of the Scottish electorate. Thus, in their assault on collectivism the reforms ran counter to one of the 'markers' of Scottish political identity. On such issues as housing not only was there a markedly different and greater pattern of state dependence in Scotland than in England, and particularly Southern England, but, as opinion poll evidence suggested, these differences were part of deeper-seated regional variations in political values (*see* Table 4.1). Furthermore, in reducing the capacity of local government to provide for the demands of collective consumption, an important bulwark against (English) centralism had been undermined – urban Scotland had been traditionally Labour and local government had acted as a 'territorial check'.

Reflecting these different value positions, the issues around which elections were fought in Scotland tended to differ from those in England. While in the 1992 election unemployment was considered the key issue throughout Britain followed by debates over the provision of collective consumption services, in Scotland the question of local government taxation, centring on opposition to the community charge (or poll tax), was

Table 4.1   Value positions on collectivism: Scotland, England and Wales, 1989

Which of these comes closest to the ideal country for you and your family?	Percentage	
	Scots	English and Welsh
A country in which private interest and a free market economy are more important	21	30
A country which emphasizes the social and collective provision of welfare	60	54
A country in which the individual is encouraged to look after himself/herself	33	38

Source: The Scotsman, 6 May 1989

consistently signalled as more important in opinion polls than was to be the case in England. Opposition to the tax had centred initially on its earlier 'experimental' implementation to Scotland, as well as its perceived unfairness. The campaign was to gather strength as a tax revolt through deliberate non-payment. Differences are also apparent too in the Scottish reaction to other reforms such as the opt-out right given to schools, releasing them from local authority financial control and providing their funding direct from central government. While English response to the legislation within the first years after the reform (in 1988) was slow, in Scotland after four years only a handful of local schools had sought to take up the right, and none had done so successfully.

As a direct reflection of the alienating of Scotland in the 1980s there was a growing demand not only for greater autonomy but also for independence, as measured in successive opinion polls. In the period immediately before the 1979 referendum only some 15 per cent of the electorate favoured independence (though a far larger proportion favoured regional autonomy), by the mid-1980s this had climbed to nearer 30 per cent and in the latter half of the decade it averaged closer to 35 per cent. Even among Scottish Conservative voters whose natural loyalties lay with the maintenance of the Union, more than half favoured greater autonomy, while overall those favouring the constitutional *status quo* were progressively marginalized to approximately a quarter of the electorate. The most striking conclusion from the opinion poll evidence was the surge in support for independence. 'In the 80s . . . despite the Scottish Nationalist Party being marginalised for the first part of the decade and despite the issue of independence being equally off the political agenda . . . the Scottish people of their own accord started making a very fundamental shift in their attitudes which reflected a far more deep-seated growing divide between Scotland and England' (Mclean, in McCrone, 1989:20).

Such opinion poll evidence needs to be interpreted cautiously. As with the rediscovered federalist term subsidiarity within the post-Maastricht debate, local autonomy has a degree both of 'natural' appeal and justification with which it may be difficult to disagree. Further, expressing a preference for greater local autonomy is one thing; whether as a specific objective it has political salience is another. Asked what were the main issues likely to influence their voting choice in the 1992 election, Scottish voters consistently placed economic or collective consumption questions before those of constitutional reform. The question of where political authority resides in a territorial sense appears to be of less influence than more material concerns.

There is no necessary contradiction between this conclusion and the argument that during the 1980s there was a re-assertion of Scottish natio-nalism which became expressed through a desire for greater political autonomy. Rather, it reflects the complex patterning of loyalties and econ-omic interdependencies within a multi-nation state. If 'new nationalists' are willing to compromise the principle of sovereignty for the perceived benefits of membership of a strengthened European Community – and voters in Scotland were consistent in favouring 'independence within a united Europe' over that of the 'wholly independent' option – it is at least plausible that the same holds for continued membership of the old multi-nation state, providing it has the institutional capacity to meet decentralist demands.

Put another way, nationalist opinion covers a broad spectrum, divisible at its simplest between those who seek separation through conviction and those whose resolve is motivated more opportunistically and materially. 'Consumption nationalists' are motivated more by the objective of winning concessions from the state and may be likely to favour continued member-ship precisely because of perceived benefits. Closer to 'old' nationalism, conviction nationalists are more willing to shoulder the economic costs of independence for the benefits of political autonomy. While such a dicho-tomy is representative of ideal-types, repeated opinion polls identified that conviction nationalists were consistently in the minority, usually less than 20 per cent of the sample. Conversely, those who favoured a 'shared sovereignty', either an independent Scotland within the EC or political devolution within the UK state, consistently numbered nearly three times the proportion of conviction nationalists. Inasmuch as consumption nationalism is the more malleable of the two types, however, such nationa-lists will be more open to other politically salient influences, the effect of which is to decentre (Scottish) national identity, and therefore the demands for constitutional reform.

De- and re-centring national identity

During the 1980s, as shown earlier, the political relationships between Scotland and the British state were to experience a substantial shift. In its attempt to restructure the British state, Thatcherism challenged Scotland's quasi-autonomous status by reforming those institutions – the health ser-vice, the legal professions and local government – which had directly contributed to the maintenance and fostering of a separate Scottish ident-ity. Even if the anti-Scottish effects were unintentional, their combined outcome resulted in the reassertion of a new Scottish identity, founded on the re-discovered concept of popular sovereignty and accompanied by the strengthening of Scottish civil society (Paterson, 1992:104–122).

While the newly constructed Scottish national identity gathered support during the 1980s, the paradox is that after contesting the 1992 election on a high-risk strategy of highlighting the need to maintain the constitutional *status quo*, the Conservative party increased its share of the vote in Scotland. Even though only marginal, the increase reflected the socially divisive effects of Thatcherism in Scotland. Thus, while the assault on collectivism was widely contested, its benefits for some were real enough. As contentious and opposed as it was, the poll tax (for example) had its supporters in Scotland, most probably from those who were tax gainers and who were willing to protest on the streets of Edinburgh against the non-paying opponents of the reform. In other words, with its emphases on individualism and consumption Thatcherism had the effect of fostering alternative, politically salient identity 'nodes', the individual and the family, and of decentring the salience of national identity. 'Comfortable' as well as 'Miserable Britain' existed in Scotland, with the former reluctant to sever links with the British state.

While the thrust of Thatcherism was to focus downwards to the individual and the family, and upwards to the British state–nation, the nationalist party strategy was to focus outwards, re-centring Scottish national identity within 'the European dimension'. In its slogan, 'Scotland's Future: Independence in Europe', new nationalism was expressed as Euro-nationalism, the ability of an independent Scotland to enter into a more beneficial negotiated sovereignty within the context of an expanding European Community. Promotion of such an idea was influenced by the spread of nationalism in Eastern Europe and the proposal that the Community, probably later rather than sooner, could be extended to include a number of the 'newly independent' East European states.

However, popular support for the re-centring of Scotland within Europe, was far from conclusive. While the opinion polls discussed previously showed that a majority of those who supported independence did so within the context of European Community membership, separatists, with the exception of a single much-publicized poll, have been consistent in being a minority. Further, Scottish identity with the European Community, perhaps reflecting its peripherality, is significantly lower than elsewhere compared to the UK as a whole and Southern England and some of the member states in particular. *See* Tables 4.2 and 4.3. Perception of the benefits of EC membership also vary regionally. *See* Table 4.4. While most, including those in Scotland, consider membership in principle to be beneficial, the perception of likely benefits for the individual vary substantially within the UK, particularly between Scotland and Southern England, and particularly bearing in mind the perceived regional implications of 1992. While a minority, although sizeable, appear to support Euro-nationalism, a much more substantial proportion are sceptical as to the personal advantages of EC membership.

Further, through playing to the dual identities of the Scots the central

Table 4.2   Politico-territorial Attachments: Scotland and English regions 1991

	Percentages[1]			
	All UK	Scotland	North of England[2]	Southern England[3]
1. Attachment to region				
very attached	54	54	63	53
quite attached	41	43	31	42
not at all	3	3	8	3
2. Attachment to UK				
very attached	58	35	59	63
quite attached	39	51	39	34
not at all	2	9	1	3
3. Attachment to EC				
very attached	6	4	7	7
quite attached	64	54	65	73
not at all	27	37	26	19

Notes: 1. Percentage values do not necessarily sum to 100 because of exclusion of 'Don't Know' and 'Did not answer' responses. 2. Northern, North West and Yorkshire and Humberside Standard Regions. 3. South East and South West Standard Regions.

Source: Eurobarometer 36, Fall 1991: Regional breakdowns.

state could turn the nationalist's argument on its head – that as part of the UK Scotland benefitted within Community negotiations by being a member of one of the large 'core' states of the new Europe. Either way, such a claim would be difficult to evaluate, though its strength for the central state was in the emphasis it gave to the advantages of British identity.

The use of British identity as a wider project of asserting the state–nation within a unifying Europe became an important marker of Thatcherism. Convinced of the merits of economic union, the limits were drawn to exclude the possibility of a federal Europe with its implications of centralization within Brussels and the loss of national sovereignty. The details of the argument are not of concern here, though its general implications were to have important bearing on how British identity was interpreted and on the sovereignty of parliament, both of which in turn were to impact on centre-periphery relations within the UK state.

Two main points are of relevance here – the reconstruction of British patriotism, and the antipathy towards federalism. Reaction to the proposal for European political union, as reflected in the famous Bruges speech given by Mrs Thatcher, and later in the post-Maastricht debate by Conservative government ministers, emphasized the primacy of Britain, its interests and national identity. In fact the appeal to British patriotism formed an essential component of New Right ideology whose 'moments' were the Falklands war and in European negotiations. A federalizing

Table 4.3   Politico-territorial attachment to the European Community: Scotland and Member States, 1991

Country		Percentages		
		Very attached	Quite attached	Not at all
All EC		12	66	16
Scotland		4	54	37
UK		6	64	27
Belgium	B	13	62	19
Denmark	D	9	69	19
Germany	G	9	72	14
Greece	Gr	15	62	19
Spain	Sp	18	66	10
France	Fr	12	66	14
Ireland	I	9	61	27
Luxembourg	L	16	65	112
Netherlands	Nl	4	74	19
Portugal	P	11	72	11

Note: 1. Percentages do not sum to 100 because of exclusion of 'Don't Know' responses.

Source: Eurobarometer 36, Fall 1991.

Europe was viewed as the most obvious threat to British identity and, more specifically, to the sovereignty of parliament (i.e. to the centralized British state). Thus, federalism as a term itself became politically unacceptable and was specifically excluded from the Maastricht treaty on the express wishes of the British.

Within such a reaffirmation of British identity the implications for Scottish nationalism were clear. Any demand for independence would have to be resisted because of its effects on the Union and the credibility of Britain in the international arena. Even the compromise of political devolution – Scottish Assembly with legislative and taxing powers – should be resisted as such a concession would become 'the first step on the slippery road' to full independence. Equally, the effect of granting political devolution to the Scots would have a 'domino effect' elsewhere in Britain, to Wales and the English regions – in other words to a substantial shift of sovereignty from the centre to the periphery. It is because of such a domino effect that the term federalism is outlawed by parties of the left, but particularly of the right in Britain.

Conclusions

As in any case study of nationalist or autonomist movements the ability to draw wider generalizations is constrained by the specificity of the contexts in which they develop. At the most basic though not very enlightening level it is no doubt true that within the modern state system the prob-

Table 4.4 Perceptions of the European Community: Scotland and English Regions, 1991

	Percentages[1]			
	All UK	Scotland	North of England[2]	Southern England[3]
1. Benefits of EC membership in general				
good thing	57	63	57	63
bad thing	15	13	14	15
neutral	21	22	21	18
2. Benefits of EC membership for the individual				
positive	53	42	54	58
negative	17	21	17	15
3. Likely benefits of 1992 for the individual				
positive	40	28	41	45
negative	10	7	10	8
neutral	36	53	32	36
4. Respondents feel European				
Often	11	1	8	16
Sometimes	20	16	21	18
Never	69	83	71	66

Notes: 1. Percentage values do not necessarily sum to 100 because of the exclusion of 'Don't Know'/'Did Not Respond' categories. 2. Northern, North West and Yorkshire and Humberside Standard Regions. 3. South East and South West Standard Regions.

Source: Eurobarometer 36, Fall 1991. Regional breakdowns.

abilities are weighed against secession being successful – to argue otherwise is to overlook the hegemony of the central state. Only where it marks the 'end of empire' or concerns a detached island territory which has little strategic or other significance to the state would it seem that secession by negotiation is the more likely outcome.

Yet to argue the Scottish case in terms of secession is to misrepresent the point. Consumption nationalism and the dual identities of the Scots as members of the British state are powerful breaks to the nationalist aspiration. As the last part of this chapter sought to show, because of the dual identity the ideological manipulation of British identity by the centre (the Crown Heartland) can be used to decentre the political salience of Scottish national identity. Ironically, though, as much as the dualism of the Scots means that Scotland has consistently stepped back from the brink of secession, the 'ultimate act of alienation' (Premdas, 1990), so it would seem that England/the British state does need Scotland.

The central problem, around which revolved both the Scottish debate and the wider issue of the relationship of the British state to the new Europe, is that of sovereignty. In the British lexicon, where European federalism was equated with centralization, somewhat contradictorily within the British state federalism was (rightly) equated with the decentralization of powers and recentring within the regions. Both represented an assault on the sovereignty of the state. In reality, however, sovereignty has drifted away from the state as internationalization of economic and political life has taken hold. The implication is that 'new nationalism', with its emphasis on 'negotiated sovereignty', provides the more flexible model for the twin forces of internationalization and localization to be accommodated in frameworks that are more supportive and positive.

References

Birch, A. (1989), *Nationalism and National Integration*, London, Unwin Hyman.

Cobban, Sir A. (1945), *National Self-Determination*, London, Oxford University Press.

Hebbert, M. (1990), 'Britain in a Europe of Regions', in P.L. Garside and M. Hebbert (eds), *British Regionalism 1900–2000*, London, Mansell: 173–90.

Held, D. (1988), 'Farewell nation-state', *Marxism Today*, December.

Hobsbawm, E.J. (1975), *The Age of Capital 1848–75*, London, Cardinal.

Hobsbawm, E.J. (1990), *Nations and Nationalism since 1780*, Cambridge, Cambridge University Press.

Jessop, B. (1992), 'From the Keynesian Welfare State to the Schumpeterian Workfare State', Paper given at Conference on the Post-Fordist Welfare State, University of Teesside, September.

Keating, M. (1988), *State and Regional Nationalism*, London, Harvester Wheatsheaf.

Lipset, S.M. and Rokkan, S. (1967), 'Cleavage Structures, Party Systems and Voter Alignments: An Introduction', in S.M. Lipset and S. Rokkan (eds), *Party Systems and Voter Alignments*, New York, Free Press.

McCartney, A. (1990), 'Independence in Europe', in A. Brown and R. Parry (eds), *Scottish Government Yearbook 1991*, Edinburgh, Unit for the Study of Government in Scotland: 35–48.

McCrone, D. (1989), 'Introduction' in D. McCrone (ed), *What Scotland Wants: Ten Years On*, Edinburgh, Unit for the Study of Government in Scotland.

Mayall, J. (1990), *Nationalism and International Society*, Cambridge, Cambridge University Press.

Midwinter, A., Keating, M. and Mitchell, J. (1991), *Politics and Public Policy in Scotland*, London, The Macmillan Press Ltd.

Nairn, T. (1989), 'Tartan Power', in S. Hall and M Jacques (eds), *New Times*, London, Lawrence and Wishart: 245–53.

Newton, K. and Karran, T. (1985), *The Politics of Local Expenditure*, London, The Macmillan Press Ltd.

Osmond, J. (1988) *The Divided Kingdom*, London, Constable.

Paterson, L. (1992), 'Ane End of Ane Auld Lang Sang: Sovereignty and the Regeneration of the Union', in A. Brown and R. Parry (eds), *Scottish Government Yearbook 1992*, Edinburgh, Unit for the Study of Government in Scotland.

Premdas, R.R. (1990), 'Secessionist Movements in Comparative Perspective', in R.R. Premdas, S.W.R. de A. Samarasinghe and A.B. Anderson (eds), *Secessionist Movements in Comparative Perspective*, London, Pinter: 12–29.

de Rougemont, D. (1983), *The Future is Within Us*, Oxford, Pergamon.
Smith, A.D. (1988), 'The myth of the Modern Nation and the myth of nations', *Ethnic and Racial Studies*, **11**, No.1: 1–26.
Smith, A.D. (1991), *National Identity*, London, Penguin.
Taylor, P.J. (1993) The Meaning of the North: England's 'Foreign Country' within? *Political Geography*, vol 12, no 2, pp. 136–155.

5

The rights of autochthonous minorities in contemporary Europe

Colin H. Williams

Introduction

We have seen in earlier chapters that one of the key elements of the 'new world order' is a greater public recognition of the rights of threatened minorities. It is as if the 'old world order' had subsumed their interests and even marginalized their existence in some societies. One consequence of this new phase in history is a plethora of demands for fair and equal treatment emanating from beleaguered minorities, especially in Central and Eastern Europe, and from indigenous groups in North America. In this chapter I wish to emphasize both the opportunities and constraints facing selected European minorities in their struggle both to reproduce their culture and to have their contribution recognized as a permanent, legitimate and democratic contribution to modern society. In Chapter 6 I shall consider the role of minorities as an issue of peace and security in modern Europe.

My central thesis is that although the recognition of minority group rights is often a major socio-political advance in European states, it is of little applied value unless and until the state also recognizes the significance of establishing the conditions whereby such rights may be exercised as a normal function of daily life. In short, the state must not only honour individual and group rights but also facilitate the development of a cultural infrastructure and socio-economic context which gives life, meaning and worth to the implementation of group rights. I shall divide my considerations into assessing the development of the recognition of cultural and language rights in Europe and then analyse the difficulties and positive lessons to be gleaned from the implementation of such rights in selected case studies. Finally, I shall suggest some avenues for future research and policy implications which will have a direct bearing on the comparative European cases we are discussing in detail in this volume.

The recognition of cultural and language rights

European history throughout its different epochs (*see* Table 5.1) is replete with examples of new initiatives being taken to legitimize the rights of national minorities, usually after periods of intense conflict, open warfare and the reconstruction of political territories. Our history is also marred by the sudden revocation of such rights when strategic, religious or ethno-linguistic exigencies dictate. We are at the threshold of just such a period of reconstruction as the twin imperatives of social justice and lasting peace force us to recognize once again the salience of national minorities in our midst.

Table 5.1 Epochs in history

The Age of Absolutism

The Age of Enlightenment

The Age of Nationalism

The Age of Statism

The Age of Transnationalism

The Age of Postmodernism

Evidence of this reconstruction abounds at all levels. At the supra-state level the parallel development of specifying the duties of states in respect of recognizing fundamental human rights has been shadowed at state and regional level by a host of reformist measures designed to allow minorities greater freedom of expression, to use their languages within the public sector and to reproduce their culture both within traditional domains and in the newer domains made possible by rapid communication and mass technology such as broadcasting and computer-aided education.

The issue of the protection of minorities has been a critical feature of both inter-state and inter-group relations in post-Napoleonic Europe. In Table 5.2 I have selected representative examples of legislation for the rights of minorities at international, state and regional level. It is evident that some states, such as Belgium, have a long history of ethno-linguistic legislation, while others, such as the UK, have yawning silences on this topic, reflecting the respective political cultures and salience of minority issues in shaping the state-formation process. (*See* Table 5.2.) This very partial selection of specific legislative acts is designed to demonstrate that we already have a varied and rich diversity of experience to draw upon in our search for comparative models of minority protection. What is new about the current period is the urgent need for flexible and effective Europe-wide

Table 5.2   Selected language and minority legislation

International level

- Historical treaties on minority rights.
- UN Covenant on Civil and Political Rights, 1966, Article 27
- CSCE Final Act, Helsinki, 1975
- UNESCO Declaration on Race and Racial Prejudice, 1978
- Council of Europe Protection of Human Rights and Fundamental Freedoms
- Standing Conference of Local and Regional Authorities in Europe, Resolution 192, 1988
- CSCE Conference Document on Human Dimension, Copenhagen, 1990
- CSCE Charter of Paris for a New Europe, 1991
- CSCE Conference Document on Human Dimension, Moscow, 1991
- CSCE Report on Experts on National Minorities, Geneva, 1991
- Council of Europe European Charter for Regional and Minority Languages, 1991

State level

- The Belgian Constitution, 1831
  Revision of Belgian Constitution, 1970 and 1980–88
- The Copenhagen Declaration, 1955
- The Constitution Act of Finland, 1919
  The Finnish Parliament Act, 1928
- The Irish Constitution, 1921
- The Spanish Constitution, 1978
- The Swiss Constitution, 1848

National/regional level

- Statute of Autonomy for the Åland Islands, 1920
  Revised Autonomy Act for the Åland Islands, 1952
  Autonomy Act for the Åland Islands, @ 1993
- The Autonomy Statute of the South Tyrol, 1948
  Amendment to the Autonomy Statute of South Tyrol, 1972
- Belgian Linguistic Laws, 1930–2
  Belgian Linguistic Laws, 1962–3
  Belgian Constitutional Reforms, 1970
  Belgian Constitutional Reforms, 1980–7/8
- Swiss Federal Constitution 1848, 1874, Article 116, modifications
- The Welsh Language Act, 1967
- Dutch Primary Education Act, 1920, revised 1937
- Basque Statute of Autonomy, 1979
  Catalan Statute of Autonomy, 1979
  Galician Statute of Autonomy, 1981
  Basic Law of the Standardization of the use of Basque, 1982

attention to minority issues and the recognition that the nation–state itself is not necessarily the best, nor most effective implementer of minority rights. New organizations and new means of monitoring and protecting against such sensitive issues as minority discrimination, genocide, anti-Semitism and chauvinistic nationalism are called for. As we shall see in Chapter 6, the security politics of the so-called 'New Europe' demand fresh initiatives

European Initiatives

As the European Community struggles to harmonize its economic and political agenda in a post-Maastricht 'federalizing' programme, one of its key deliberations is how to overcome the need for rapid mutually intelligible communication without simultaneously threating the survival of lesser-used languages. The dominance of English, French, German and Spanish necessarily encourage language spread and the cultural–ideological diffusion of values, behaviours and orientations associated with these powerful, global languages (Williams 1993: 115–128). The establishment of a linguistic hegemony allows speakers of selected global languages to transcend traditional state boundaries and social conventions and communicate directly with more and more people in such diverse fields as science and technology, mass culture and entertainment, sport, administration and religion.

One of the abiding characteristics of the contemporary world is this simultaneity of communication demanding different languages at different scales in the functional hierarchy of the Tower of Babel. However, for speakers of threatened languages such trends may be interpreted less as an opportunity and more as a restriction on their communicative competence. Recent attention at EC level has been focused on the need to harmonize state and community policies so as to construct appropriate structures and language régimes. This is a pressing issue, for the wider question of language legitimacy among the official EC languages makes many political representatives wary of further complicating European politics by also addressing the needs of non-official, non-state languages and their speakers. However, roughly one in seven or about fifty million citizens in the EC have a mother tongue which is not the main official language of the member state in which they live. Admittedly not all of these citizens would be described as speaking a minority language; consider the role and status of German in Italy, Denmark and Belgium, for example. But a large proportion would qualify as speaking a language which is under considerable threat and likely to decline if remedial action is not taken very soon.

The European Bureau for Lesser-Used Languages, established by the European Parliament and located in Dublin since 1984, has categorized the various language communities as follows:

1. Small independent nation–states whose languages are not widely used by European standards and which are not official, working languages of the European Community (e.g. the Irish and Letzeburgers).

2. Small nations without their own state (e.g. the Welsh, the Bretons, and the West-Frisians) who reside in one or other member-state.
3. Peoples such as those in item 2 who reside in more than one member-state (e.g. the Catalans, the Occitans who can be found in France, Spain and Italy).
4. Trans-frontier minorities (i.e. communities within one country who speak the majority language of another, be that country a member-state of the EC or not (e.g. the German-speakers of North-Schleswig, the Slovenes of Trieste, the Francophones of the Vallee d'Aoste). (O'Riagain, 1989: 511).

The constituent language groups are represented in Table 5.3 and Figure 5.1. They vary tremendously in their size, constitutional recognition, socio-economic levels of material well-being, internal cohesion and susceptibility to contraction and decline. However, despite their many individual problems, which I would not wish to underplay, collectively they face a brighter future than any other time in the post-War period for a number of reasons. First, several initiatives taken in the past decade have brought the common plight of Europe's minority cultures to the attention of key decision-making bodies who have established in turn representative agencies to promote the use of lesser-used languages.

Thus the European Community's Bureau for Lesser-Used Languages has in a very short time mobilized a large number of previously disparate and often overlapping organizations to cooperate in its general aim of safe-guarding and promoting minority cultures. It has pursued three broad strategies as described by its Secretary General Donall O'Riagain:

1. To press for the bringing into being of legal and political structures which would protect lesser-used language communities;
2. To engage in and promote work programmes which would be of practical assistance to those it is endeavouring to serve;
3. To facilitate an exchange of information and experiences between the various lesser-used language communities and thus help bring about a greater sense of collective awareness. (O'Riagain, 1989: 514).

Through its international links and national representative committees the Bureau has been very active in the following areas. It has prepared reports for the European Parliament on the necessity for legislation permitting constituent language groups to make more use of their language in formal affairs, and on the cultural aspects of minority life. Further initiatives have involved a comparative analysis of pre-school education in the EC's lesser-used languages, a project on primary school education, the preparation of an EC map of the lesser-used languages and several investigations into the relationship between the media, particularly broadcasting and lesser-used languages. These activities are means of sponsoring research findings which feed in to practical policies and also permit the cooperation and closer understanding of shared problems, thus raising the general standard of discussion and prescription for the resolution of these problems.

Table 5.3 Western Europe's lesser-used languages

Country	No. of languages	Languages
Belgium	1	German
Denmark	1	German
France	7	Basque
		Breton
		Catalan
		Corsican
		Dutch
		German/Alsatian
		Occitan
Germany	4	Danish
		East Frisian
		North Frisian
		Polish
Greece	4	Arvinite
		Macedonian
		Turkish
		Vlak
Ireland	1	Irish
Italy	11	Albanian
		Catalan
		Croatian
		French (Franco-Provencal)
		Friulan
		German
		Greek
		Ladin
		Occitan
		Sard
		Slovene
Netherlands	1	West Frisian
Luxembourg	1	Letzebuergesch
Portugal	0	
Spain	4	Basque
		Catalan
		Gallego
		Occitan
UK	5	Cornish
		Gaelic
		Irish
		Scots
		Welsh

Source: Williams (1991), *Language Survival*: 14

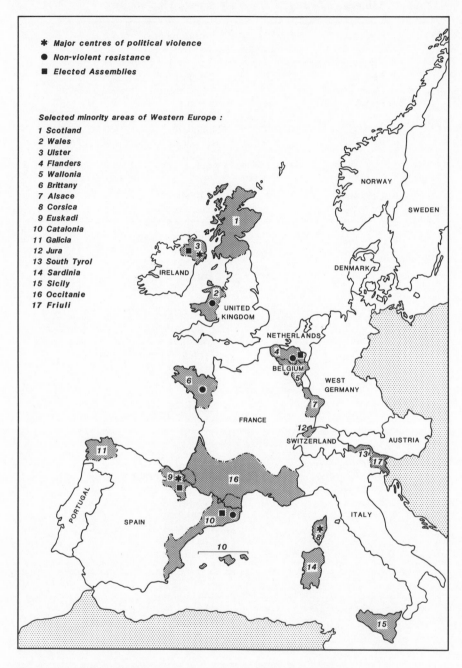

Figure 5.1 Selected minority areas in Western Europe, 1988

Source: Williams, 1991, p. 14.

Parallel initiatives have been taken by the Council of Europe, through its Conference on Local and Regional Authorities of Europe, which has drafted a Charter on European Regional and Minority Languages, and the UN Commission on Human Rights, which is preparing a universal declaration of the rights of members of national, ethnic, religious and linguistic minorities (O'Riagain, 1989: 515). In addition there has been a proliferation of interest groups, quasi-political organizations and lobby associations to promote the activities of, for example, the Federal Union of European Nationalities or the Bureau of Unrepresented Nations in Brussels.

However, the most significant 'new actor' has been the Council for Security and Cooperation in Europe (CSCE) which has focused on minorities as a result of the profound political changes and ethnic challenges in Central and Eastern Europe. After initiating a concern with fundamental individual rights following the Helsinki Declaration of 1975 the CSCE process is now currently engaged in constructing a comprehensive framework for the protection of national minorities. At its Copenhagen meeting, June 1990, it declared that the participatory states would commit themselves to the following aims:

(40)   The participating States clearly and unequivocally condemn totalitarianism, racial and ethnic hatred, anti-semitism, xenophobia and discrimination against anyone as well as persecution on religious and ideological grounds. In this context, they also recognize the particular problems of Roma (gypsies).

They declare their firm intention to intensify the effort to combat these phenomena in all their forms and will therefore:

(40.1) take effective measures, including the adoption, in conformity with their constitutional systems and their international obligations, of such laws as may be necessary, to provide protection against any acts that constitute incitement to violence against persons or groups based on national, racial, ethnic or religious discrimination, hostility or hatred, including anti-semitism;

(40.2) commit themselves to take appropriate and proportionate measures to protect persons or groups who may be subject to threats or acts of discrimination, hostility or violence as a result of their racial, ethnic, cultural, linguistic or religious identity, and to protect their property;

(40.3) take effective measures, in conformity with their constitutional systems, at the national, regional and local levels to promote understanding and tolerance, particularly in the fields of education, culture and information;

(40.4) endeavour to ensure that the objectives of education include special attention to the problem of racial prejudice and hatred and to the development of respect for different civilizations and cultures;

(40.5) recognize the right of the individual to effective remedies and endeavour to recognize, in conformity with national legislation, the right of interested persons and groups to initiate and support complaints against acts of discrimination, including racist and xenophobic acts;

(40.6) consider adhering, if they have not yet done so, to the international instruments which address the problem of discrimination and ensure full compliance with the obligations therein, including those relating to the submission of periodic reports;

(40.7)   consider, also, accepting those international mechanisms which allow
         States and individuals to bring communications relating to discrimination
         before international bodies. (Copenhagen Conference, June 1990: 10–11).

A major breakthrough occurred when from 1 to 19 July 1991 a Meeting of
Experts on National Minorities was held in Geneva under the CSCE
auspices. Its purpose was to:

hold a thorough discussion on the issue of national minorities and of the rights of
persons belonging to them, with due attention to the diversity of situations and to
the legal, historical, political and economic backgrounds.

It included:

• an exchange of views on practical experience, in particular on national legislation, democratic institutions, international instruments, and other possible
  forms of co-operation;
• a review of the implementation of the relevant CSCE commitments and consideration of the scope for the improvement of relevant standards;
• a consideration of new measures aimed at improving the implementation of the
  aforementioned commitments.

Significantly the CSCE meeting recognized that its recommendations
required a reconceptualization of the sovereignty of the state, at least in so
far as the respect of its constituent minorities was concerned. It recognized
that external agencies had a legitimate interest in the internal affairs of
a particular state concerning the upholding of national minority rights. I
quote their new stance:

Issues concerning national minorities, as well as compliance with international
obligations and commitments concerning the rights of persons belonging to them
are matters of legitimate international concern and consequently do not constitute
exclusively an internal affair of the respective State (CSCE Expert Meeting on
Minorities, Geneva, July 1991).

Theoretically this is a very useful safeguard against abuse. In selected
cases we know from our reading of recent history that such a precedent
might be used to justify direct involvement through physical force or
economic coercion in the name of the beleaguered minorities at risk.
However, the emphasis of the CSCE process on participatory democracy
and constructive dialogue is to be greatly welcomed. A recent Minority
Rights Group report (1991) highlighted the issues by publishing a summary
of these implications for public affairs and the exchange of ideas
and information which offers a broad schemata of the types of practical
implementation necessary to translate titular rights into effective action.

On minority participation in public affairs:

Aware of the diversity and varying constitutional systems among them, which
make no single approach necessarily generally applicable, the participating States
note with interest that positive results have been obtained by some of them in an

appropriate manner by, inter alia: advisory and decision-making bodies in which minorities are represented, in particular with regard to education, culture and religion;

- elected bodies and assemblies of national minority affairs;
- local and autonomous administration, as well as autonomy on a territorial basis, including the existence of consultative, legislative and executive bodies chosen through free and periodic elections;
- self-administration by a national minority of aspects concerning its identity in situations where autonomy on a territorial basis does not apply;
- decentralized or local forms of government;
- bilateral and multilateral agreements regarding national minorities;
- for persons belonging to national minorities, provisions of adequate types and levels of education in their mother tongue with due regard to the number, geographical settlement patterns and cultural traditions of national minorities;
- funding the teaching of minority language to the general public, as well as the inclusion of minority languages in teacher-training institutions, in particular in regions inhabited by persons belonging to national minorities;
- in cases where instruction in a particular subject is not provided in their territory in the minority language at all levels, taking the necessary measures to find means of recognizing diplomas issued abroad for a course of study completed in that language;
- creation of government research agencies to review legislation and disseminate information related to equal rights and non-discrimination;
- provision of financial and technical assistance to persons belonging to national minorities who so wish to exercise their right to establish and maintain their own educational, cultural and religious institutions, organizations and associations.
- governmental assistance for addressing local difficulties relating to discriminatory practices (eg. a citizens' relations service);
- encouragement of grassroots community relations efforts between neighbouring communities sharing borders, aimed at helping to prevent local tensions from arising and address conflicts peacefully should they arise; and
- encouragement of the establishment of permanent mixed commissions, either inter-State or regional, to facilitate continuing dialogue between the border regions concerned.
- the participating States are of the view that these or other approaches, individually or in combination, could be helpful in improving the situation of national minorities on their territories.

On the free flow of information and exchange of ideas:

- they will take effective measures to promote tolerance, understanding, equality of opportunity and good relations between individuals of different origins within their country.
- in access to the media, they will not discriminate against anyone based on ethnic, cultural, linguistic or religious grounds. They will make information available that will assist the electronic mass media in taking into account, in their programmes, the ethnic, cultural, linguistic and religious identity of national minorities.
- they reaffirm that establishment and maintenance of unimpeded contacts among persons belonging to a national minority, as well as contacts across frontiers by persons belonging to a national minority with persons with whom they share a common ethnic or national origin, cultural heritage or religious

belief, contributes to mutual understanding and promotes good-neighbourly relations.

- they therefore encourage trans-frontier co-operation arrangements on a national, regional and local level, inter alia, on local border crossings, the preservation of and visits to cultural and historical monuments and sites, tourism, the improvement of traffic, the economy, youth exchange, the protection of the environment and the establishment of regional commissions.

- they will also encourage the creation of informal working arrangements (eg. workshops, committees, both within and between the participating States where national minorities live, to discuss issues of, exchange experiences on, and present proposals on, issues related to national minorities).

On the implementation of CSCE commitments:

- the participating States note that appropriate CSCE mechanisms may be of relevance in addressing questions relating to national minorities. Further, they recommend that third meeting of the Conference on the Human Dimension of the CSCE consider expanding the Human Dimension Mechanism. They will promote the involvement of individuals in the protection of their rights, including the rights of persons belonging to national minorities.

- with a view to improve their information about actual situation of national minorities, the participating States will, on a voluntary basis distribute, through the CSCE Secretariat, information to other participating States about the situation of national minorities in their respective territories, as well as statements of national policy in that respect. (quoted in Minorities and Autonomy in Western Europe, 1991, Minority Rights Group).

Armed with such emphases on democratic participation in public affairs, on representation within decision-making bodies at all levels from the local to the state and encouraged to participate in an informed dialogue, members of Europe's national minorities may look forward to a far more constructive and promising future. However, reliance on this form of supra-structural definition of rights and obligations alone could provide a false dawn of optimism, if it is not accompanied by a parallel sub-structural reform of many aspects of public life in multi-cultural societies.

In a recent volume (Williams, 1991) I argued that there was often a time-lag between the formal recognition of cultural rights and the implementation of such rights as a social norm among the respective populations of the modern state. I also argued that cultural rights had to be set within a far wider socio-economic context if they were to be meaningful. This is not to suggest that cultural rights in central Europe need be delayed or compounded by the difficulties in establishing the appropriate socio-economic context, merely a cautionary reminder that there are several layers in the processes of recognising the rights of national minorities, layers that have to be addressed and constructed simultaneously, for it is not a logical, evolutionary process that we are describing, but one which is too often fired by emotions and passion and thus needs to be tempered by reason, struggle and planning.

Minority groups, conscious of their relative powerlessness, have tended to argue on moral grounds that their right to have a separate language or religious status in the modern state are an expression of universal human rights. They echo the 19th-century liberal call for tolerance and equality for disadvantaged groups, and assert that the modern multi-cultural state not only has an obligation to guarantee them freedom from oppression, but also freedom to expression and participation. This new conception of freedom and social rights places a responsibility on the state to construct the conditions of possibility whereby a minority culture may be permitted to operate in formal, public domains. Hence the current thrust of minority-language agitation in Western Europe has been for bilingual educational provision, for simultaneous translation services in legal and public administration services, for official recognition of language rights both on the statute book and in the market place. That such proposals are nearly always accompanied by both conflict and counter-claims that cultural pluralism is inefficient or subversive of state integrity should come as no surprise (Williams, 1991: 10).

We recognize that legislating for the freedom to use a minority language in several domains has been a major political breakthrough in many of the states of Western Europe. This was the battle of the 1960s and 1970s. The challenge facing such minorities in the 1990s is to transform the legal recognition institutionalized in the past two decades into actual routine social behaviour. This involves reform at two levels. First, many minority-language speakers have to be encouraged to make use of the new opportunities which are now available. Paradoxically this is not as self-evident as one might expect. After decades or centuries of being socialized into accepting that their culture is second-rate and of limited utility in a burgeoning world economy, many within the minority communities are reluctant to take advantage of the opening of new domains, whether in formal education or in dealings with local and civil authorities in the autochthonous tongue. Reversing this status differential and inducing more self-confident use of the lesser-used language is clearly far more difficult in some contexts, such as Breton and Arberesch, than in others, such as Catalan. Secondly, in order to allow these new domains to function, there has to be corresponding reform of the public sector to enable bi- or multilingual practices to be instituted. There is little justice in legislating for the use of the minority language in the courts of law, for example, if there are not also facilities for simultaneous translations. Similarly, the employment and training of personnel must be a key factor in the success of bilingual reforms. Initially it often happens that the demand for language usage in a wide range of domains threatens to outstrip the supply of competent bilinguals in specialist fields. Thus we are led to conclude that the recognition of minority language rights places a new obligation on the modern state to provide the context within which such rights may be exercised. This context should be seen from an holistic perspective for it involves all aspects of the local state's apparatus if language equality is to be a norm. Conventionally, attention has been focused on formal education as the chief agency of language reproduction, but increasingly we are recognizing the potency of regional planning, of economic development and of social policy in structuring the conditions which influence language vitality.

Elsewhere in this volume I have argued that the effectiveness of such organizations is enhanced by a second trend in European political life, namely the recognition that a Federal or United Europe, however conceived, is likely to be more democratic and more responsive to the needs of its citizens. Traditionally the call for a reconstituted Europe of the People, rather than a Europe of the Nation-State, has come from Nationalist parties and Liberals interested in regional devolution and electoral reform. More recently both Social Democrats and Green Party members across Europe have also added their support for a decentralized Europe, based upon its constituent regions. Indeed the ecologists have taken up the central plank of nationalists in arguing for a devolution of power to lower levels in the political hierarchy. Their motivation may be different from nationalists, but the effect may bring about remarkably similar results if enacted in a reformed Europe. Too often the struggle of language minorities has been overly associated with nationalist political mobilization. Increasingly though we are seeing a realignment of the political ranks which will have far-reaching normative consequences for minority groups (Williams, 1991).

I also argued that a third promising trend was inherently ambiguous for it is now commonplace to suggest that mass technology has so empowered international languages such as English or French, that they become irresistible forces in the modern world and contribute to the spread of ideologies, values, modes of behaviour, style and economic impulses in our inter-related world system. Beginning with print capitalism, which Anderson has demonstrated conferred 'economic advantage, social position and political privilege' on new languages of power, we have witnessed the 'possibility of a new form of imagined community, which in its basic morphology set the stage for the modern nation' (Anderson, 1983: 49). Rapid communication methods have enabled the cultural values of imperial states in both the 19th and 20th centuries to set the agenda of world politics and global aspirations. Television and mass air transport have created a 'shrinking world', a 'global village', but they have also threatened the very survival of minority cultural groups by exposing them to external influences and realizable alternative life-styles.

However, it is not the technology itself which threatens, but its social control and political determination. Thus within Catalonia, Euskadi and Wales we have seen the rapid development of radio and television services operating within the national language and serving as a focus of ideas, news, entertainment and discussion which has far-reaching normative consequences for the lesser-used language. Similarly, in the field of bilingual education, the introduction of computer-aided learning in the weaker languages, the preparation of a diverse set of teaching materials across the curriculum and the interaction between educators and administrators which relatively inexpensive software now affords, is a major breakthrough in making the best material available to staff and pupils. I recognize that often the stumbling block to the full implementation of such programmes is the cost of releasing full-time teachers/researchers to develop such initiatives, but even so the computerization of knowledge within the lesser-used language is a healthy embracing of modern technology. In time, when speech-wise computers will enable the identification of thousands of words and the adoption of models of speech blocks in any language, it is possible that lesser-used languages will be employed more generally within the public administration and commercial life of hitherto disadvantaged communities.

The fourth and most vital trend is the renewal of commitment and sense of urgency which animates many within the communities we are discussing to act for the collective good of their fellow nationals. To date most of the successful programmes of language reform, whether in education, the media or the workplace, have been extensions of ventures which were pioneered by committed volunteers who gave of their time, energy and resources to the cause they most valued. A second stage has been the institutionalization of the bilingual or mother tongue practices advocated by the pioneers. The fact that such practices are in the hands of professionals drawn from within the lesser-used language communities, has induced critics to suggest that there are both class implications and tendencies towards positive discrimination arising from this new situation. Opponents interpret the rise in influence of the lesser-used language as a necessary diminution of power of the majoritarian language, and at times in this cause immigrants are in the front line of attack, either as victims of retrospective language legislation or as champions of majoritarian state rights. It is understandable therefore that immigrants are often seen as the active advance guard of an army of potential invaders/colonizers into the threatened heartland. This is why they are seen as an insidious threat for they both personify a challenge to the existing local order and represent the larger social whole which has so often discriminated against the minority language.

However, as we shall see, this crude zero-sum conceptualization of immigrants as active agents of state integration is neither a helpful nor particularly accurate description of the various situations in contemporary Europe (Williams, 1992). There are many splendid and prosaic examples of immigrants who have fully adjusted to the local order through sociolinguistic absorption into the community becoming the virulent champions of minority group rights and cultural defence.

Implementation

Remarkable as it may seem, given the attention to international law and the rights of minorities in the first part of this chapter, there is ample testimony in Western Europe to argue that many minorities have achieved substantial improvement in their positions without recourse to specified group or individual rights. Clearly I am not arguing that we should jettison the search for a comprehensive legal regime on minority rights, merely alerting to the fact that where social protest and a responsive state apparatus conjoin, there exists the possibility of extending the use of a minority culture into hitherto new and novel social domains.

If we conceive most minority demands as a manifestation of socio-political struggle then we can usefully summarize the experience of selected European minorities in terms of a five stage process (Table 5.4). Many linguistic minorities, such as the Vlaks and Arberol in Greece, are at the very early stage of conceiving themselves as a legitimate language grouping. Others, such as the inhabitants of Occitanie and Friuli, are at the mobilization stage. Still others such as Gaelic-speakers in Scotland and Bretons in France are searching for a legitimacy to their demands. It is at stage four, institutionalization, and stage five, parallelism/normalization, that we see the more mature expression of minority ambitions. These are best represented by the Flemish, Basque, Catalans, Frisian, Irish and Welsh cases.

Table 5.4   Language survival: five foci of social pressure for language change

1. **Idealism:** the construction of a vision of a fully rehabilitated 'threatened' language, this is the issue of making language and nation coterminous.

2. **Protest:** mobilizing sections of the population to agitate for a social reform/revolution in the promotion of the lesser-used language.

3. **Legitimacy:** securing a generalized acceptance of the normalacy of exercizing language rights in selected domains.

4. **Institutionalization:** ensuring that the language is represented in key strategic agencies of the state (i.e. the law, education, and public administration).

5. **Parallelism/Normalization:** extending the use of the language into the optimum range of social situations (i.e. the private sector, entertainment, sport and the media).

The potential for implementing cultural/linguistic rights is enormous. Here I merely alert to the central domains of access to the media, education, public administration and the law as the most promising avenues for recognizing new rights. I am conscious however that it is in the private/commercial sector that the full realization of such rights will need to be addressed.

Mass culture and access to the media

Ever since the diffusion of print capitalism and mass literacy, members of Europe's linguistic minorities have been calling for greater access to and control over the mass media, recognizing that the media, together with education, public sector administration and the law were the institutional bases for cultural reproduction. The Arfé Report adopted by the European Parliament in 1981 and the Kuijpers Resolution of 1987 have reinforced this perspective, leading to a more formal emphasis on the provision of the requisite infra-structure for lesser-used languages to be represented within the mass media. However, as we are aware, guaranteeing access to the media is often a sensitive and politically volatile move.

Often the values, ideas and messages imparted through the lesser-used language circulation network are at variance with the state's majority; hence the unwillingness of government to guarantee access to minority voices in the media. Yet without access to the media, which overarch space and distance and re-combine and re-unite disparate speakers, it is doubtful if relatively weak and embattled minority communities can survive intact (Williams, 1992). Although majorities are often suspicious of minority involvement in mass communication, fearing their usurpation by an unrepresentative section, such participation is essential to the furtherance of pluralist democracy. Thomas recently encapsulated the nub of the question when he advised that:

Media in a given language provide the forum within which shared experience and shared problems are discussed, often from very different standpoints. Outsiders in the majority group often perceive a minority as having a single, monolithic, highly politicized stance and many resist the establishment of media in the minority language, fearing that the air-waves will be dominated by a single point of view. Media are an essential part of democracy in whatever language or size of language they operate. Indeed in those areas of the EC where literacy in the lesser-used language is poor because of past discrimination in the education system, radio and television in their own language can have the special function of admitting to the spoken democratic debate people who are neither very fluent in the state language nor very literate in their own (Thomas, 1989: 4).

This is an important justification for the role of media, especially in multilingual societies generally, as within Central, Eastern and South-Eastern Europe. The transition to democracy is a fragile enough phenomenon for strong cultures; for the weaker it could pose a further threat, as I have alerted elsewhere for:

If the new cultural order of 'unity in diversity' is to become a reality in the future Europe, then much greater attention to the implications of 'development from below' . . . (including mass technology and access to the media) . . . needs to be stimulated; otherwise participatory democracy in the new Europe will be yielded to the tyranny of the majority in the name of progress and development, the watchwords of the centralising state and of its dominant elite (Williams, 1990: 244).

A further feature is the economic aspect of the development of the mass media, both in terms of job creation in a diverse set of related occupations and in the export potential of televisual material. This is a vital feature if members of the minority community are to be employed in the private, commercial sector where too often the language is excluded. Clearly this has important social psychological, language status planning and behavioural implications for a specialized division of labour within the lesser-used language community. The media not only transmit material, they also help establish new norms, new domains and new perceptions which seek to extend the hitherto restrictive domains of most languages (Thomas, 1989: 6; Williams, 1989: 46–8).

This question of legitimization of new domains and identity reformulation is crucial. If the media in lesser-used language are able to provide a mix of local, regional, national and international material then they can be an 'important means of internationalizing the consciousness of their own group. That is an important function, for just as no culture can survive without institutions of its own, so no culture can survive as an autarchy, impervious to outside influence. If cultures are unique, they are so because each culture stands at a unique cultural crossroads, not on a unique cultural island' (Thomas, 1989: 6). This platform is the means both to launch and to receive contributions from the wider world and thus becomes a pivotal agency for national minorities.

Specific examples of the success achieved by determined minorities would include popular literature, newsprint capitalism and radio–television broadcasting in Catalonia, Euskadi and Wales, and the cross-fertilization of ideas and practice which these nations enjoy through membership of the European Broadcasting Union. Let me illustrate by reference to the UK.

Television broadcasting in Wales and Scotland

The statutory provisions relevant to the Fourth Channel in Wales were contained in the Broadcasting Act of 1981. The Welsh Channel was an independent authority responsible not to the IBA, but via the Home Office to Parliament. Its first transmission was on 1 November 1982 and since then it has established itself as a central agency for the transmission of Welsh culture and as a reflector of Welsh social life. S4C operates a partnership with BBC, HTV and independent producers as programme suppliers. This in turn has not only spawned a plethora of programmes but also new training and career opportunities for a wide variety of occupations, further strengthening the utility of Welsh in new domains. Currently some 27 hours of Welsh-medium programmes are broadcast per week, but inevitably, as the average number of English-language hours taken from Channel Four has risen from 47 hours per week in 1984 to around 134 hours per week in 1991, the Welsh proportion has dropped steadily from 32.7 per cent in 1984 to an estimated 16.7 per cent in 1991. S4C's estimated expenditure for 1989–90 was £51.5 million, of which programme costs account for about 88 per cent of total funds and operating costs some 9.5 per cent (S4C, 1989). S4C audience research suggests that the service reaches about 80 per cent of the total potential Welsh-speaking viewers, and about 55 per cent of all viewers in Wales.

The principal problems of S4C in the short- to medium-term are a gradually reducing share of advertising revenue; increased competition from new channels (e.g. C5 and C6); increasing penetration of satellite broadcasts; search for new talent and maintenance of the highest standards of performance and broadcasting skills. Apart from seeking to broadcast to both Welsh and English speakers in Wales, S4C is also active on an international scale in co-operative arrangements with overseas television services and independent producers. It is particularly active in the

European Broadcasting Union in relation to the influence of new technology on small-scale countries and lesser-used language communities. With a decade of experience to date it is instrumental in diffusing information and practice on minority broadcasting elsewhere in the world. Despite a halting start, this reform has been an overwhelming success and one I would recommend to other demographically and regionally significant minorities. It is certain that the emerging private broadcasting systems of Eastern Europe will learn from collaborative ventures with companies such as Agenda, Barcud and S4C.

In Scotland, the broadcasting of Gaelic-medium programmes is less well developed. Currently the BBC, STV and particularly Grampian cover the regions but at a relatively modest level and with little real power to act as a safeguard for the language. Recently as a result of strong lobbying, the government has announced an £8 million injection of capital for independent Gaelic-medium broadcasting and this is interpreted as a significant fillip to the extension of Gaelic in new domains. If the Welsh experience is used as a base, then new opportunities both for programme development and career development will strengthen the role of Gaelic. In addition to obvious entertainment and current affairs broadcasting, the television service could be an important boost to distance learning Gaelic-medium education and act as a catalyst to the wider spread of the language in the nation.

Being politically and demographically stronger, the Catalan situation is even more impressive in terms of broadcasting programmes through the medium of Catalan where it has become a majority language. Although there are many scheduling and technical lessons to be learned from Catalonia, a more realistic comparison for the larger minorities in Central Europe is with the Basque and Welsh experience of mass media communication.

Educational rights

There is a significant literature on the education of linguistic and cultural minorities (for a good survey see Churchill, 1986). This is not the occasion to review that corpus of writing, or to repeat previous detailed analyses (Williams, 1989). Here I merely want to make three vital points about education:

1. Next to the family it is the single most important agency for cultural reproduction, socialization and identity formation. It therefore seems desireable where possible for minorities to receive a significant proportion of their formal education through their mother tongue or preferred language.
2. Investment in minority education presumes a tolerant, plural society. It also presumes that the level of investment should be commensurate with the goals of the minority education programme. That this is hardly ever the case in reality is self-evident, but, at the very least, members of minority groups deserve co-equal treatment so that they are not sub-

sequently disadvantaged in adulthood. Schooling should be related to the wider social context and not perceived as either a preservationist element of the threatened culture, or as a detached agency for within-group control and sustenance.

3. Even in successful cases of educational reform, such as Catalonia, Euskadi and Wales, members of the minority community may still prefer to communicate in the majority language in many domains. We should not be surprised or cynical about reports which conclude that Catalan or Welsh children speak to their school friends in Castillian or English, or that after leaving school many of them will use the predominant state language.

This is a function of a complex process of psychological adjustment, new domain construction and the obvious reality that these bi- or multi-lingual children/students inhabit a society wherein two or more languages are in constant competition with each other. This in no way detracts from the inherent utility of promoting lesser-used languages within formal education, which is a notoriously difficult task but an integral expression of group maintenance.

Rather than survey good practice within this educational field I have decided to set the educational experience within a framework of minority group planning for my homeland Wales. This is offered as an example of the formal infra-structure which would need to be in place in order to honour the rights of 'equal validity' enshrined in The Welsh Language Act of 1967 and reinforced under the new Welsh Language Bill of 1993. My central point is that formal language planning is now a necessary accompaniment to the declaration of minority rights, but that it is not a self-evident process or one that can be readily transferred from one political context to another. Figure 5.2 is offered as an exemplar of the manner in which a well organized minority can campaign for new domain construction for language and cultural representation in society. It is a potential, not an actual representation of how I would see language planning being organized in my home country of Wales (Williams, 1989).

Here I want to argue that formal language planning is not only politically necessary but also economically sound. Too often within minority communities there is a plethora of well-intentioned but ineffective language support agencies. Their central thrust if often muted because of internal fragmentation, overlapping responsibilities and duplication of effort, materials and aims. What is needed is a holistic framework within which the disparate elements would be co-ordinated (Williams, 1991). In the near future we are likely to see the passing of a New Welsh Language Act with far-reaching normative and legislative consequences. One of these will be the need for short- and medium-term national language strategies under the auspices of The Welsh Language Board and its affiliated agencies to serve the approximately 500,000 current Welsh speakers. However, I also recognize that by advocating such bureaucratic developments I am tying the Welsh culture closer than ever to the dictates of the local state, a trend I have cautioned against in the past. In the new world order it must be

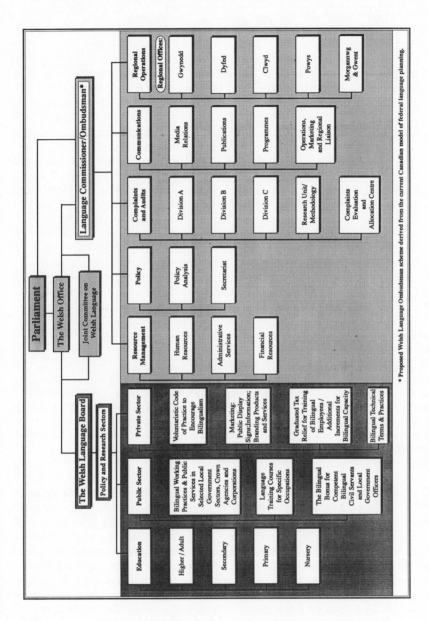

Figure 5.2 A Language planning framework for Wales

concluded that this is a necessary relationship for only the resources of the local state can sustain a fully comprehensive minority culture in an advanced industrial state.

Future directions

It is evident that the potential for inter-group conflict is enormous in a continent undergoing such profound transitions. The current conflict between Serbia and Croatia is the latest sad manifestation of ethnic rivalry, federal–regional cleavages and the absence of an overarching state ideology. The search for security and for principles whereby conflict is neutralized or at least minimized is vital. The experience of selected societies, particularly Canada and Belgium, has led Nelde, Labrie and Williams (1992) to argue that linguistic conflicts can be partially neutralized if the principles elaborated upon in Table 5.5 are followed. What is significant here is the treatment of the territorial protection of minority interests. We are witnessing the erosion of all-encompassing territorial regions (i.e. formal regions), and their replacement by functional spaces which may or may not correspond to a legally binding administrative unit. This is part of the dual process of globalization and localization which is such a pertinent feature of contemporary life. Strict adherence to the territorial principles of language planning and minority protection seem less relevant now than hitherto. We conceive identity less in terms of 'cultural islands' and more in terms of 'cultural cross-roads' (Thomas, 1989 quoted in Williams, 1992). Summarizing these trends Mlinar argues that:

the traditional territorial identities based on *continuity, homogeneity*, and clearly (physically and socially) identifiable *borders* are now being threatened. Does this mean that we are approaching the end of territorial identities as such or is it more a question of their transformation and (re) construction? It is increasingly unlikely that a territorial unit can continue to *preserve* its distinctiveness on the basis of frontal insulation ("dissociation" or "delinking"), while there is an increasing probability that distinctive identity may be *formed* as a unique crossroad in the flow of people, goods and ideas (Mlinar, 1992: 2).

Thus sensitivity to place, to new identity formation, to the mutual respect and guarantee of cultural rights for all citizens in a state should inform our planning. Sectoralism and exclusivity appear to have had their day. But such sentiments do not accord with the wishes of certain minority groups who seek through territorial autonomy precisely those exclusive group rights recently denied to them by hegemonic majorities and central state powers. While in some respects contemporary Europe is exercizing its new openness in cross-border relations, by fluidity and flexibility in market exchanges, in other respects there is a greater insistence than ever on becoming *maitre chez nous* and a dominant local majority. Hence the whole pressure for a reconstituted Europe of the peoples rather than a Europe comprised of mythical but powerful nation–states. Hence the return to localism, to autarchy, to grassroots politics and social–ecological reform.

Table 5.5   Four principles for neutralizing conflicts

The Canadian and Belgian examples show that linguistic conflicts can be partially neutralized insofar as:

1   The introduction of the territoriality principle is limited to a few areas like administration and education.

2   The institutional multilingualism that emerges leads to the creation of independent unilingual networks which grant equal opportunity of communication to minority and majority speakers and which exclude linguistic discrimination connected with speakers of the prestige language.

3   Measures of linguistic planning are not exclusively based on linguistic censuses carried out by the respective governments; they should, rather, genuinely take into account the situational and contextual characteristics of the linguistic groups.

4   Linguistic groups in a multilingual country are not judged primarily quantitatively. Because they are in a minority situation, they should, on the contrary, be awarded more rights and possibilities of development than would be due to them based on their numbers and their proportion to the majority (for example, a lower number of pupils per class should be accepted for the minority).

Source: Nelde, Labrie and Williams, 1992

Hence too the inherent dynamism unleashed in the call for liberty in Central and Eastern Europe.

If minorities are not to be marginalized, or worse till typified as the scapegoat for many of society's ills, then as we argue in Table 5.5, point 4, dependent peoples should be awarded 'more rights and possibilities than would be due to them based on their numbers and their proportion to the majority'. In contemporary Europe two sorts of counter-argument are posed to this positive development of a minority's cultural infra-structure. The first, often raised in the Czechlands, Slovakia, Hungary and Poland, argues that the prime requisite of the democratic state is to treat all its citizens equally, regardless of ethnic, national or linguistic origin. Minorities should not need 'extra rights' if the democratic guarantees are in place. For as Vaclav Havel reminds us:

It seems to me that these collective rights can be accepted and included in the legal system only when we do not understand them as something beyond. As if there were some civil rights that are equal for everybody and then there are some special rights for some special groups of citizens which the others do not share. It is not the case. The right for freedom of speech, the fight to keep their individual culture, the right to education, all these are the essential human and citizen rights and in the case of minorities, i.e. communities with their own traditions, spiritual, historic, social and with their own language background, can these general rights be well ascertained when they are allowed to be exerted within that frame and in that

Table 5.6   Eight key questions on territory and language

1   Can an autochthonous culture survive without its own territory?

2   Do the advances in technology liberate minority cultures from the confines of tradition, habit, routine behaviour and localism?

3   Are there measurable thresholds beyond which it is both uneconomic and untenable to advance the scope and scale of technological developments for minority cultures, if the necessary infra-structure is lacking? If so, what are they and to which forms of technology do they apply?

4   Need radio and television always follow, rather than precede, comprehensive educational reform where the lesser-used language is recognised within the local system?

5   Should language rights be predicated on the territorial or the personality principle of language planning?

6   What are the class implications of developing a bureaucratic technical intelligentsia within the minority culture?

7   Are elitism, a new professional/technocratic intelligentsia and a burgeoning bureaucracy, the necessary progeny of the recent marriage between language activists and the local/central power brokers?

8   What role does the European Community, the Council of Europe, CSCE and the European Bureau for Lesser-Used Languages have in facilitating inter-group networking on the media, group rights and cultural reproduction?

environment that are genuine to them. And I think that these instrumental functions belong to the collective rights (Vaclar Havel, 1991).

This citizen democracy stance is understandable in a political climate which stresses the state as a co-ordinator of change rather than as the instigator or creator of a new binding order and social reality following 40 years of state intervention under totalitarianism. But such pristine democratic principles of co-equality, of majoritarian tolerance, of freedoms under the law to reproduce identity, do not guarantee or satisfy minority aspirations in West European societies. In Central and Eastern European societies there is even less consensus about the nature of mass society, let alone the legitimacy of selected minorities in multi-ethnic societies.

A second objection relates to resources as well as to political will. It is argued that some societies can barely afford the cost of mass education and citizen socialization within the majority culture. How can they afford to provide, for example, a Hungarian-medium University in Slovakia, restitution of Turkish language rights in Bulgaria following their denial under Todor Zhivkov's regime, or primary-level instruction in the mother tongue of Lipovanions, Tatars, Ceangai, Secui, Svabi, Sachsons in Romania? Such objections should be taken seriously, and sympathetically for constructing democracy and socio-economic development is indeed an expensive, if

Table 5.7   Seven key research areas summarized

---

1   Comparative cross-national research on the application of territoriality and personality principles of language planning.

2   Social Survey analyses to identify actual language behaviour by domain and group characteristics, to supplement aggregate census data.

3   Identification of various social communication networks and their relationship to institutional support agencies.

4   Audits of the bilingual nature, operation and policy objectives of major public institutions.

5   Future expectations of the range of opportunities available to bilinguals in their employment in both public and private sectors.

6   The wide question of the perceptions held by consumers, agencies and educationalists as to what constitutes an appropriate place for proficiency in the threatened language.

7   The deep question of relative cultural autonomy, group relations and the increasing dependence of the language on state provision and control.

---

necessary, process. Minority concerns are too often marginalized as economically wasteful of scarce resources and regarded as an essentially private matter from which the state would be well advised to withdraw. The common argument runs that if people are so concerned with their own identity and the reproduction of their culture they should devize ways and means of financing and nurturing their language, religion and folk ways. This is a well-established charge against minority participation in the public, formal life of the state. It is but a short step from saying that the state has no obligation to support such minorities to saying that such minorities have no permanent right of residence in the state and should depart forthwith. When minority activists press for their demands in the face of state centralist assimilation, they are accused of being recidivists, separatists, traitors and anti-pathetic to the state ideal. If full participation in multi-ethnic societies is to be realized then remedial action to counter long-term structural discrimination against minorities must be instigated. It is simply not good enough for a ruling elite to argue that society cannot afford to cater for its own minority population. The truth is that in these troubled times democracies cannot afford to disregard their obligations to constituent minorities.

Clearly the timing, precise nature and range of available institutional support will vary tremendously from society to society, depending upon the vagaries and exigencies of each situation. We are not naive enough to expect newly democratic societies to promise minorities a blissful future, only to disappoint because of shortages of resources, personnel and infra-structure. That scenario would only increase the relative discontent and frustration already felt by many minorities. However, some judicious mixture of formal cultural-economic planning, together with means of neutralizing conflict appear to be a *sine qua non* of the security politics of Europe today.

We have been arguing that structural changes in society, together with the spread of social market economies, necessitate mutual tolerance, open boundaries and the reconstruction of identities in an increasingly techno-logical age of instant communication and individualism. Where does this leave our original concern with language reproduction and territory? In my previous writing I have argued that territory is not only contextual, not only a scene for the playing out of socio-economic factors, but is itself a significant source of symbolic and resource power. Its possession and control is often deemed vital to the very survival of specific groups. However, territorially-rooted group identities are facing extreme press-ures which serve to devalue place and regions within the spatial hier-archy of power and action. In Table 5.6, I raise eight key questions pertaining to these issues which I believe are worthy of further consideration.

Finally, what is to be done by the intellectual community and govern-ment agencies in terms of key research areas? In Table 5.7 I signpost seven broad areas which need urgent attention if the rights of minorities are to be instituted more generally throughout Europe. Substantive answers to these questions would quicken our awareness of the dynamic relationship between cultural reproduction, technological change, citizen participation and the modern interpretation of a democratic society. Many of our most pressing global problems such as mass starvation, social inequality and ecological pollution seem to defy conventional solutions because the poli-tical will is often absent to alter radically the system which gives rise to such problems. In terms of protecting the cultural, linguistic and religious rights of European minorities many of the practicable solutions are avail-able and have been successfully grafted on to the political system of selected states to provide a tolerable existence for many – majority and minorities alike. Socio-political conflict is neither a necessary nor an inevi-table product of this relationship. I would argue that the principles and practical measures for satisfying legitimate minority demands are well understood. The real challenge facing us today is to determine how best to implement such principles as state policy in as wide a set of social domains as is feasible in each specific context. In an age of increasingly complex social organizations, where questions of citizen identity, respon-sibility, obligation and expectation are continually being re-formulated, it would be foolish to deny the legitimacy of minority rights and thereby to add one further layer of difficulty to the management of our common European home.

Acknowledgements

This is a revised version of 'The Cultural Rights of Minorities', the Plenary Opening Address to the Bratislava Symposium 'Minorities in Politics', 13–16 November 1991, organized under the auspices of the then President of the Czech and Slovak Federal Republic, Vaclav Havel.

References

Churchill, S. (1986), *The Education of Linguistic and Cultural Minorities in the OECD Countries*, Clevedon, Multilingual Matters.

Council of Europe (1991), *European Charter for Regional and Minority Languages*, Strasbourg, Council of Europe.

Foreign and Commonwealth Office (1991), *Charter of Paris for a New Europe*, London, HMSO.

Havel, V. (1991), Opening Speech to the Conference on Minorities in Politics, Bratislava Castle, 13 November.

Mlinar, Z. (ed.), (1992), *Globalization and Territorial Identities*, Aldershot, Avebury.

Nelde, P. Labrie, N. and Williams, C.H. (1992), 'The Principles of Territoriality and Personality in the Solution of Linguistic Conflicts'. *Journal of Multilingual and Multicultural Development*, **13**, No. 5, 1–20.

O'Riagain, D. (1989), 'The EBLUL: its Role in Creating a Europe United in Diversity', in T. Veiter, (ed.), *Federalisme, régionalisme et droit des groupes ethnique en Europe*, Vienna, Braumuller.

Palley, C. et. al. (1991), *Minorities and Autonomy in Western Europe*, London, Minority Rights Group.

Siguan, M. (1990), *Linguistic Minorities in the EEC: Spain, Portugal, Greece*, Brussels, O.O.P.E.C.

Thomas, E.M. (1989), *News and Information Networks for the Lesser-used Language Communities* Aberystwyth, Mercator Project.

Thornberry, (1991a), *Minorities and Human Rights Law*, London, Minority Rights Group.

Thornberry, P. (1991b), *International Law and the Rights of Minorities*, Oxford, Clarendon Press.

Williams, C.H. (1989), 'New Domains of the Welsh Language: Education, Planning and the Law,' in G. Day and G. Rees (eds), *Contemporary Wales*, Vol. 3: 41–76.

Williams, C.H. (1990), 'Political Expressions of Under-development in the West European Periphery', in H. Buller and S. Wright (eds), *Rural Development: Problems and Practices*, Aldershot, Avebury.

Williams, C.H. (ed.), (1991), *Linguistic Minorities, Society and Territory*, Clevedon, Multilingual Matters.

Williams, C.H. (1992), 'Identity, Autonomy and the Ambiguity of Technological Development', in Zdravko Mlinar, (ed.), *Globalization and Territorial Identities*, Aldershot, Avebury.

Williams, C.H. (1993), 'Global Language Divisions', in T. Unwin (ed.), *Atlas of World Development*, London, Belhaven.

6
Issues of peace and security in contemporary Europe

Colin H. Williams and Stephen W. Williams

1989 will undoubtedly go down in European history as a turning point ranking alongside 1789, 1848, 1919 and 1945 in its significance. While we might not be witnessing the 'end of history' as envisaged by Fukuyama (1989, 1992) we are certainly in uncharted waters without the support of tested navigational aids. In terms of peace and security the present conjuncture provides a constellation of opportunities and risks, the final outcome being difficult to determine with any degree of certainty. As Antonio Gramsci noted in another context 'the old is dying and the new cannot be born – in this interregnum there arises a great diversity of morbid symptoms'.

This chapter seeks to evaluate the changing nature and adequacy of the emerging security architecture of Europe. Specific attention is paid to the issue of minorities and to their role in the restructuring of the territorial foundation of post-communist Europe. The implications of the dismemberment of Yugoslavia for this new security order are particularly profound as they represent the re-assertion of fundamental questions of identity, territory and authority in the European state system.

The emergence of a bipolar system

The bipolar Cold-War system which existed from the late 1940s to 1989 replaced the classical European state system which emerged at the end of the 15th century:

From 1500 onwards, for over four centuries, Europe was characterized by a constant process of diplomatic manoeuvering and frequent conflict between states. During this period, despite the wars which occurred, almost all of the European countries managed to maintain their existence. This was largely the result of the successful working of a continuously shifting, but generally maintained balance of power amongst the main European states. The patterns of power altered cease-lessly but the fundamental structure of relations between the European states persisted (Baylis, 1992: 385).

This European balance of power system was severely shaken by the events leading up to World War I (the creation of a powerful unified Germany) and the termination of the War itself (the necessity for the intervention of the USA as an 'external' balancer). However, the system was provided with a prolonged lease of life by the Versailles Treaty of 1919 and the operation of an ineffectual League of Nations; the latter possessing neither enforcement powers nor any real machinery for collective security. As Kennedy has noted:

The United States would not join the league. The Soviet Union was treated as a pariah state and kept out of the league. So too were the defeated powers, at least for the first few years. When the revisionist states commenced their aggression in the 1930s they soon thereafter left the league (1989: 374).

By 1940 the failure of traditional power-balancing systems was all too apparent with Germany once again within reach of achieving hegemony in Europe. Only a combination of American, Soviet and British resources were capable of inflicting defeat on Germany in 1945. As Baylis observed, 'the Second World War finally revealed the failure of the old European system to perform its essential task of maintaining an internal balance and the independence of its member states' (Baylis, 1992: 387).

In the aftermath of World War II the USSR and the USA emerged as the principal actors in the European theatre. However, the preoccupation of rebuilding a war-torn continent provided a temporary focus for common concern and delayed the establishment and intensification of the split between the two blocs. Nevertheless, by 1941 Churchill could make his famous (and for some self-fulfilling) pronouncement that 'from Stettin in the Baltic to Trieste in the Adriatic an Iron Curtain has descended across Europe'. And certainly by 1948 the Cold War took on a rising curve with the Berlin blockade. In 1949 the North Atlantic Treaty Organization (NATO) was created and Germany's bifurcation was confirmed (see Figure 6.1 and Table 6.1). In 1955 West Germany was integrated into the NATO structure and the Warsaw Pact was created in the same year, ostensibly as a consequence of this. In an ironic twist brought about by the disinte-gration of the balance-of-power system, the freezing of ideological pos-itions and their etching into the political geography of Europe, a new European system emerged. This consisted of 'a bipolar set of relationships which taken as a whole constituted a state system encompassing not only the superpowers whose actions created it but the European states as well' (Deporte, 1986: 116). The security system of Cold War Europe was predi-cated, therefore, on the division of the continent into hermetically sealed blocs, and in many respects was completely unlike previous power arrangements. First, as stated previously, it was a bipolar system domi-

Figure 6.1   Pre-1989 Eastern Europe

Source: Short, J. (1982), *An Introduction to Political Geography*, London, Routledge.

nated by the two superpowers. In an economic context the USA was truly a global power and this position was reinforced by its nuclear superiority. On the other hand the Soviet Union commanded the largest conventional armed forces on the continent. Second, the division of Germany and the integration of the successor states into opposing alliance structures provided a satisfactory solution to the 'German question'. Third, the role of nuclear deterrence fundamentally changed the rules of the game of the international system, and the 'balance of terror' became a pivotal element of the European security system.

In the opinion of many commentators the so-called 'long peace' of the

Table 6.1   The Major Cold War Alliances

The North Atlantic Treaty Organisation (NATO)

The North Atlantic Treaty was signed in Washington on 4 April 1949. This action brought North America into military alliance with, in particular, the states which had formed the 'Western European Union' a year earlier. The key article of the treaty included the statement that 'an armed attack against one or more of [the parties] in Europe or North America shall be considered an attack against them all.'

Membership

1949	Belgium	Luxembourg	Italy	United States
	Canada	Netherlands	1952	Greece
	Denmark	Norway		Turkey
	France	Portugal	1955	West Germany
	Iceland	United Kingdom	1982	Spain

In 1966 President De Gaulle withdraw France from the integrated military command and NATO headquarters were moved from Paris to Brussels. Since the Turkish invasion of northern Cyprus in 1974, the relationship of Greece with NATO has also been somewhat stormy.

The end of the cold war saw no enthusiasm in NATO for disbanding the alliance, mainly because of the unpredictability of political developments in the Soviet Union, but also because of the usefulness of the alliance organisation in coordinating collective responses to 'out-of-area' threats.

The Warsaw Treaty Organisation (WTO)

The 'Warsaw Pact', as it was usually known, was concluded between the Soviet Union and its East European satellites in the Polish capital on 14 May 1955. 'In case of armed aggression in Europe', its signatories assured of 'immediate assistance . . . with all means which appear necessary, including the use of armed force.' A United Military Command with headquarters in Moscow was established. Ostensibly created in retaliation for the granting of sovereignty to West Germany and its integration into NATO, formally the Pact represented little more than a multilateral synthesis of the series of bilateral treaties between Moscow and its satellites which had existed in most cases for nearly a decade; arrangements for Soviet control of their forces were also at least three years old by this time.

Membership

Albania	Hungary
Bulgaria	Poland
Czechoslovakia	Romania
East Germany	Soviet Union

Having sided with China in the latter's dispute with Moscow, in 1962 Albania was excluded from Warsaw Pact meetings and withdrew in 1968.

In the late 1980s the collapse of communism in Eastern Europe spelled the end for the Warsaw Pact. In 1990 East Germany ceased to exist and in February 1991 the remaining six members formally dissolved the military wing of the Warsaw Pact at a meeting in Budapest.

Source: Berridge, G.R. (1992), *International Politics: State, Power and Conflict since 1945*, Hemel Hempstead, Harvester Wheatsheaf.

post – 1945 period (Gaddis, 1986) can be attributed to the positive resonances associated with the characteristics noted above. Mearsheimer, for example, argues that 'the absence of war in Europe since 1945 has been the consequence of three factors: the bipolar distribution of military power on the continent; the rough military equality between the two states comprising the two poles of Europe . . .; and the fact that each superpower was armed with a large nuclear arsenal' (Mearsheimer, 1990: 6). Mearsheimer's central argument is that the bipolar structure provided discipline, predictability and stability, the final outcome being that wars were prevented from occuring. The realist underpinnings of Mearsheimer's conclusions can certainly be debated (Hoffman, et al, 1990); nevertheless it is the case that the bipolar system created a military structure which was based on well defined alliances with clear commitments and doctrines. Kaldor provides a deft summary of the evolution of NATO strategy in Europe, identifying three principal phases:

. . . the 'tripwire strategy' associated with massive (nuclear) retaliation; 'flexible response', introduced in 1967; and the increasing emphasis on warfighting (both nuclear and conventional), associated with the deployment of Cruise and Pershing missiles, and later with 'deep strike' concepts. All these strategies start from the premise which mirrors the Second World War experience, that Western Europe depends on the technological superiority of the United States for defence against a Soviet blitzkrieg attack across the North German plains (Kaldor, 1990: 203. See also Freedman, 1989; McInnes, 1991).

On the ground the starkest manifestation of the bipolar system was the Central Front (see Figure 6.2). Here, the fundamental NATO precept of the 'forward defence' of West Germany right up to the inner German border led Farringdon to conclude that 'nowhere else are the limits of operational space and time so narrowly defined, and nowhere is political and military movement fraught with such heavy consequences' (Farringdon, 1989).

A new security architecture for Europe?

Despite the weaknesses and risks inherent in a bipolar system, bipolarity during the period from 1945 to 1989 did result in the longest period of 'peace' in European history. For many, the revolutions of 1989 and the subsequent disintegration of the Soviet Union following the abortive coup in 1991 has resulted in Europe resuming its 'normal' path of multipolarity. The critical issue is, of course, how best to respond to these changes in Europe's landscapes. At the risk of oversimplification two broad positions can be identified. The pessimists fear that the end of bipolarity signals a return to a more fractious multipolar Europe, where problems hitherto suppressed will erupt into violence (see Mearsheimer, 1990, for example). On the other hand, the optimists do not fear the return of multipolarity, arguing that many of the causes of war evident in the first half of the 20th century have been eliminated or significantly reduced and welcome the opportunity for the emergence of a pan-European security order (see Kupchan and Kupchan, 1991; Van Evera, 1990).

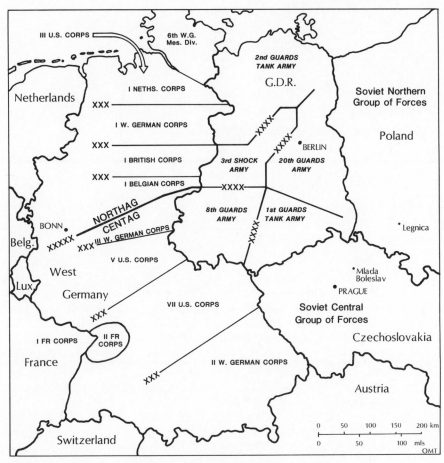

Figure 6.2   The Central Front: major formations

Source: Farringdon, H. (1989), *Strategic Geography*, London, Routledge.

Independent of this debate, however, it is the case that 'the changes in Europe confirm the fact that menaces today are of an utterly different character compared to those of the Cold War period. The main challenge for the future is uncertainty and its related risks' (Rotfeld, 1992: 580). Some of these risks are summarized in the *Statement on the Defence Estimates* (HMSO, 1992) and include the still massive nuclear (strategic and tactical) and conventional arsenals of the former Soviet Union; the uncertainties associated with the effects of the successor orders in Central and Eastern Europe to establish or strengthen democratic institutions and rebuild economies; the management of national, ethnic and related territorial tensions. Clearly the major challenge to the stability of the European is from the structural transition and constellation of problems associated with the break up of the former Soviet Union. In addition, there are issues outside

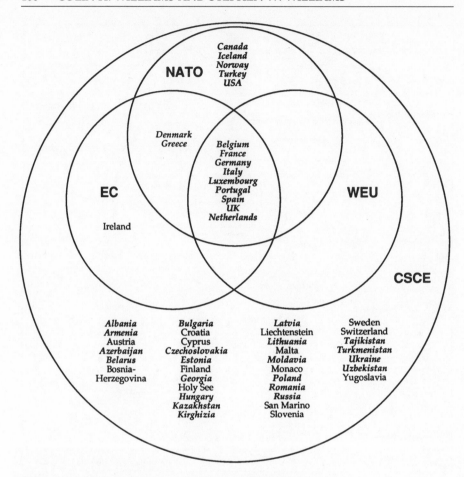

Members of North Atlantic Co-operation Council as at 5 June 1992 in Bold

Figure 6.3 Security in Europe: membership of international organizations

Source: HMSO (1992), *Statement on the Defence Estimates*, London, HMSO.

Europe which, although not presenting an immediate threat, are cause for concern (for example, the proliferation of ballistic missiles and nuclear, chemical and biological weapons). As Legge notes, 'in contrast to the single monolithic threat of the past we now face a range of risks which are multifaceted, multidimensional and very difficult to predict' (Legge, 1992: 11–14).

Of course the primal question is what is the most appropriate structure for managing peace and security in Europe as we approach the end of the millennium? Within this context the current 'buzz' words are a 'new European security architecture' and the importance of 'interlocking institutions'. According to Kinkel (1992: 5) the future security architecture of Europe will consist of three complementary levels (*see* Figure 6.3).

1. The Atlantic level, consisting of the Atlantic Alliance and its Cooperation Council, which extend far into Eastern Europe and Asia.
2. The core is the European Community and the emerging European Union, with the Western European Union as an integral component.
3. The comprehensive all European level which brings together the 52 member states of the Conference on Security and Cooperation in Europe (CSCE).

The North Atlantic Treaty Organization (NATO)

Kinkel refers to NATO as 'the most successful alliance in history' (1992: 3). However, despite the alliance's strength, there are dissenting voices concerning its future relevance. Johnson, for example, is of the firm belief that 'NATO in its present form is anachronistic and will disappear' (1992: 45). Some of the reasons advanced for this judgement include the following. First, with the disappearance of the Warsaw Pact, NATO neither has a visible opponent nor a well defined area to defend. Without such an existential threat there is no basis for formulating military plans. Second, the remaining threats are not of a military nature and therefore do not require military solutions. Third, at a theoretical level, alliances in general are created to face a specific threat or threats. Without a clear focus there is no glue to hold the armies together and alliances disintegrate (see Chernoff, 1992).

A majority view, however, holds that NATO's immediate future is not in doubt and that it will be a major component in the new security architecture. As Clauss argues, 'NATO is a critically important building block. It is in fact the only functioning security alliance in the world and continues to form the backbone of European security' (1992: 3). As Deputy Supreme Allied Commander Europe he would say that anyway, wouldn't he? Nevertheless, there are legitimate reasons why NATO should occupy a central position in the new security order. First, it guarantees the link between Euro–Atlantic defence and pan-European security. The North American commitment cannot be taken for granted and requires an institutional anchor for it to survive. Second, through its involvement in arms control and confidence-building negotiations. Third, of all international organizations NATO is the only one which can provide for its members military security to military threats. As Baylis (1992: 403) points out the Gulf War and the crisis in ex-Yugoslavia are timely reminders that military force remains an important feature of international relations in the post-Cold-War world.

Significant changes in NATO's role and missions in the new security environment have been made as a consequence of both the 1990 London Summit and 1991 Rome Summit. At the London Summit five principal action points emerged:

1. The establishment of a new relationship with the countries of Central and Eastern Europe.
2. The elaboration of a new military strategy.

3. A determination to strengthen the CSCE.
4. A commitment to pursue the arms control process beyond the conventional forces in Europe treaty.
5. The encouragement of a European security identity and defence role (see *NATO Review*, 1990).

The Rome Summit confirmed that these commitments had been kept. in particular, it was announced that the North Atlantic Cooperation Council (NACC) would be the institutional basis for contacts between NATO and Central and East European countries (*see* below). At a military level NATO's 'new Strategic Concept' was unveiled and the re-defined objectives of the Alliance in the context of the changed European security environment were encapsulated in four so-called 'core security functions':

1. To provide one of the indispensable foundations for a stable security environment in Europe.
2. To serve as a transatlantic forum for consultations on any issues that affect the Allies vital interests.
3. To deter and defend against any threat of aggression against the territory of any NATO member state.
4. To preserve the strategic balance within Europe.

In addition the military posture of the Alliance was significantly overhauled to reflect the increased emphasis on crisis management (and the need therefore for highly mobile standing forces), reduced manpower, and the political desirability for multinational forces. At the operational level a comprehensive in-place linear defence posture based on forward defence was no longer required. This was replaced by a triad of reaction forces, main defence forces and augmentation forces (for more detail see Legge, 1992 and Clauss, 1992). However the final structure is still in some doubt:

NATO has always been a compromise between the military desirable and the politically possible. One consequence has been too many headquarters and too many staff offices . . . The alliance has now got most of its new organisation in place. Although still smaller than the old one, it will still be much larger than it needs to be for the number of men at its command. The alliance will still have two levels of authority below the overall European command; one would be plenty . . . the expense and awkwardness of the present plan makes it look, at best, a temporary arrangement (*Economist*, 1992).

Prior to the Rome Summit it seemed possible that certain countries in Central and Eastern Europe would be accorded observer status at NATO meetings (see Taylor, 1992). However, unsurprisingly, this suggestion soon lost favour. Nevertheless, at the Rome Summit the North Atlantic Co-operation Council (NACC) was established, consisting of 37 members, being a forum for consultations between NATO and countries in Central and East Europe and Central Asia (see Worner, 1992). Hoise (1992) considers the NACC to be a 'framework for a new security culture', although a less generous interpretation might consider it to be yet another 'talking shop'. According to Worner the principal advantage of the NACC is that by giving the non-NATO members 'a common security anchor in our Western structures, we have helped to prevent the formation of competing alliances in Central and Eastern Europe. The NACC has given the countries of Central and Eastern Europe an instrument for addressing their security concern and for identifying multilateral solutions' (1992: 6). More specifically to date the NACC, has considered a wide range of issues including: the sharing of NATO expertise in the transformation of domestic systems and structures; the discussion of key security issues (e.g. the question of nuclear weapons in the former Soviet Union) and; acted as a forum for maintaining the momentum and integrity of existing treaties (e.g. START and the CFE). Furthermore, it has addressed various practical issues such as the creation of defence-oriented armies and the civilian control of armed forces.

In addition, the announcement in December 1992 that the NACC will be involved in peacekeeping operations has provided it with a more significant security function. The intention is that the countries of NATO and the former Warsaw Pact will cooperate in joint peacekeeping operations to deal with future European crises such as in ex-Yugoslavia if called upon by the CSCE or the UN (*The Guardian*, 1992, 19 December). The brief of the NACC could be considered overambitious but 'its acceptance within NATO does show that the organisation, at the working level, is cognisant of the problems ahead and anxious to discuss practical steps towards solutions' (Johnson, 1992: 34).

The West European Union

One of the more sensitive issues which preceeded the signing of the Maastricht Treaty concerned the question of how far the political union should extend into the area of defence and defence policy in addition to the wider areas of foreign and security policy. As Menon *et al* (1992: 99) observe, 'the distinction among these four categories is a matter of almost theological dispute – reflecting the sensitivity of extending the integration of the EC's civilian external relations into areas of high politics that the United States considered the proper domain of the Atlantic Alliance under US leadership'.

However, the Maastricht Treaty did go beyond the concerns of foreign policy formulation into the realms of defence policy. The key institution in this context is the Western European Union (WEU) which was created a year before NATO and was established as a collective defence organization partly to integrate a re-armed West Germany into Western defence planning. The recent rejuvenation of the WEU dates from the early 1980s, particularly in the context of debates concerning the nature of financial burden-sharing and the nature of a European Pillar in the Alliance (see Bathurst, 1992). Investment in the two Gulf conflicts and participation with humanitarian aid to the Kurdish refugees in Northern Iraq also raised the WEU's profile. The signing of the Maastricht Treaty in February 1992, has thrust the WEU into a pivotal position with respect to the emerging

European security architecture. Thus, one of the key objectives of the Treaty on European Union was identified as 'the implemenation of a foreign and security policy including the eventual framing of a common defence policy, which might in time lead to a common defence'. Furthermore, the European Union was empowered to request the WEU, 'which is an integral part of the development of the Union, to elaborate and emplement decisions which have defence implications' (Menon, *et al*, 1992).

In effect the WEU is being touted as the hyphen in the EC–NATO relationship. This position was made clear in the 'Petersburg Declaration' of the WEU Council of Ministers in June 1992, which stated that the organization is defined as the 'defence component of the European Union and . . . the means to strengthen the European pillar of the Atlantic Alliance'. It is equally clear, however, that NATO will be the senior partner in any relationship, as the following statement from the North Atlantic Council meeting in December 1992 attests:

We reaffirm the importance of maintaining the Allies' existing obligations and commitments of forces to NATO and we emphasise in this regard that the primary responsibility of forces answerable to WEU will remain NATO's collective defence under the Washington Treaty.

The definition of the WEU as both the security identity of the European Union and the European Pillar of the NATO Alliance is intuitively attractive. Nevertheless, there may well be practical problems associated with the orchestration of these two functions. Although the details have yet to be established, the WEU will certainly have mission of its own (Bathurst, 1992). Initial discussions suggested that a satisfactory division of labour could be based on NATO forces operating within the NATO area while the WEU would be involved in operations outside. This arrangement, however, looks increasingly meaningless as NATO has been given the go-ahead to be involved in out-of-area activities under the auspices of both the NACC and CSCE. This is despite the fact that such activities are limited by Article 5 of the North Atlantic Treaty. Further complications have arisen as a result of the expansion of the already existing Franco–German brigade into a corps (within the framework of the WEU) to which other WEU members have been invited to contribute. The French refer to this cell as the 'Euro-corps' which would form the embryo of a European army. Not for the first time this represents an alternative French perception of matters European: for them the WEU was a first step along the road towards a single European armed force which was both distinct and separate from the USA. Nevertheless, agreements have been made between the French and German chiefs of staff and the Supreme Allied Commander Europe on the conditions under which the Euro-corps is to be used in the context of the Atlantic Alliance. As Manfred Worner, NATO Secretary General, states, 'to operate meaningfully, (the WEU) would need to be able to use NATO's assets or NATO's armed forces in cases where NATO does not choose to act. We have offered our assets to the WEU and such a double-assignment does not pose any problem so long as the priority for NATO is clearly maintained' (Worner, 1992: 5). And yet, one cannot but recognize an element of truth in Wollacott's caustic observation that 'the creative use of the concept of double and triple hatting . . . meant that a German sergeant in the European corps can be regarded as a NATO trooper, a Western European Union soldier, or Lotharingian grenadier, depending on which day of the week it is, or whether or not there is an 'r' in the month' (Wollacott, 1992).

The Conference on Security and Cooperation in Europe (CSCE)

If there is to be a keystone in the new European security architecture, then the CSCE would appear to be the most likely candidate (see Kupchan and Kupchan, 1991, for example). As Snider observes the CSCE is part of a new European peace order based on 'neo-liberal institutionalism', whereby the Hobbesian tendencies inherent in the break up of the old European order 'can be mitigated by an institutional structure that provides legitimate and effective channels for reconciling conclicting interests' (Snider, 1990: 15). Currently, its membership consists of 52 West, Central and East European states, the countries of the ex-Soviet Union plus the USA and Canada. In essence it provides the framework for a security organization stretching from Vancouver to Vladivostock and has recently been recognized as a regional organization by the United Nations under Chapter VIII of the Charter.

The CSCE came into being in 1975 (and had a membership of 35 countries) with the signing of the Helsinki Final Act. At that time its principal purpose was to function as a forum for overcoming the artificial division of Europe. Specific CSCE activities provided a series of rules to guide the behaviour of states and to build confidence between the two military alliances. Specific CSCE activities covered a host of issues: political–military confidence building measures; human rights; and scientific, cultural and educational cooperation. Nevertheless, as Johnson (1992: 33) has observed: 'following greater than expected success, the CSCE process led an episodic and somewhat erratic life; the great powers being obviously reluctant to give permanence to a body which they had created only for certain immediate purposes'. However, following the events of 1989 the CSCE process was transformed from a forum which attempted to ameliorate the hostility and suspicion between two opposing blocs to one which could provide the focus for a pan-European security order, based on the principles of common security and non-provocative defence. As a consequence of the Charter of Paris for a New Europe, signed on 21 November 1990, which recognized the formal termination of the Cold War, the CSCE was institutionalized, its membership widened and the process given a new impetus by being assigned new and important tasks. A Conflict Prevention Centre was created in Vienna, an Office of Free Elections was established in Warsaw, and a small Secretariat set up in Prague. However, the optimism which followed the Charter of Paris was short-lived as the CSCE's political efforts in the context of the Yugoslavian civil war and the problems of national minorities proved to be disappointing. As Ghebali observes, 'the CSCE had been reshaped to meet the needs of a Europe that was seen as having overnight, merely as a result of the collapse of communism, become *democratic, peaceful* and *united* to use the words of the Charter of Paris' (1992: 3). Many of the issues underlying this judgement (including the lack of operational resources and weaknesses in the CSCE's institutions and structures) were addressed during the 1992 Helsinki meeting. At this meeting a new set of Helsinki accords were signed entitled 'The Challenge of Change'. The stated purpose of these accords is to transform the CSCE into an instrument capable of preventing wars and promoting political stability and economic progress across the continent.

In the context of operational security capabilities three principal decisions are of importance. First, with the creation of a High Commissioner for National Minorities it is intended that certain types of conflict could be prevented at an early stage. In essence it provides an 'early warning' function which would prevent national minority tensions from developing into conflict. Second, and in a sense more significant, the CSCE was empowered to conduct peacekeeping (but not peace enforcement) operations in line with UN practice. In pursuit of this the CSCE is able to call upon the resources and expertise of NATO, WEU, EC and the CIS. The role of NATO in this context generated a certain amount of debate. France in particular did not wish to see a direct linkage between NATO and CSCE as it was the USA's preference that NATO should become the CSCE's military arm.

Eventually, a compromise was reached on the basis of a verbal fudge whereby NATO was 'willing to support on a case-by-case basis . . . peacekeeping activities under the responsibility of the CSCE'. The third innovation was the future involvement of the CSCE in the area of disarmament negotiation rather than just the negotiation of confidence-building measures. Consequently, a Forum for Security Cooperation has been established which will focus on a wide range of disarmament issues, and in addition will provide a framework for consultation, cooperation and dialogues on a wide range of security issues (see Ghebali, 1992).

There are clearly problems remaining, and perhaps one of the most important is the CSCE's 'concensus rule'. This states that decisions must be unanimous, which means each government has a veto. As Ghebali observes, this is 'a cause of unwieldiness at best, or paralysis at worst' (1992:7). A promising development, however, is that the unanimity rule has been suspended under certain circumstances, allowing measures to be taken against states violating the Helsinki Final Act or the Charter of Paris.

The future success of the CSCE cannot be taken for granted. However, the 1992 Helsinki accords have gone some way towards transforming its image and reality from a 'debating club or a forum of never-ending negotiations' (Rotfeld, 1992: 582) to one which at least possesses the means to develop a concrete policy.

Although the CSCE provides an attractive focus for an all – embracing pan-European security institution we should be suitably circumspect in pursuing this as a realistic goal at the present time, as the following reservations suggest:

will it be capable of supporting the 'heavy traffic' of European security on 'good days and bad'?

it studiously ignores the prevalence of national self-interest and the chronic nature of ethnic and national rivalries. It is, therefore, naive, idealistic, Utopian and impractical.

the conceptual fuzziness of many of the terms used to characterise the new peace order. Thus what precisely is meant by a 'Common European Home' and a 'Europe Whole and Free' – reification or reality?

these ideas are in fact dangerous, seductive and delusory leading statesmen to abandon 'the tried and tested security structures of the post-war period . . . in order to adopt some ill defined concept of 'collective security' (Hyde-Price, 1990: 232–8; see also Baylis, 1992).

With reference to this latter, critical, issue Joffe has made the following acute comment:

Collective security (CS) is a nice idea, a mutual insurance society that does not depend on alliances, blocs and enemy images . . . One serious flaw is that CS has been tried before – and that it has failed miserably in each case (p.37) . . . A key conceptual weakness of CS is that the principle of 'one for all and all for one' requires all members of the system, or at least the great powers to treat aggression or the threat of aggression as the supreme evil, against which all other values are dwarfed'. States, however, follow their own interests; and they are loathe to sacrifice their particular interests on the altar of abstract justice. This is the irreducible reason why CS systems tend to 'bipolarise' at the moment of truth, its membership taking sides not against one single aggressor, but lining up behind either of the two combatants. For the same reason, states rarely, if ever, agree on the identity of the 'aggressor', which is the *conditio sine qua non* of collective sanctions (Joffe, 1992: 39).

The more realistic goal, therefore, is the creation and effective operation of a system of interlocking institutions based on, and bound together by, a concern for 'common security' but with clearly differentiated areas of competence. In this context Rotfeld's suggestion (1992: 582) for a General Treaty on Security and Cooperation in Europe would appear to be a sensible step forward. Without such a general agreement (supported by detailed operational protocols) the clear danger is that 'interlocking' could easily slide into 'entanglement' at best, and impotence at worst. One only has to recall that despite the deliberation of the principal security organizations the slide into war in the Balkans was not averted.

Minorities as an issue of peace and security

It is axiomatic that at a time of profound structural change in European society, when the spread of social market economies simultaneously opens new opportunities and closes old privileges, that greater attention than ever before is paid to the role of minorities in the construction of the new European order. We recognized the salience of the minority issue for state formation and identity reconstruction in the introduction to this volume. Here we want to pursue several sub-themes of that larger relationship as they influence political stability and the search for peace.

The long-term effects of the revolutionary year of 1989 are yet to be discerned. However, although few would deny the liberating potential of democracy in former totalitarian Stalinist states, neither should we under-estimate the difficulties involved in this great structural transition from a dictatorship and a command economy to a legally-binding representative democracy. Our new security policies, let alone humanitarian action, must still confront the consequences of the re-partition of Europe following the Versailles peace conference of 1919 when the Wilsonian principle of national self-determination created not only the new 'nation-states' of Czechoslovakia, Bulgaria, Romania, (See Figure 6.4) but also sealed the fate of minorities within minorities within these new borders.

So much of our present woe is due to the unravelling of the Versailles and Trianion Treaties, but so much could also have been predicted had the political fathers, such as Lloyd George and Clemenceau given the minori-ties question greater heed in a Central and Eastern European geo-strategic settlement.

The post-Versailles-Treaty's search for national congruence and the homogenizing tendencies of these new states led to two fateful periods of suspicion, discrimination, assimilation and expulsion. The first period, from 1919 to 1939 saw a flowering of virulent, chauvinistic nationalism which impressed itself into the landscape as much as into the hearts and minds of ordinary folk. Thus Bucharest, in celebration of the Allies' victory constructed French-style 'national monuments', such as the Arc de Triomphe on Souseaua Kisdeff, designed by Petru Antonescu. But the city like the country was soon plunged into the familiar trinity of economic crises, bitter political conflict and the rise of fascism in the form of the Iron Guard, under the leader Corneliu Codreanu until his execution in November 1938. A similar pattern was repeated elsewhere in Central and Eastern Europe, although for Germany itself it was difficult to create a national and republican iconography in the immediate post-Versailles Weimar Republic. When the imperial eagle was stripped of its crown and coat of arms on republican coins and emblems, the new state's enemies argued that this 'bankrupt vulture' (*Pleitegeier*) epitomized the new spiri-tual and material impoverishment of the state. As Harold James (1989: 122) has demonstrated the 'Weimar had rejected the old, but found it difficult to create a new political style. Though Germany had a republican form of government, the central state was still called the Empire (*Reich*), with a Reich Chancellor, Reich government, Reichstag (parliament), Reich postal service and so forth'. The transition from Empire to Republic produced a plethora of practical political difficulties, but all of these were conditioned by the insistence that, despite being defeated in World War I, Germany was still a Great Power with commensurate ambitions, shackled but for the present.

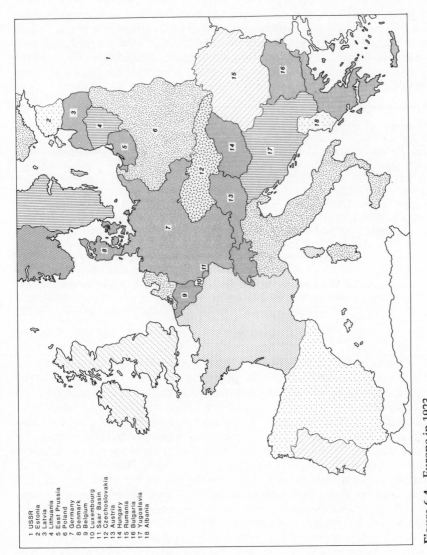

Figure 6.4   Europe in 1923

Source: Treharne, R.F. and Fullard, H. (1976), *Muir's Historical Atlas*, London, Philip.

1 USSR
2 Estonia
3 Latvia
4 Lithuania
5 East Prussia
6 Poland
7 Germany
8 Denmark
9 Belgium
10 Luxembourg
11 Saar Basin
12 Czechoslovakia
13 Austria
14 Hungary
15 Rumania
16 Bulgaria
17 Yugoslavia
18 Albania

Further tensions arose between the construction of a limited state sovereignty and the drift towards highly polarized politics. This was exacerbated by the Allies' (particularly French) insistence that the German economy be geared towards repaying reparation costs. Successive crises, of both an economic and political nature, threatened to de-stabilize Weimar democratic practice because it was only by repaying reparations, according to James (1989, p.132) that Germany would be able to think about a return to real sovereignty. The implications of limited sovereignty and economic underperformance were wide reaching for all, but particularly for Jews and other targeted foreigners, as James succinctly argues:

The dilemma of Weimar politics could be put as follows: it was important to have someone to blame – preferably a foreigner. It was also important to assert Germany's Great Power status – and that meant not allowing foreigners to intervene. In that case, how could foreigners be blamed? The idea of the great nation, together with the history of nineteenth-century economic strength, made it difficult to live with the realities of vanished prosperity and the traumas of a nation that was no longer great. There was a great risk that the collected political venom of Germans would turn on internal targets – and particularly on the Jews. 1919 and 1924 were partial triumphs for the sovereignty and Great Power principles; but it was not until the end of reparations in 1932 that the foreign shackles vanished altogether, and with them disappeared the limiting and stabilizing factor in German politics. A Hitler government before this date could have done little damage because of the limitations, imposed from abroad, on its room for manoeuvre. At any time after this date, however, any government – and particularly a Nazi one – could prove immensely powerful and ferociously destructive. (James, 1989: 135).

The details of the Nazi period and the ensuing World War are too well known to bear repeating here, though it is salutary to remind ourselves that features such as warfare, mass murder and post-war demographic and territorial readjustment have a compelling influence on the structure of the world order, the formation of European states and the plight of the beleaguered minorities. We have argued elsewhere that the preparation for warfare, and the effects of mass war are the most under-researched aspect of majority-minority relations (Williams, 1991: 1–43). But for Germany, in particular, modernization and nation–state formation were also contributions to a new European order after 1871. When they discovered, to their cost, that the international order would not brook an adventurous, virile newcomer and when the state became in turn a broken empire, following 1918, they could not offer as an excuse the fact that they had been bullied by coercive neighbours, as did many of the smaller nations. For 'when national ideologues looked for constraints on Germany's room for manoeuvre, when they realised that the nation could not do all that it set out to do, they concluded that the fault lay in internal weakness. The national strength had been sapped by some domestic difficulty, perhaps by an enemy from within' (James, 1989: 214). Fifty years on, echoes of the same search for the 'enemy within' haunt parts of Germany, particularly former

East Germany, where Jews, Turks, Gypsies, Romanians and other 'foreigners' are being harrassed and victimized by the resurrected popular front of the violent right.

If in the period from 1871 to 1939 Germany epitomized a new force for the destabilization of the old world order, in the second period from 1945 to 1991 she provided a model of the ambiguities inherent in the super-power era. On the one hand, the legitimacy of the German Federal Republic was strengthened at each successive stage of the development of the European Community. With the Franco–German political alliance as its cornerstone, the European Community, Council of Europe, C.S.C.E. and other trans-national organizations sought to bind Western Europe and North America closer together in an international economic order based upon capitalist inter-dependence. But a divided Germany was also the symbol and the substance of the Cold-War era because 'politics and geography made Berlin the gravest and most persistent source of tension in the nuclear age' (Newhouse, 1989: 65).

During the second period from 1945 to 1991 under the banner of revolutionary socialism Communist leaders abused the original Marxist–Leninist principles and substituted a harsh Stalinist repression whereby national cleavages were often exploited and cultural diversity was limited to circuses and operas, safe havens for control and subsidy by the centralizing state. With hindsight, some are arguing that the larger super-power conflict, discussed above, 'kept the lid' on sporadic ethnic 'bush-fires' but that now that the controlling influence of the Red Army and its allies has been lessened, such conflicts are likely to escalate and spread.

One consequence of the new world order in Eastern Europe is that territorial disputes and ethnic harmonization are once again matters of great political concern. But with the 'liberation' of oppressed peoples and their 'return to Europe', the problems of multi-ethnic societies cannot be solved by the old formulaic search for national congruence through territorial means. This does not stop chauvinistic nationalism creating new tensions in old places. We recognize that there are new waves of anti-Semitic, anti-gypsy, anti-foreign sentiment sweeping the former DDR, Czech-lands and Slovakia. Poland, the Ukraine and Romania. They have their counterpart in calls by extremists for the expulsion of Turks from Germany, Magyars from Slovakia, Croats from Serbia, Jews and Roma (Gypsies) from Romania, and Russians from the Baltic States.

The issue of the protection of minorities, as we saw in chapters 2 and 5, has been a critical feature of both inter-state relations and of individual initiatives since post-Napoleonic Europe. Table 5:2 indicates some of the more salient legislative acts of the past two decades and is designed to suggest that we already have a varied and rich diversity of experience to draw upon in our discussion of minority rights and security politics (Williams, 1991). What is new about the contemporary period is the urgency of the need for flexible and effective Europe-wide attention to the minority issues, and the recognition that the nation-state is not necessarily the best nor the most effective implementer of minority rights. New organizations and new means of monitoring and protecting against such sensitive issues as racial discrimination, genocide, anti-Semitism and over-stimulated nationalism are increasingly essential.

The operation of these new organizations will ultimately depend upon how the international community addresses the question of ethnic conflict in Central and Eastern Europe. A key feature influencing the emergence of ethnic politics has been the failure of the former communist regimes to develop a sense of legitimacy. The abiding feature of mass consciousness in these societies has been the lack of popular confidence and trust in public authorities and a greater fear of the future now that the old assumptions about social security and co-equality of all citizens have been challenged. With the collapse of the Soviet Union and its subsidies to maintain the Council for Mutual Economic Assistance we hear the urgent cry to 'rejoin' Europe and all its institutional organs. 'Yet, the prospects for full and formal membership in bodies such as the European Community and the Council of Europe are limited, thus forcing East Europeans to place primary stress on their ethnic communities. They recognize that their political survival will be a function of an ability to consolidate a domestic consensus rather than a product of international ties' (Bowers, 1992: 5).

In Western Europe it is argued that the only effective way to defuse ethnic conflict in Central and Eastern Europe is to spread the blanket of democracy over such peoples as quickly and effectively as possible. Thus special consideration is given to the more 'progressive' societies of the Czech Republic and Slovakia, Hungary and Poland to encourage their full participation in the EC. But we must be cautious of the implications of the pace of change. The very act of embarking upon rapid structural change to a free market economy with full representative democracy can in fact accelerate ethnic conflict. Not only because of the withdrawal of subsidy and guaranteed prices for fixed income citizens, a powerful material argument for the *ante status quo*, but also because for some groups in society, the legitimacy of the host nation-state and of the post-War boundaries are the subject of acute opposition. The decoupling of the Czech-Slovak Federation is not merely a domestic issue for those two national groups. It has implications for separatism elsewhere, for the question of the rights of the Hungarian minorities, for boundary changes, for ecological management of the Danube system, for defence and security structures, for popular trust in the army as a state institution. In short, long-subsumed sources of grievance and tension have emerged to challenge the nation-state system. Yet rather than argue for the erosion of the state, or for a transfer of sovereignty to some higher level (e.g. Brussels *vis à vis* the EC) the pressure is for the grounded constitution of a pluralist democracy, with interest groups and opposition movements thirsty for real participation within the state system itself. Few would have credited the fragility of the former totalitarian system. They would rather have stressed a normal pattern which transferred power automatically from Stalin to Brezhnev, from Gottwald to Husak, from Ulbricht to Honecker, from Rakosi to Kadar, from Gomulk to Jaruselski (Leonhard, 1990: 28). In the face of a withdrawal of Soviet guarantees for the future, civic resistance and reforming politicians effected a largely non-violent transition from the known to the unknown. But one of the certainties of the unknown is the necessity of the open state in Central and Eastern Europe. It may be under attack and challenge in the western part of our continent but the state will be reinforced as the principal political insitution in any enlargement of the European Community, precisely because it remains the focus of aspiration and the locomotive of collective action.

It is, of course, a dangerous illusion to assume that Eastern Europe will necessarily follow the same political economic path as Western Europe merely because the continent is now united under the banner of democracy. But being free does allow some states to deal with old problems in novel ways. One very promising method is to encourage trans-frontier cooperation in new regional economic systems. Trans-frontier cooperative ventures, such as the Alps-Adria and Carpathian-Tisa projects, promise to be a significant development for three reasons. First, they permit the increased harmonization of and investment in essential infrastructure such as communication links, trade flows, and economic development. Secondly, they highlight the frontier regions of the constituent nation-states as zones of open exchange, rather than as barriers to contact. Too often in the past such frontiers have been subject to population transfer, de-industrialization, neglect and underinvestment, precisely because they were 'suspect' or strategically sensitive regions. Thirdly, the creation of such functional regions can contribute to new forms of identity and behaviour based upon shared experience rather than state socialization. In truth many of the people who inhabit such functional regions either share more in common with neighbours across state boundaries than they do with fellow citizens or are desirous of opening up their region to strengthen ties of common bonds to fellow ethnics or irredentist minorities abroad. Such tendencies also serve to reduce the emphasis on the solution of problems within a national framework. Economically we are urged to conceive of Europe as an increasingly 'free' geographic area, while politically and juridically we continue to advance the cause of the nation–state ideal by using its administrative apparatus as the basis of data collection and of problem-solving.

The Carpathian–Tisa region occupies a pivotal space at the intersection of five states (see Figures 6.5 and 6.6) and could literally be said to be comprised of five peripheries. It has a complicated political and ethnic past best illustrated by reference to one region, the Zakarpatskaya Oblast in the western Ukraine. It was established on 22 January 1945 as an administrative unit, bounded by the Lvov/Ivano Frankovsk regions of the Ukraine and by four international states. Prior to the World War I it was part of Hungary; between 1918 and 1939 it was part of Czechoslovakia. Transcarpathia was divided between Ruthenia and Hungary when Hitler invaded Czechoslovakia and was incorporated into the Soviet Union after its occupation by the Soviet Army in the autumn of 1944 (Kinnear, 1991).

The region has long been an area of out-migration, a process accelerated since 1887 when a large group of Transcarpathians emigrated to North America swelling the approximately 800,000 who emigrated during the late 19th and early 20th century. Today emigration fears are once more being

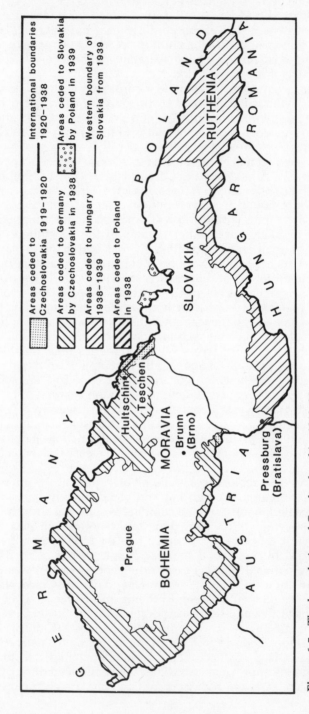

Figure 6.5   The boundaries of Czechoslovakia, 1919–39

Source: Tägil, S. (ed.) (1977), *Studying Boundary Conflicts*, Lund, Esselte Studium: 200. Reproduced with permission.

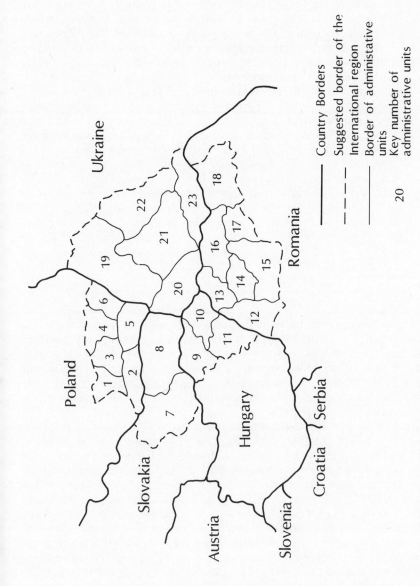

Figure 6.6 The Carpathian–Tisa Region

Source: Tóth, J. (1993) reproduced with permission.

expressed within the region. Approximately 2000 Transcarpathians per annum out-migrate, mainly through marriage with Hungarians and Slovaks and it is argued that both socio-economic and social–psychological factors predispose young residents to consider migrating (Kinnear, 1991). In order to counter this trend and to restore cultural confidence, knowledge, transferable skills and a new economic orientation the constituent regions are seeking to foster trade cooperation, to bolster the free movement of population within the region and to reduce the sources of ethnic conflict through regional development.

However, whilst at the macro-level the new post-communist era allows considerable latitude to foster inter-state economic and political relations, at the meso-level it has thrown up new sources of tension which challenge the ethnic order of Transcarpathia. In a series of trenchant publications, Professor P.R. Magosci (1978; 1992a; 1992b) has demonstrated how the native Carpatho-Rusyns were officially excised under all communist regimes (save for the Vojvodina region of former Yugoslavia).

Prior to the communist era, brief periods of relative autonomy had been guaranteed the Subcarpathian Rus by the Paris Peace Treaty (10 September 1919), the Trianon Settlement (4 June 1920) and by the Czechoslovak constitution (29 February 1920). But it was strategically advantageous for Stalin to declare that the Rus population was really Ukranian thereby legitimizing the annexation of the Subcarpathian Rus in 1945 as part of the Soviet Union. This had at least four long term consequences. It sealed the fate of the Rus population for 40 years as Ukranians. It forestalled the anticipated return of the region to Czechoslovakia, contrary to what had been agreed throughout the War. It gave a huge military advantage to the Soviet Union in the deployment of its forces on the strategically essential edge of the Hungarian plain, from which it was able to influence events in Central Europe. It facilitated large-scale population movements and ethnic transfers in the Transcarpathian region. Thus, for example, the identification of Polish Lemkos as Ukranians made it easier for the government to deport them.

Magosci notes that the deportations took place in two phases. Between 1945 and 1946 about 200,000 Lemko Rusyns 'voluntarily' took up the offer to resettle eastward in the Ukraine in exchange for Poles who moved west within the new postwar boundaries of Poland. The remaining 80,000 Lemko Rusyns, mostly in the western Lemko region, were forcibly deported in 1947 (Magosci, 1992a: 221). In Slovakia during the 1950s and 1960s a rapid degree of Slovakisation and national assimilation helped the Rusyns to separate themselves from their pejorative Ukranian identification. For the Rusyns in Slovakia the choice was simple, 'if one could not be a Rusyn, better declare oneself a Slovak than a Ukranian (which among other things was associated with the hated East') (Magosci, 1992a: 225).

For the Rusyns the new world order was a time for revival and reconstruction. In 1990 five new Rusyn organizations had been established. Initially they were cultural and ecological in orientation but quickly developed a political thrust to put forward the following demands: 'that Rusyns be recognized as a distinct nationality; that a Rusyn literary language be codified and eventually used in schools as a medium of instruction; that Rusyns be guaranteed full rights as a national minority in the countries where they live or, in the case of Transcarpathia, that Rusyns be recognized as the dominant indigenous nationality' (Magosci, 1992a: 216). Current pressure is aimed at convincing members of the CSCE that they are obliged to recognize the Rusyns or Lemko Rusyns (in the case of Poland) as a distinct national minority and construct an appropriate infrastructure for them to realize their goal of becoming a vibrant group once again and a bridge to facilitate the economic development of the Carpathian–Tisa region. Like many other rediscovered peoples in Europe they are seeking national autonomy in some form of reconstructed sovereign state system.

Trans-frontier regions such as Carpathia–Tisa, Alpia–Adria, and emerging or reconstituted regions focused upon the Baltic Sea, the Black Sea and the Western Mediterranean, promise much in the restructuring of Europe. Potentially they are capable of emulating the more successful elements of trans-frontier cooperation between the European Community and selected neighbours such as Switzerland and Austria. But they are also constituents of a new set of European actors commensurate with the emergence of 'transregionalism'. Often referred to as 'a Europe of regions' comprising groups of states, of regions across states, of cross-border networks and transborder functional associations at many levels. At one level 'transregionalism' can be interpreted as an opportunistic extension of normal open intercourse between people in a manner more reminiscent of mediaeval Europe than of that of the late 19th century sovereign national spaces. At another level it can be interpreted as a structural challenge to the notion of territorial sovereignty, the key variable maintaining the system of states in the modern world. Indeed some have argued that in the fluid, indeterminate and transitional period we experience today, the very essence of politics is itself an open question. Reflect on Walker's observation that there is a:

difficulty of speaking about *politics* in the late twentieth century, about what concepts like political community, obligation, freedom, autonomy, democracy or security can mean in the context of contemporary rearticulations of space and time. This may seem abstract to those who have learnt to treat the abstractions of an earlier era as the very stuff of common sense and brute reality. It would presumably seem like a rather familiar theme to someone like Machiavelli (Walker, 1989: 45).

One of the enduring themes of this volume is that the nation-state ideal is being challenged from a variety of sources. Conceptually, it may be argued that this is an imprecise formulation, and what we need to do is to separate out those challenges which relate to sovereignty, and its exercize, and those which relate to the particular national flavour of the state. Waever (1991) quoting Mayall (1990) shows how the old territorial state order was challenged by the national idea in the 19th century. A compromise, which led to the continuation of the international system in a modified form, superimposed the ideal of national sovereignty on the old order's territorial sovereignty.

In the current political flux created by the collapse of the Cold War, the distinction between the territorial state and the nation state has some intriguing consequences. At least in Europe, nationalism seems to be outliving the territorial state into which it was born. Sovereignty is older than *national* sovereignty (before that it was dynastic), thus the national idea has so far always existed as a *modification* of a deeper structure, the state system based on territorial status with ultimate sovereignty (Waever, 1991: 20).

This deeper structure is also undergoing profound modification as we saw in Chapter 1. The collapse of space and time has emphasized a switch from a political geography of sovereign units to a post-modern geography emphasising flows. Thus nodal cities interact more with each other than they do with lower order centres within their own national spaces, and former imperial capitals such as Berlin, Paris or London become 'europolises' or modern city states exercising discretionary power and responsibilities far beyond the closed cosmologies of local government. Similarly whole regions, as we saw in chapter 3, interact with others on a European scale, diminishing the significance of territorial, national borders. New actors are emerging at all levels and this will undoubtedly place extra strain on an international state system designed to cope with the reality of 1648, not the 21st century. Transnational regions, among other new actors, strike at the heart of the old order, namely the organizing principle of international politics, the 'principle of separation of units' (Ruggie, 1983). In contemporary Europe one of the key questions influencing peace and security concerns the issue of what kind of units make up the system. Waever argues that new actors have been discussed in international relations for a long time, but they acted in a system comprised of sovereign states. 'Now, we have to rethink the principle of differentiation of units and thereby the nature of a new system' (Waever, 1991: 30).

A Balkan tragedy

Long perceived as the 'powder keg of Europe', the Balkan region has once again suffered the tragic emergence of transnational ethnic antagonism and political disintegration which threatens the peace and security not only of Europe but of significant sections of the Islamic realm. The dismemberment of Yugoslavia can be considered as the first major revision of the Trianon Treaties (Koch, 1991). Additional developments might include a greater fragmentation of either the Czech or Slovak Republics, Hungarian revisionism, a greater Albania, a disputed Macedonia, a Romanian–Moldavian union and an increased military role for Turkey in policing parts of the former Ottoman Empire. Does the desire of East European nations to form constituent peoples of a Democratic Europe necessarily mean that while we strive in Western Europe for supra-state integration, in Eastern Europe the nation–state ideal is the highest form of political ambition? Are restyled federations, confederations and multi-ethnic polities a thing of the past in former Hapsburg, Ottoman and Tzarist lands? If the Yugoslav federation cannot survive the transition from communism to nationalism, what chance does any other ethnically-heterogenous state in the region have of resisting the appeal of national self-determination? Does the new world order necessarily presage a period of ethnic conflict and territorial readjustment in Central and Eastern Europe?

Larrabee (1992) argues that such historical conflicts had been held in check by bipolarity and bloc politics. During the Cold War security politics in the region were given a measure of stability as the Balkans were divided into blocs, with non-aligned Yugoslavia acting as a strategic buffer between East and West. The political geography of the post-Cold-War world has upset this delicate balance. The old bipolar order has given way to regional disorder and ethno-territorial conflict. The disintegration of former Yugoslavia may be just the start of the Balkanization of the Balkans. If so, what are the security implications and the lessons to be learned for ethnic accommodation and the preparation for peace.

Implications for peace and security

If the superpowers were more than adequately prepared for a major conflict on European soil during the Cold War, their successor-organizations and alliances are woefully unprepared for the Yugoslav-type conflict which threatens to become the norm in the foreseeable future. Many commentators have observed that the Yugoslav crisis underscored the absence of effective institutional mechanisms for dealing with such conflicts, especially as the new European security structures were in transition and could not bring themselves to intervene in the crisis at an early juncture. Recent works by Larrabee (1992), Rotfeld (1992), Bowers (1992) and Zametica (1992) allow us to suggest the following long-term implications for European security. First, despite the myriad challenges to the form and function of the sovereign nation-state, it is still perceived by stateless nations as 'a panacea for their grievances, real or imaginary, and as the vehicle for their ambitions' (Zametica, 1992: 76). The pursuit of national interests remains the most powerful force in international relations, and is capable of being judged positively or negatively dependant upon the political context. While the secessionist challenge of a stateless nation is seen as destabilizing and thus negative, the integrationist experiment of the European Community is regarded positively because it harnesses and harmonizes national interests. Zametica offers a refreshingly caustic judgement when he claims that 'the international community, which is just a collection of nation-states, would be hypocritical to condemn the phenomenon of nationalism among those nations still seeking statehood in order to have the luxury of pursuing their national interests through independent choice' (Zametica, 1992: 77).

A second lesson is perhaps the harder to learn, namely that the principle of national self-determination must not be applied selectively by the international community. The EC was partial in recognizing Croatia and assuming that the Serbs in the republic were a minority, not a nation, 'even though the whole point about the Serbo-Croat conflict in Croatia was that the Serbian community insisted on retaining its status as a nation' (Zametica, 1992: 77). By seeking to support both the principle of self-determination (Croatia's) and state sovereignty, the EC appeared to be denying the right of reunification of all Serbs who wished to live together in one state. There was a simultaneous reinforcement of the ideal of national self-determination (Croatia's) and of a multi-ethnic plural state (former Yugoslavia). This partiality has been echoed in a more general manner by Dr Geza Jeszenszky, the Hungarian Minister for Foreign Affairs, who argues that:

In Central and Eastern Europe, the genuine democrats know that human rights are indivisible, that self-determination cannot be applied selectively, that the use of force, particularly military force, is unacceptable for settling political and national differences. Unfortunately . . . it is quite natural to find many who eagerly repeat the new catchwords of democracy and that of the CSCE process, but who want democracy at best only for their kin and cannot bring themselves to apply it to those whose political beliefs, religion, language and national consciousness are different from their own (Jeszenszky, 1992: 10).

A third lesson is to ask the question when is a minority a nation? Who decides, in times of acute conflict, if minorities are entitled to human rights and nations entitled to pursue national self-determination? When Serbia sought to suppress Kosovon rights it was to prevent their secession, in similar manner 'When the Croats excluded the Serbs from their constitution of December 1990 as a constituent nation in the republic, they knew perfectly well that they were thereby creating an argument for stopping a minority from seceding' (Zametica, 1992: 78). Post-communist nationalism and chauvanistic patriotism have both fired the movement for national independence, but as the Hungarians say 'a patriot defends rights, whereas a nationalist violates rights'. The failure of the international community to distinguish between patriotism, minority grievances and over-stimulated nationalism as the motor for ethnic change in former Yugoslavia has been a grave influence on its differential treatment of the constituent parties to the conflict.

A fourth lesson is that existent frontiers should not be considered inviolable for they often reflect a previous generation's experience of conflict and repression rather than the popular will of the nationals concerned today. This is not an excuse for 'ethnic cleansing' nor a mandate to ignore legitimate frontiers in the quest for ethnic *lebensraum*. Rather it is a recognition that frontiers are functional reflections of reality, and when that reality changes so should frontiers. Zametica points to the paradox of the EC action in recognizing that frontiers are expendable when no one was fighting in Slovenia, and inviolable when the frontiers of Croatia were still a cause of war. 'In the case of Bosnia-Herzegovina, a member of the CSCE with theoretically inviolable borders, the conflict of principles was thrown into ever starker relief, since it was doubtful whether there existed a majority-driven quest for the building of a nation-state'. His solution to the question of disputed borders is to hold a boundary plebiscite, and even if this produces at least one discontented nation, it would reduce the fear of mass genocide, refugee flows and open conflict. However, it is doubtful whether in a current or future post-Yugoslav context, a peaceful referendum on boundary divisions could be binding, unless there were provision for boundary readjustment every decade or so, as has existed in Finland in relation to the designation of its Swedish-speaking districts. In a post-modern world it is salutary to reflect that the designation of an arbitary line on a map or on the landscape can arouse such warring passions, but then one's perceived identity and life changes are often at stake in such divisions!

The fifth lesson from the Yugoslav conflict reinforces the need for an early warning response to crises from the international community. The EC sought to mediate in the crisis after the intervention of the Federal army in Slovenia in June 1991, but internal dissension as to the aims, role and scale of peace-keeping forces rendered it ineffective, and it lost an oppor-tunity to prevent the conflagration from expanding into other regions. During the second half of 1991 the EC yielded its leadership to an active UN involvement, comprised of a well equipped but politically-confused peacekeeping force. In humanitarian terms this presence has been most useful, but in terms of crisis management and resolution, it has yet to prove its worth.

Most commentators agree that the main threat to European security comes not from Russian military power but from the post-communist ethnic and territorial conflicts, particularly in South-Eastern Europe. However, the pre-eminent security organization in Europe, NATO, has hitherto played hardly any role in the crisis. Juridicially, Yugoslavia falls outside the NATO security area, as defined by Article 5 of the NATO Treaty. Politically, the USA did not want to become directly involved, except through its membership of the UN, CSCE and NACC. This has led some critics to question the relevance of NATO in the new world order. Larrabee (1992: 45) asks 'whether the current definition of NATO's respon-sibility accords with the new realities in the post-Cold War period?' NATO's response is to outline the new European Security architecture which sees 'three mutually reinforcing pillars, which have been consoli-dated to provide the support for structured links and a process of effective, consistent co-operation in which NATO, in particular, the linchpin of the entire system, will interact with the other institutions involved – first and foremost with the Western European Union (WEU) and with the CSCE' (Colombo, 1992: 3).

However, neither the WEU nor the CSCE proved capable of acting swiftly. It is true that the CSCE, in particular, served as a necessary forum for crisis dialogue, but with 51 members the CSCE has become too unwieldy to act on the basis of unanimity. A necessary reform, according to Larrabee, would be to introduce a system of qualified majority voting to enable it to take swift and decisive action. This would be rendered less urgent if respect for minority rights and the impermissibility of changing borders by force were made binding principles of the CSCE. But to be truly effective in the management and resolution of conflict, the CSCE would need to be able to muster considerable forces at short notice to act as a rapid-reaction corps. Whether or not the bulk of such a corps were pro-vided by NATO, the UN or the WEU, there is a certain logic in arguing that

European conflicts should be mediated by a primarily European peace-keeping force.

Conclusion

In concluding this chapter it is necessary to address a broader geopolitical question which has been embedded in much of the previous discussion. Given the decisive influence of the two superpowers on European affairs over the past 40 years, how important will their role be in the 'new Europe'? In the case of the ex-USSR the key player is clearly the Russian federation. It is perhaps fair to say that recent discussions have indicated a certain lack of direction in the general area of foreign and security issues. Nevertheless, a number of broad currents have been identified (Steele, 1993). The principal division of opinion is between those who want a close relationship with the West (and especially a desire for a partnership with the USA) and those who want a balance between Russia's westward-oriented policies and a new focus on Asia. Steele refers to this as a 'radical shift' involving the creation of an international consortium including China, Japan, the two Koreas, the US and Australia. As Steele argues:

the argument is as new as it is provocative, and no one should be amazed if it becomes the orthodoxy in a few years time. Although he was picked for other reasons, Russia's new Prime Minister, Victor Chernomyrdin, with his background in the gas wealth of Siberia, may be one sign of a coming change (1993: 13).

Depending on one's prejudices, the involvement of the USA in the European theatre has either been intrusive or essential. However, what cannot be doubted is that during the 20th century the influence of the USA has been crucial, and in the case of the World Wars I and II decisive. According to Powell, continued involvement will be crucial to future growth and prosperity. Thus he reassures Europe, 'do not be disturbed by the debates you see in Washington and across the United States concerning our role in Europe. The advocates of isolationism – those who say, "come home America" – will not prevail' (Powell, 1992: 7).

So much for rhetoric! However, in a more objective analysis Treverton espouses a similar view, but adds the significant rider that 'Europe will be a test case for the broad question about America's role: can the US participate creatively in enterprises it does not dominate?' (1992: 119). This domination was brought about by the Cold War; such exigencies have now disappeared. Nevertheless, alternative but less 'momentous' transatlantic projects exist which will cement, and in some instances possibly extend, American involvement (rebuilding Eastern Europe, coordinating out-of-area actions, managing the global economy). A more controversial suggestion reaffirms the view that 'America's pressing business now lies at home, not abroad' (Treverton, 1992: 133) and that the USA should not pursue new transatlantic projects.

At the military level American involvement will continue. However, with the reduction of troop numbers from 300,000 to 100,000 its position as *primus inter pares* can no longer be automatically assumed. Nevertheless, in a recent Pentagon report it is argued that this level of deployment is sufficient to pursue the vital interests and associated military requirements of the USA, *viz* the necessity for a 'forward presence', meeting NATO commitments and providing a basis for the power projection of American troops out of the NATO area (Snider, 1992/93: 25). Clearly the USA's European involvement will be predicated upon the wider foreign policy and national interest concerns. As the next three chapters demonstrate, there is a strategic shift in American orientation and relative power to influence global events; it may be possible to predict that in the medium-term a partial withdrawal from the European theatre may lead to a more equitable partnership between American and European interests in determining *Pax Europa*.

As the preceding discussion has indicated, the security challenges facing Europe in the near – and mid-term are fairly clearly delineated. These include *inter alia* the balance between pan-Europeanism and Atlanticism; relative integration in the West and disintegration in the East; the movement towards a multipolar environment and multidimensional threats; the tension between the increased need for effective diplomatic and political interventions and the tendency for conflicts to take the military option; the struggle between anarchy and interdependence. One could go on. However, the basic message seems to be that the dissolution of the Manichaean certainties of the bipolar order has bequeathed a world where uncertainty rules. Perhaps there is some truth after all in the postmodernist appellation that 'anything goes'. However, whether this is a cause for celebration or regret is left appropriately ambiguous.

References

Bathurst, B. (1992), 'Western European Union: a Military Perspective', *RUS1 Journal*, October: 8–11.

Baylis, J. (1992), 'Europe Beyond the Cold War', in J. Baylis and N.J. Rengger (eds), *Dilemmas of World Politics*, London, Clarendon Press.

Bowers, S.R. (1992), *Ethnic Politics in Eastern Europe*, London, RISCT.

Chernoff, F. (1992), 'Can NATO Outlive the USSR?', *International Relations*, **XI**, No. I, 1–16.

Clauss, D. (1992), 'Allied Command Europe: a Time of Change', *RUS1 Journal*, June: 1–5.

Colombo, E. (1992), 'European Security at a Time of Radical Change. *NATO Review*, June: 3–7.

Deporte, A.W. (1986), *Europe between the superpowers*, New Haven, Yale University Press.

The Economist (1992) 'NATO Slims Slightly', 5 September: 49.

Farringdon, H. (1989), *Strategic Geography*, London, Routledge.

Freedman, L. (1989), *The evolution of nuclear strategy*, London, The Macmillan Press Ltd.

Fukuyama, F. (1989), 'The End of History?' *National Interest*, Summer. 3–18

Fukuyama, F. (1992) 'The End of History and the Last Man. London, Penguin.

Gaddis, J.L. (1986), 'The Long Peace: Elements of Stability in the Postwar International System', *International Security*, **10**, No. 4, 99–142.

Ghebali, V.Y. (1992), 'The July Helsinki Divisions – a Step in the Right Direction, *NATO Review*, **4**, August: 2–8.

Gramsci, A. (1971), Selections from the Prison Notebooks. London, Lawrence and Wishart.

The Guardian (1992) 'New Peace Keeping Alliance Extends NATO Power to the East, 19 December.

HMSO, (1992), *Statement on the Defence Estimates*, London, HMSO.

Hoffman, S., Keohane, R. and Mearsheimer, J. (1990), 'Back to the Future Part II', *International Security*, **15**, No. 2.

Holst, J. (1992), 'Pursuing a Durable Alliance in the Aftermath of the Cold War, *NATO Review*, August: 9–13.

Hyde-Price, A. (1990), *European Security Beyond the Cold War*, London, RIIA.

James, H. (1989), A German Identity, 1770–1990. London: Weidenfeld and Nicolson.

Jeszenszky, G. (1992), 'Nothing Quiet on the Eastern Front'. *NATO* Review, June: 7–13.

Joffe, J. (1992), 'Collective Security and the Future of Europe: Failed Dreams and Dead-ends', *Survival*, April/May: 36–50.

Johnson, P. (1992), 'The Hinge of Opportunity: a Security System for Europe, *New European*, **5**, 1–56.

Kaldor, M. (1990), *The Imaginary War*, London, Basil Blackwell.

Kennedy, P. (1989), *The Rise and Fall of the Great Powers*, London, Fontana.

Kinkel, K. (1992), 'NATO's Enduring Role in Europe', *NATO Review*, **40**, No. 5: 3–7.

Kinnear, R. (1991), 'The Trans-Carpathian Region as a Case study', paper presented to the Bratislava Symposium on Minorities in Politics, 13–16 November.

Koch, K. (1991), 'Back to Sarajevo or beyond Trianon?' *Netherlands Journal of Social Sciences*, **27**, No. 1: 29–42.

Kupchan, C.A. and Kupchan, C.A. (1991), 'Concerts, Collective Security and the Future of Europe, *International Security*, **16**, No. 1: 114–161.

Larrabee, F.S. (1992), Instability and Change in the Balkans, *Survival*, **34**, No. 23: 31–49.

Leech, J. (1991), *Halt! Who Goes Where. The Future of NATO in the New Europe*, London, Brassey's.

Legge, J.M. (1992), 'NATO's New Strategic Concept, *RUSI Journal*, June: 11–14.

Leonhard, W. (1990), 'From Moscow to Berlin and Points West', *Encounter*, **LXXV**, no. 2: 26–28.

McInnes, C. (1991), *NATO's Changing Strategic Agenda: the Conventional Defence of Central Europe*, London, Unwin Hyman.

Magosci, P.R. (1978), *The Shaping of National Identity: the Subcarpathian Rus, 1848–1948*, Boston, Harvard University Press.

Magosci, P.R. (1992a), 'Carpatho-Rusyns: Their Current Status', in J. Plichtova, (ed.), *Minorities in politics*, Bratislava, European Cultural Foundation.

Magosci, P.R. (1992b), 'Carpatho-Rusyns: a New or Revived people?' in L. Matejka (ed.), *Cross currents*, **11**, New Haven, Yale University Press.

Mayall, J. (1990), *Nationalism and International Society*. Cambridge, University Press.

Mearsheimer, J. (1990), 'Back to the Future: Instability in Europe After the Cold War, *International Security* **15**, No. 1, pp. 5–56.

Menon, A., Forster, A. and Wallace, W. (1992), 'A Common European Defence', *Survival*, Autumn: 98–118.

NATO Review (1990) 'Documentation Section: Text of the London Declaration', **4**, August.

NATO Review (1992), 'Documentation section: Text of the Alliance; new strategic concept', **6**, December.

Newhouse, J. (1989), The Nuclear Age, London, Michael Joseph.

Nystrom, K. (1984), 'Regional Identity and Ethnic Conflict: Croatia's Dilemma', in S. Tägil (ed.), *Regions in upheaval*, Lund, Esselte Studium.

Oakey, R. (1991), 'People with Problems', *Planet*, **84**, 717.

Powell, C. (1992), The American Commitment to European Security; *Survival*, Summer: 3–11.

Rotfeld, A.D. (1992), 'European Security Structures in Transition. *SIPRI Yearbook 1992*, Oxford, Oxford University Press.

Ruggie, J.G. (1983), 'Continuity and Transformation in the World Polity: Towards a Neo-realist Synthesis, *World Politics*, **35**: 261–85.

Snider, D.M. (1992) 'US Military Forces in Europe: How Low Can We Go', *Survival*, Winter: 24–39.

Steele, J. (1993), The Bear's Necessities, *The Guardian*, 4 January.

Tägil, S. (ed.), (1977), *Studying Boundary Conflicts*. Lund, Esselte Studium.

Taylor, T. (1992), 'NATO and Central Europe: Problems and Opportunities in a New Relationship', *RIIA Discussion Paper*, **39**.

Tóth, J. (1993), 'Regionalism and Minorities in Hungarian Perspective', *Discussion Papers in Geolinguistics*, **22**, Stoke-on-Trent.

Treharne, R.F. and Fullard, H. (1976), *Muir's Historical Atlas*. London, Philip.

Treverton, G.F. (1992), America: Stakes and Choices in Europe, *Survival*, Autumn: 119–35.

Van Evera, S. (1990), 'Primed for Peace: Europe after the Cold War', *International Security*, **15**, No. 3, 7–57.

Waever, O. (1991), 'Territory Authority and Identity, Working Paper', Florence, European University Institute.

Walker, R.B.J. (1989), 'Ethics, Modernity and the Theory of International Relations, Working Paper', Princeton, Princeton University.

Walker, R.B.J. and Mendlovitz, S.H. (1990), *Contending Sovereignties: Redefining Political Community*, Boulder and London, Lynne Rienner.

Williams, C.H. (1989), 'The Question of National Congruence', in R.J. Johnston and P. Taylor, (eds), *A World in Crisis*? Oxford, Blackwell.

Williams, C.H. (1991), Linguistic Minorities: West European and Canadian Perspectives, in C.H. Williams (ed.), *Linguistic minorities, Society and Territory*, Clevedon, Avon Multilingual Matters.

Williams, C.H. (1992), 'On the Recognition of Minorities in Contemporary Greece; *Planet*, **94**: 82–90.

Wollacott, M. (1992), 'Europe's Tank-driven Arsenals in the Grip of Elephantiasis', *The Guardian*, 30 May.

Worner, M. (1992), 'A Vigorous Alliance – a Motor for Peaceful Change in Europe', *NATO Review*, **6**, December: 3–9.

Zametica, J. (1992), *The Yugoslav conflict*, London, Brassey's.

7

Trading blocs or a world that knows no boundaries? The British–American 'Special Relationship' and the continuation of the post-War world economy

John Agnew

No country was as willing as Britain to be a participant in the 1991 'Gulf War' against Iraq. Elsewhere in Europe and in Japan there was considerably greater elite and popular equivocation. For example, a MORI poll of 10 January 1991 found that 75 per cent of Britons thought force should be used against Iraq, if its troops were not removed from Kuwait. Only 18 per cent disagreed. In contrast, polls taken around the same time showed 70 per cent of Germans, 53 per cent of French respondents, 51 per cent of Italians, and 46 per cent of Americans opposed to war. The House of Commons voted 453 to 57 on 15 January 1991 in favour of the government's war policy. This recalls both Britain's colonial past and its former activities as a global 'policeman' and the 'special relationship' between Britain and the USA that has made Britain, during its decline from world power, into the most steadfast ally of its successor as conductor of world affairs. A writer for the most consistent mouthpiece of Anglo-American Atlanticism, *The Economist* magazine captures the essential sentiment:

Take two films. One is about the passing of cold-war comradeship, fading American interest in Europe and an uneasy British conversion to European union. The other is about an alliance restored, in an old colonial stamping-ground, for as good a cause as you get, with those continentals dodging and weaving. Guess which cinema the British will flock to (*The Economist*, 1991).

This chapter has two objectives. The first is to attempt to explain the peculiarity of the 'special relationship' in the context of the transition to

American hegemony within the world economy. Theories of hegemonic succession have trouble in accounting for the absence of war as the USA replaced Britain as the dominant world power. In emphasizing the economic and ideological continuity between the two, this chapter disputes those perspectives that see hegemony in exclusively realist (national–territorial) terms; as if each hegemony was mutually exclusive and without common substantive content. The second objective is to outline the continuing importance of the special relationship today, in its mythic as well as material dimensions, in relation to the prospect of a more integrated Europe and a more Pacific- and Americas-orientated USA. The Britain–USA nexus is critical in relation to the possibility that the most economically developed countries of the world economy may form into competing trading blocs (North America, European Community, and East Asia). It represents a continuing commitment to globalization and a world with fading national economic boundaries, as pressures mount everywhere in favour of protectionism and a re-territorialization of economic activities on a national basis, especially in Europe and the United States (Fieleke, 1992).

Hegemonic succession

Certain periods in modern world history can be seen as marked by the presence of a hegemony or a system in which a set of norms, values and interests emanating from a particular state regulate the behaviour of other states. To most theorists of international relations, however, hegemony is synonymous with dominance or coercive power. The ability to enforce hegemony is equated with it. There is consequently an identity between the dominant state's economic–military power and its hegemony. Once its economic–military potential begins to fade so does its hegemony. Hegemonic succession is therefore a process whereby one territorial state replaces another, usually through victory in war, and establishes its own system of regulatory rules. In long-cycle, world-system, hegemonic stability, imperial overstretch, and other 'fixed process' views of hegemonic succession, this process is invariant over time and in relation to the identity of the states involved in succession (Agnew and Corbridge, 1989: 266–88). Thus, in one well-known account, hegemony passed from Spain to the Netherlands to Britain and on to the USA (Wallerstein, 1984). Today we stand poised for another transfer of hegemony, probably to Japan (on why this is unlikely even when assumptions about the invariant nature of the process of hegemonic succession are unchallenged see Haber, 1990). Even those accounts which adopt a Gramscian conception of hegemony, with its acknowledgment of the importance of ideas in cementing power relations, tend to focus on the socialization of weaker powers by the new hegemon rather the possibility of substantive continuity with the old one (e.g. Ikenberry and Kupchan, 1990).

The two most widely acknowledged periods of global hegemony, as opposed to periods of competitive rivalry or ones of limited geographical hegemony, are those of Britain in the mid–19th century and the USA since 1945 (Cox, 1987). Without access to the historical record and condemned to a library of international relations texts one would expect the British–American succession to have been one of overt conflict followed by coercive dominance. Certainly, one can find evidence for latent conflict and, in the 1890s, even for the possibility of war. After World War II the USA did exercize a degree of economic coercion over Britain as a direct result of its colossal presence in a world economy largely reduced to a shambles. But what is remarkable about the shift in hegemony from Britain to the USA is not just the lack of conflict between the two states but the equanimity and sense of inevitability with which the shift in the centre of international gravity was accepted in Britain.

One obvious answer to this, of course, is that the alternatives, German or, later, Nazi and Japanese, and, finally, Soviet territorial empires, were even less acceptable. What is less obvious is why this was the case. Discussions of hegemonic succession or transitions in the geopolitical order usually imply that states under challenge can choose among a range of possible allies or 'tilt' towards a potential partner to maintain their relative dominance. Thus after World War II Britain could have allied with the Soviet Union or formed a European block to balance against its erstwhile American ally (e.g. Taylor, 1990). What this effectively ignores is why subsidiarity to the USA was so acceptable. One answer to this might be that 'liberal democracies' such as modern Britain and the USA do not go to war with one another (e.g. Doyle, 1984) and, hence, the British government was willing to accept subordination rather than engage in conflict over hegemonic succession with a similar kind of state. There may well be something to this, especially as the two countries had been such recent and close wartime allies against a group of self-consciously 'authoritarian' states. But liberal democracies need not necessarily share a particular view of how the world beyond their respective national boundaries should be organized. Yet, I would claim, this is exactly what has bound Britain and the USA together. The USA represented an essential continuity in significant respects of the content of the hegemony that Britain had itself exercized previously. So even as the territorial identity of its sponsor changed, and along with it some of its substance, there was a continuation of a hegemony committed to reducing barriers to trade, encouraging currency convertibility, stimulating international investment, and opposing regional trading blocs.

It is important to emphasize therefore that hegemony is not just about the acquisition and deployment of power but also about the uses to which power is put. The British–American succession was peaceful and largely consensual because the material and symbolic commitments that Britain had built up historically could continue to be realized under American auspices. The internationalist elite that emerged into prominence in the USA during the 1930s and 1940s was convinced that the Depression they had experienced was a product of interstate rivalry and protectionism (Maier, 1978). Moreover, there was a persistent 'Wilsonian' vision of world order in the dominant American political imagination, following the ideas of President Woodrow Wilson for institutionalizing international cooperation under American auspices. It was an article of faith with powerful figures such as Cordell Hull, one of President Franklin D. Roosevelt's Secretaries of State, that 'economic relations were all-important for peace. In particular, all restrictions on the free flow of goods and money were anathema . . . economic blocs inevitably lead to political rivalry, militarism, and war'. Hence, in Hull's ideal world, free trade was to be accompanied by free convertibility of money and freedom for investments and capital movements' (Calleo, 1973: 210).

Britain, dominated economically then as now more by its financiers than by manufacturing or agrarian capitalists and politically by the key roles of the Treasury and the Bank of England rather than by more domestically-orientated government departments in economic-policy making, was a natural ally to the USA in rebuilding an open world economy (Ingham, 1984). This does not mean that in Britain and the USA there were no groups then or since hostile to internationalism (the themes of 'America first' and isolationism have appeared periodically in American presidential elections from 1948 to 1992; they have become especially strong in recent years with the perception of American economic 'decline' relative to other countries that appear to be more internally-orientated and with fewer foreign military and political obligations, especially Japan). In the immediate post-war years, however, isolationism and autarchy did not constitute strong political currents in either country (Rupert, 1990: 71–96). Neither does it mean that the British and American hegemonies should be regarded as completely equivalent. Major differences involve, for example, the central role of transnational corporations and the split between geopolitical (East–West) and economic competition in American hegemony when compared to that of Britain (Mjoset, 1990: 21–47). Most importantly, however, there were compromises between American and British political elites in designing a post-war political–economic order, represented most clearly by the Bretton Woods agreement of 1944, that incorporated elements of both global *laissez-faire* and global economic management. The British, above all in the person of Keynes, actively sought the middle ground between international free trade and national capitalism by extending ideas about domestic economic regulation by government into the international realm. In this way Britain and the USA together shaped the basis for American hegemony (Ikenberry, 1992).

The British state was in many respects already internationalist in orientation when called upon to help define and serve the new cause as it was formulated in the years from 1944 to 1947. This did not happen overnight some time between 1944 and 1947 and in response to American coercion over Britain's dollar shortage at the end of World War II. It was a long established feature of a country with a large and lightly administered empire, massive overseas investments, and a major exposure to international trade. Neither a 'Little England' nor Britain as the centre to a European bloc was ever on the cards in the 1940s. Indeed, it was a future Labour party minister, Sir Stafford Cripps, with, one might presume, a greater propensity than representatives of other political groupings to imagine a new domestic political economy for Britain with lesser international involvements, who, on 27 June 1940, first laid out the political–economic arguments for creating 'Anglo-America'. Stolen later by Churchill in his famous 'Iron Curtain' speech of 5 March 1946, it indicates how widely accepted across the British political spectrum was the idea of the USA and Britain as partners in a 'common' enterprise.

The 'special relationship'

The term 'special relationship' finds its origins in wartime collaboration and implies, especially in its usage by Churchill and later British politicians, something more than an ordinary alliance founded on a temporary confluence of interests. But Atlanticism, the belief that the British Empire and the USA could together bring peace and justice to the world, has roots in the early years of the 20th century. Largely a British phenomenon, like reference to the 'special relationship' itself was to be later, Atlanticism spanned the political divide from the radical right through the racist 'Pan-Anglo Saxons' and the benign English Speaking Union to all shades of liberal and even socialist opinion.

Christopher Hitchens, in the funniest if not the most scholarly study of the special relationship, points to a certain elite bonding between Britain and the USA as the root of the phenomenon. Common literary, cultural, historical, and emotional images form a 'stock of allusion and reference' that constitute a 'joint mythology' that has been 'semi-institutionalized' in 'the Rhodes Scholarships, in the joint-stock aspect of Wall Street and the City of London, and through an unwritten but well-observed partnership in diplomacy' (Hitchens, 1990: 360–1).

'The wrinkles and crevices of the "special relationship" ' (Hitchens, 1990: 361) are certainly revealing of the peculiar relationship that has long existed between British (or, rather, English) and American elites. Each can not unreasonably claim to know the other (or rather what the other reads, watches, and perhaps thinks) better than it does the elites of other countries. But, contrary to the idealism of the old Atlanticists, there was never an automatic 'Anglo Saxon alliance'. Though it draws on older images and myths, the special relationship is very much a product of World War II and its aftermath. Contemporary interest in it derives largely from the question of whether it can survive in a world that finally appears to have put World War II to rest.

The special relationship can be seen therefore as a concept invented and used by British politicians from the Dark Days of 1940 onwards to use the historically-sedimented sentiment that joined the USA and Britain as a means of arresting the relative decline of British power. To Churchill, the USA and Britain bound in 'familial closeness' as equal partners could act together to create a new force in the international system, Anglo-America or Pax Anglo-Americana (Ryan, 1987). Nazi, fascist, and Japanese propaganda contributed to this vision by explicitly linking the two countries as indistinguishable 'plutocracies'. But whatever the British role in bringing about the Cold War, in one interpretation the implication being that Britain could somehow have leapt into a Soviet or other alternative alliance (Taylor, 1990), in American eyes Britain was not an equal partner. The USA was not about to pursue specifically British policies, especially ones relating to perpetuation of the Empire, under the rubric of Anglo-America.

The 'reality', then, was that Britain had to accept whatever help the Americans chose to offer. Living beyond its means, Britain in the 1940s was not in a position to do other than treat its least menacing potential foe as its greatest ally. This was because the 'new world' that the USA offered was in many respects a continuation of the old one that Britain itself represented.

With the exception of the period of the Suez crisis in 1956, which showed clearly how much the structural power had shifted from Britain to the USA, the special relationship became an important rhetorical device that British politicians could use to indicate their continuing importance in world politics. The Americans wanted a dependable European ally and co-contributor to global policing, especially East of Suez. Until 1961 summits were always of the Big Three rather than the Big Two. American governments were willing participants in the illusion that Britain was still a Great Power (Dimbleby and Reynolds, 1988).

Immediately after World War II most European states were concerned with national economic recovery and re-establishing the national identities that had been fractured by wartime divisions into groups of fascists and anti-fascists, collaborators and resisters (on the persistence of these concerns in France, the other European country with global political pretensions, see, for example, Rousso, 1991). Only in Britain was foreign policy formulated from the start after World War II in global terms. This reflected the history of Britain's role in ordering world affairs and the lack of impact of the war upon domestic political divisions. British politicians, both Labour and Conservative, were also concerned that the USA should not withdraw from the international system as it had done in the 1920s (Barker, 1983). We can smile at this today, knowing what we know about the constellation and the balance of domestic political forces in the USA in the 1940s. But at that time and in the light of historical analogy it was not unreasonable for British political leaders to worry that they would once again be abandoned to their role as stabilizer and supporter of 'world order' without the assistance of the now immensely more wealthy and powerful USA.

This did not reflect some 'ideological' aberration (and in this usage a manifestation of 'false consciousness' about Britain's 'real' place in the world) or constitute a 'mere' rhetorical device without practical substance as it is usually presented. Britain had economic interests to protect that had come to be defined in terms of maintaining the world order that Britain and the USA had brought and would continue to bring to the world economy. As a result of the 'post-War settlement' described previously, governing elites in Britain and the USA developed similar understandings of, and orientations towards the world economy. In practice this is what the 'mythic power' of the special relationship, in its invoking of ties of folk kinship and common feeling, has been about naturalizing and preserving. Not until the late 1950s did the economic and political attraction of Europe begin to outweigh somewhat Britain's widely spread trade and investment interests elsewhere and their associated internationalist orientation. Even then the draw of Europe, as seen from both London and Washington, was that British membership of the EEC would link Europe more tightly into the 'free world' economy rather than Britain into Europe. As Miriam Camps expressed this perspective around the time of Britain's first application for EEC membership:

The reflection that the shortest, and perhaps the only, way to a real Atlantic partnership lay through Britain's joining the Common Market seems to have been a very important – perhaps controlling – element in Mr Macmillan's [the British Prime

Minister at the time] own decision that the right course for the United Kingdom was to apply for membership (Camps, 1964: 336).

It was precisely this attempt to try to maintain the special relationship while applying for EEC membership that President de Gaulle found unacceptable and led him to reject Britain's application. If the purpose of the new Europe, reasoned de Gaulle, was to build a new superpower to rival the two giants 'why did it need be permanently intertwined with the Americans?' (Beloff, 1963:173). The British objective was and remains largely different: the pursuit of multilateral free trade and the defence of the capitalist world economy as it has developed under British and American leadership. Britain's applications to the EEC and its ultimate membership in the organization are the result of a perception that these objectives would be threatened by an EEC without Britain in it. The USA consistently advocated British membership on these grounds. Even as the EEC proved an economic success for its members in the 1960s and the myth of the British economy as the strongest in Europe had to be abandoned in the face of the evidence, the major attraction of the EEC remained, and the main cause of friction between Britain and other members became the British commitment to the Atlantic Alliance as the basis to international stability.

To Stephen George, in a brilliant historical review of Britain's strained relationship with the European Community, British governments have been persistently hostile to the ideal of European union as espoused by the founders of the 'European idea' in the aftermath of World War II. The American and global connections have remained paramount. As a consequence, 'the relationship between the EC and the United States, and the relationship of the EC to the wider world order, have been frequent sources of disagreement with the Community, in which Britain has often been seen as the US Trojan horse, or at least as the awkward partner' (George, 1990: 41).

But the 'mythic power' of the special relationship has not only been important to British politicians in developing their post-war role in the world. It has also had importance in British domestic politics. A range of surveys show that in general Britons are closer in social and political attitudes to Americans than they are to 'other' Europeans. The major transatlantic differences relate to the role of the state in welfare provision and the political efficacy of citizens (Davis, 1986). There are definite limits therefore to the importation into Britain of an American model of domestic political economy, as Mrs Thatcher discovered in her loss of leadership of the Conservative Party in 1990. But other 'foreign' models drawing from Europe may fare no better, such as the 'German' one discovered by elements in the Labour Party in 1991. Even though there was widespread fear in the early 1980s of the warlike propensities of the Reagan administration (Whiteley, 1985: 95–119), polls have consistently reported British respondents as ranking the USA as 'Britain's Best Friend in the World' by a huge margin over the alternative choices (O'Duffy 1991). *See* Figure 7.1. British governments can be assured that when they invoke the special relationship, a significant proportion of public opinion both understands and approves.

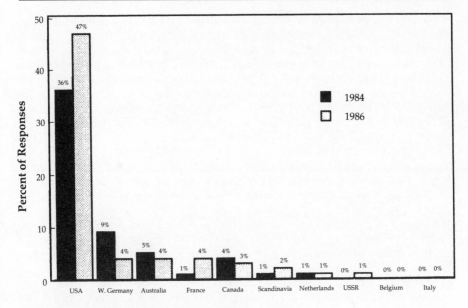

Figure 7.1 Britain's 'Best Friend in the World'
Souce: Gallup Political Index, 1984, 1986.

The contemporary situation

The setting in which the special relationship must be invoked has changed considerably since Britain joined the EEC in 1973 and especially as a result of the 1992 programme for further integration. In particular, British economic interaction with Europe has increased markedly: for example, 52 per cent of British trade in 1989 was with the EC, compared to 36 per cent in 1973. There has been a parallel expansion of the proportion of Britons thinking that the EC 'is a good thing': from 31 per cent in 1973 (excluding Northern Ireland) to 50 per cent in 1989 (Franklin with Wilke, 1990: 14). At the same time, the USA has tilted increasingly towards Germany as its main European ally, perhaps because of its greater economic weight and importance in financing American trade and federal budget deficits and because of the shifting balance of trade and investment flows, away from Europe and towards the 'Pacific Rim'. American trade growth, especially growth in exports, has been much greater with East Asia than with Europe. (A point largely missed, incidentally, by the growing band of 'Japan bashers' in the USA.) The prospects for growth also appear to be greater in that direction than across the Atlantic (Gordon, 1990–91).

All these changes would appear to bode badly for the continuing 'mythic power' of the special relationship. However, there are at least four elements of Britain's relationship to the world economy that are likely to maintain, if not to enhance, the global importance of the special relationshipand to help keep Britain as the 'awkward partner' within the EC.

First is the persisting significance of Britain as an American and extra-European, particularly Japanese, trading and investment 'partner' within a world economy in which the outline of three regional trading and investment blocs is beginning to take shape (UNCTC, 1991). Of the EC countries in 1988 only Britain had a level of *per capita* imports from the USA comparable to Japan and the countries of East Asia: $342, compared to $606 for Taiwan, $344 for Japan, and $298 for South Korea. Germany had a figure of $272, France $243, and Italy $134 (Gordon, 1990–91: 52). American direct investment has long favoured Britain and this continues. In 1990 41 per cent of total US direct investment in the EC went to Britain. Germany, the closest competitor, had only 14.9 per cent. In the same year 37.6 per cent of total Japanese direct investment in the EC was in Britain. Much of this is market- or consumption-rather than product-cycle or production-related; directed towards gaining access to European markets but combined with the appeal of Britain's lower labour costs and history of social and political 'stability'. Surveys of firms suggest that cheaper factors of production, in particular labour, are not in themselves the major attraction (Economics Focus, 1991). Market access is much more important.

Europeans, most especially Britons, have long been used to heavy foreign direct investment, particularly from the USA. Indeed, Britain can reasonably be characterized as 'a rentier economy in reverse', importing rather than exporting capital, as foreign businesses acquire an increasingly dominant role in the British economy in advance of the movement towards a more tightly integrated and potentially more exclusionary EC economy after 1992. *See* Figure 7.2. This continues an old trend, if at an increased pace since the mid-1980s. In the late 1980s, however, the major novelties in the world economy were explosive growth in Japanese investment, mainly direct rather than portfolio, in both Europe and the USA, and large-scale European investment in the USA. Although Japan registered the highest rate of growth in foreign direct investment in the period from 1983 to 1988, the USA and Britain still have the largest overseas stakes (Julius, 1990). At the same time, although regional ties of trade and investment have increased within the EC, East Asia, and between the USA, Canada, and Mexico, in the 1980s between-bloc trade and investment were commensurate or bigger. For example, Japanese direct investment in the EC rose from $1.9 billion in 1985 to $9.1 billion in 1988 and in North America from $5.5 billion to $22.3 billion in the same period, while its East Asian direct investment increased only from $2 billion to $8.2 billion (Frankel, 1991). In 1992 the hysteria in the American press about regional trading blocs and the rise of the Pacific Rim at the expense of Europe and North America seemed to represent an imagined rather than a real economic geography. The EC countries have experienced the greatest increase in regionally-biased trade (the EC ratio of intra-regional to share of world trade went from 1.28 in 1980 to 1.77 in 1989 compared to a decrease in this ratio from 2.18 to 1.85 for the East Asian countries of ASEAN, Hong Kong, South Korea, and Japan over the same period). To limit this trend towards a closed EC trading bloc is why a British 'fifth column' within the EC is vital to the continuation of the American vision of an 'open' world economy.

Figure 7.2 Three Aspects of Direct Investment into Britain (a) Foreign Direct Investment, Britain (b) Direct Investment into Britain (c) Inflows of Foreign Direct Investment

a)

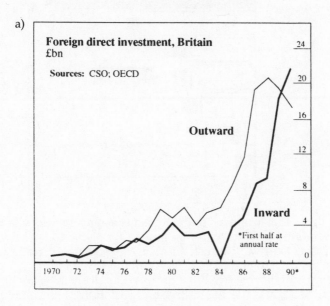

b)

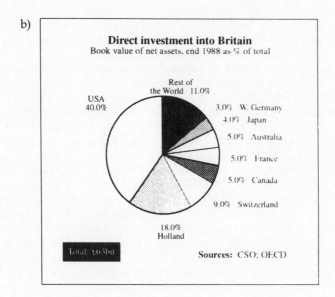

c)

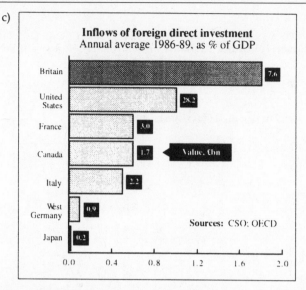

Inflows of foreign direct investment
Annual average 1986-89, as % of GDP

Sources: CSO: OECD

Second, the spatial 'frontiers' of the British economy have long lain outside rather than inside the country (for an interesting discussion of why this has been so, relating to its early industrialization, dependence on trade, and long-term global financial role, see Heim, 1991). In this respect Britain's experience was a precursor to the massive burst of American direct investment overseas beginning in 1950s and the 1960s. British capital in the 19th century became increasingly dependent on limiting international impediments to the flow of trade and investment. Even today British direct investment in the USA far outstrips that emanating from other countries. Japan is still a distant third. In addition, British GNP has been consistently higher than British GDP for many years, reflecting the relative importance of international transactions in British economic accounts. Some other countries have only recently caught up with or overtaken Britain (e.g. Germany) (*Economist*, 1991).

Within the councils of the EC, British representatives together with the Dutch are consistently the greatest supporters of a liberal trading posture for the EC, as illustrated by their positions on the external implications of the 1992 programme and the Uruguay Round of the GATT negotiations (Franklin with Wilke, 1990: 48). If anything, the liberalization of international access to British financial institutions in the 1980s, turning Britain (more accurately, the City of London) into an offshore banking centre, has reinforced the role of Britain within a world economy that extends well beyond the shores of Europe (Llewellyn, 1992: 429–68). In the late-1970s international financial business had begun to bypass London, partly because of arcane rules and regulations (*Economist*, 1991). The removal of exchange controls in 1979 exacerbated this trend as New York's more freewheeling financial institutions drew business away from London (Coakley and Harris, 1983). But after 1986, in Susan Strange's words, London has become 'a kind of adventure playground for British and other European banks as well as American ones to profit from uncontrolled intermediation between dollar depositors and corporate or public borrowers of large Eurocurrency loans' (Strange, 1990). It is as a financial and insurance centre that Britain is now most attractive to Japanese and American capital: 53 per cent of American ($20.6 billion) and 41 per cent of Japanese ($5.7 billion) direct investment in European finance and insurance in 1989 was in Britain (London). These absolute figures are substantially larger than those for American and Japanese direct investment in other sectors (Economics Focus, 1991). They reflect the fact that, as of 1989, 59 per cent of the total assets of banks in Britain were denominated in foreign currency. In terms of volume of assets, the foreign-currency business of banks operating in Britain was substantially larger than sterling-denominated domestic business (Llewellyn, 1992: 429). This balance of international to domestic banking assets is not true of any other major national economy.

Establishing the historical basis to the political–economic predominance in Britain of finance capital orientated overseas is beyond the scope of this chapter. The roots probably lie in the persisting influence of those practising 'the English ideology' of making money cleanly and pragmatically rather than through 'planned' industrial activity, as much as through the direct economic importance of the City of London within the modern British economy (Ingham, 1984). It is important to note, however, that since 1945 New York has proved unable to assume the position of preeminence within the international financial system that London had previously exercized. The scale of the American domestic economy, the lack of a centralized banking structure, and powerful representation of industrial interests in Washington have prevented the emergence of a thoroughly internationalized financial centre. At the same time, British governments faced with persisting problems with their manufacturing industries have chosen to maintain economic policies and political priorities favourable to London as a global financial centre (Ingham, 1984). There is some truth to Nairn's claims, therefore, that 'after Empire Britain did not shrink to being a nation–state but its true self "a City–state" ' and 'the City regards itself as separate from the country at large' (Nairn, 1988: 240–1). The persistence of the City of London's global financial role has required considerable sacrifice by the British economy as a whole (Taylor, 1991).

The integration of Britain's financial sector into the very fibre of the national political regime can be shown in two examples. One is the movement of many government, especially military, personnel into 'City' employment after official retirement (Ingham, 1984). Another is the central value placed by British governments upon international political 'stability'. The vulnerability of financial markets, banking, and insurance to 'external shocks' turns even minor political and economic changes anywhere in the world into potential political–economic disasters. Consequently, 'stability' is seen as an absolute good and a fundamental goal of British foreign policy irrespective of the consequences for foreign places and their populations.

The political–economic elements intrinsic to persistence of the special relationship have been accompanied by the particular ideological orientation of a large section of the British population. This is the widespread British hostility to a tightly integrated European Community. One important manifestation of this has been popular opposition to European monetary union. Some of the hostility undoubtedly results from the history of British involvement in the world economy with its championing of free trade, overseas investment and colonial commitments. But much of it results from the sense of a British (or rather English) exceptionalism that finds expression in the 'Dunkirk spirit', celebrating the unique features and eccentricity of the Britain that 'stood alone' in 1940 (among other things its 'superb' if amateurish civil service and constitutional monarchy are regarded as illustrative of the avoidance of the 'political excesses' to be found elsewhere), and the absence of the institutional 'corporatism', state insinuation into 'the nooks and crannies' of private life, that is often seen in popular British opinion as afflicting 'continental' Europe (Coker, 1990–91).

The lack of much historic political or cultural interaction with continental Europe, except in wartime, is probably of importance in understanding this attitude. Since the Norman invasion Britain has not been occupied by or merged with any other pre-existing state. But this has been a common experience elsewhere in Europe. The British gaze has been overseas, towards the Empire or its remnants and the settler colonies it spawned, and the unique games that they all play, rather than towards the 'foreigners' who begin at Calais and their mysterious ways.

Fourth, and finally, is another ideological dimension to the special relationship. This is the widespread, perhaps increased, commitment in Britain to the tenets of the liberal internationalism, free trade and currency convertibility, that have been at the heart of American hegemony since World War II. It is undoubtedly the case that certain elements of the original 'package' that were most national in orientation, in particular Keynesian demand management and the allowance of public ownership of 'key' industries, had been largely discredited by the 1990s, partly as a result of the total increase in globalization of economic activities, capital has become increasingly mobile, and partly because of American governments' attempts in the 1970s and 1980s to regulate the economy by manipulating the world monetary system to its advantage and imposing limits on autonomous government action elsewhere (Parboni, 1984; Cafruny, 1990: 97–118). These external constraints have become the givens or constants of economic policy-making in the 1990s.

For example, in the late 1960s and in the 1970s British economic policies that were designed to stimulate a revival of manufacturing industry through national industrial and regional policies stand in popular consciousness as reminders of British vulnerability to external economic shocks as national economic autonomy was held hostage by recurrent monetary crises. The first Mitterrand government's (1981) disastrous experiment in France with unilateral domestic stimulative policies (involving massive capital flight) offered perhaps a final demonstration of the apparent redundancy of national fiscal and monetary policy, if not labour and investment policies (Garrett and Lange, 1991), in an increasingly globalized world economy. For an argument that this outcome was not inevitable but, rather, the product of government mismanagement see Singer (1988). The advent of the Reagan and Thatcher governments in the USA and Britain in 1979–80 gave tremendous impetus to the apparently 'realistic' view of a 'boundaryless' world economy in which capital would flow unimpeded to where it generated the highest rates of return.

It is no historical accident that these governments and the models they provided for neoliberal reforms all over the world were elected in the USA and Britain, the two countries that have successively provided the world economy with its central guiding imperatives and which in the past, if less obviously today, seemed to profit politically if not always economically from practising them. There is much more cultural–economic depth, therefore, to the 'special relationship' than the linguistic and literary–cultural affinity or 'anglophilia' documented by Hitchens (1990).

Conclusion

Britain's geopolitical position between the American connection or Atlanticism on the one hand, and the European connection or Europeanism on the other, is often seen as the result of a chronic failure to choose. From this point of view the 'special relationship' has been merely a rhetorical device adopted by British politicians to maintain the illusion of Britain's continuing importance as a Great Power. As a consequence Britain has lost out in effectively establishing its presence and voice in Europe.

This perspective is deficient in three respects. First, the special relationship has had cultural–economic substance to it. In effect, there was no choice between 1945 and 1947. Britain and the USA have represented a particular vision of the world and associated practices that today are often understood in their consequences by the term 'globalization'. Even if their territorial economies may increasingly suffer from it (e.g. on the USA, Agnew, 1987), dominant groups and the bulk of public opinion in both Britain and the USA still remain committed to 'a world that knows no boundaries', to borrow a phrase from an advertisement for the American brokerage firm Merrill Lynch. Of course, whether this will continue indefinitely is moot.

Second, partly as cause and partly as consequence, the special relationship fits the evolution of Britain's real economy away from manufacturing and into services, especially financial ones, that serve global rather than just regional or national markets. Britain's historical experience and the recent experience of the USA are more closely parallel in this regard than is that of Britain and its European partners.

Third, the special relationship continues to represent in the globally significant context of Europe and the North Atlantic what the Cold War was really about: creating and maintaining a world economy (a 'free world') in which trade and capital movement would be unimpeded to the greatest extent possible. American hegemony, as with British hegemony before it, has had substance to it. It has never been about just more national power or more national wealth. Power was allied to particular purpose. But without an ally in Europe such as Britain, American hegemony would not have been possible. That remains the case today. If the special relationship does die out, and there are no obvious understudies for the British role, then so too might a major prop of American hegemony. As long as Britain is the American 'Fifth Column' within Europe, then Europe itself may not become one of the blocs or 'fortresses' that the inventors of the special relationship and the Cold War so dreaded.

Fifty years on and at the end of the Cold War, Britain finally has a meaningful choice, one it did not have in 1945: to continue its ambiguous role as an

American intermediary in Europe or to opt fully for a Europe that may well operate on territorial–autarchic rather than liberal–internationalist principles. However, the persisting mythic power (not 'mere rhetoric') of the special relationship and its material correlate in Britain's global economic role signify that, when viewed from Britain, the Atlantic Ocean still remains geopolitically narrower than the Straits of Dover.

References

Agnew, J. (1987), *The United States in the World-economy*, Cambridge, Cambridge University Press.

Agnew, J. and Corbridge, S. (1989), 'The New Geopolitics: the Dynamics of Geopolitical Disorder', in R.J. Johnston and P.J. Taylor (eds), *A world in crisis? geographical perspectives*, Oxford, Basil Blackwell.

Barker, E. (1983), *The British Between the Superpowers: 1945–50*, London, The Macmillan Press Ltd.

Beloff, N. (1963), *The General Says No: Britain's Exclusion from Europe*, Harmondsworth, Penguin.

Cafruny, A. W. (1990), 'A Gramscian Concept of Declining Hegemony: Stages of US Power and the Evolution of International Economic Relations, in D. P. Rapkin (ed.), *World Leadership and Hegemony*, Boulder, Co, Lynne Rienner.

Calleo, D. P. (1973), 'The Political Economy of Allied Relations: the Limits of Interdependence, in R. E. Osgood, *Retreat from Empire? The First Nixon Administration*, Baltimore, The Johns Hopkins University Press.

Camps, M. (1964), *Britain and the European Community, 1955–63*, London, George Allen and Unwin.

Coakley, J. and Harris, L. (1983), *The City of Capital: London's Role as a Financial Centre*, Oxford, Blackwell.

Coker, C. (1990–91), 'Dunkirk, and Other British Myths', *The National Interest*, **22**: 74–82.

Cox, R. (1987), *Production, Power, and World Order: Social Forces in the Making of History*, New York, Columbia University Press.

Davis, J.A. (1986), 'British and American attitudes: Similarities and Contrasts', in R. Jowell et al. (eds), *British Social Attitudes: the 1986 Report*, Aldershot, Gower.

Dimbleby, D. and Reynolds, D. (1988), *An Ocean Apart: the Relationship Between Britain and America in the Twentieth Century*, New York, Random House.

Doyle, M. (1984), 'Kant, Liberal Legacies and Foreign Affairs', *Philosophy and Public Affairs*, **12**: 205–35, 323–53.

Economics Focus (1991), 'Those Perfidious Japanese', *The Economist*, 20 April: 65.

The Economist (1991), 'Back to the Bulldog Stuff', 19 January: 51.

The Economist, (1991), 'Alphabet Soup', 21 September: 33.

The Economist, (1991), 'Five Years Since the Big Bang', 26 October: 23–6.

Fieleke, N. S. (1992), 'One Trading World or Many: the Issue of Regional Trading Blocs', *New England Economic Review*, May–June: 3–20.

Frankel, J. (1991), 'Is a Yen Bloc Forming in Pacific Asia?' *Amex Bank Review*, November: 2–3.

Franklin, M. with Wilke, M. (1990), *Britain in the European Community*, London, Royal Institute of International Affairs.

Garrett, G. and Lange, P. (1991), 'Political Responses to Interdependence: What's "Left" for the Left?', *International Organization*, **45**: 539–64.

George, S. (1990), *An Awkward Partner: Britain in the European Community*, Oxford, Oxford University Press.

Gordon, B. (1990–91), 'Who Really Buys American?' *The National Interest*, **22**: 48–56.

Haber, D. L. (1990), 'The Death of Hegemony: Why "Pax Nipponica" is Impossible', *Asian Survey*, **30**: 892–907.

Heim, C. E. (1991), 'Dimensions of Decline: Industrial Regions in Europe, the US, and Japan in the 1970s and 1980s', paper presented at The Social Science History Association, Annual Meeting, New Orleans, November. Available from the author, Amherst, MA Department of Economics, University of Massachusetts.

Hitchens, C. (1990), *Blood, Class, and Nostalgia: Anglo-American Ironies*, New York, Farrar, Straus and Giroux.

Ikenberry, G. J. (1992), A World Economy Restored: Expert Consensus and the Anglo-American Postwar Settlement', *International Organization*, **46**: 289–321.

Ikenberry, G. J. and Kupchan, C.A. (1990), Socialization and Hegemonic Power, *International Organization*, **44**: 283–315.

Ingham, G. (1984), *Capitalism Divided? the City and Industry in British Social Development*, New York, Schocken.

Julius, D. (1990), *Global Companies and Public Policy*, London, Frances Pinter.

Llewellyn, D. T. (1992), Competition, Diversification, and Structural Change in the British Financial System, in G.G. Kaufman (ed.), *Banking Structures in Major Countries*, Boston Kluwer.

Maier, C. (1978), The Politics of Productivity: Foundations of American International Economic Policy after World War II, in P. Katzenstein (ed.), *Between Power and Plenty: Foreign Economic Policies of Advanced Industrial States*, Madison, University of Wisconsin Press.

Mjoset, L. (1990), 'The Turn of Two Centuries: a Comparison of British and US Hegemonies, in D.P. Rapkin (ed.), *World Leadership and Hegemony*, Boulder Co. Lynne Rienner.

Nairn, T. (1988), *The Enchanted Glass: Britain and its Monarchy*, London, Chandos.

O'Duffy, B. (1991), 'As Others See Us 1: Italy and Italians according to the British', *Relazioni Internazionali*, **55**: 86–97.

Parboni, R. (1984), *The Dollar and its Rivals*, London, Verso.

Rousso, H. (1991), *The Vichy Syndrome: History and Memory in France Since 1944*, Cambridge MA, Harvard University Press. Original French second edition (1990), *Le syndrome de Vichy: de 1944 à nos jours*, Paris, Editions du Seuil.

Rupert, M. E. (1990), Power, Productivity, and the State: the Social Relations of US Hegemony, in D.P. Rapkin (ed.), *World Leadership and Hegemony*, Boulder Co Lynne Rienner.

Ryan, H. B. (1987), *The Vision of Anglo-America: the US–UK Alliance and the Emerging Cold War, 1943–1946*, Cambridge, Cambridge University Press.

Singer, D. (1988), *Is Socialism Doomed? The Meaning of Mitterrand*, New York, Oxford University Press.

Strange, S. (1990), 'Finance, Information and Power', *Review of International Studies*, **16**: 259–74.

Taylor, P. J. (1990), *Britain and the Cold War: 1945 as Geopolitical Transition*, London, Frances Pinter.

Taylor, P. J. (1991), 'The English and their Englishness: 'a curiously mysterious, elusive and little understood people', *Scottish Geographical Magazine*, **107**: 146–61.

UNCTC (1991), *World Investment Report 1991: the Triad in Foreign Direct Investment*, New York, United Nations Centre on Transnational Corporations.

Wallerstein, I. (1984), *The Politics of the World-economy*, Cambridge, Cambridge University Press.

Whiteley, P. (1985), 'Attitudes to Defence and International Affairs', in R. Jowell and S. Witherspoon (eds), *British Social Attitudes: the 1985 Report*, Aldershot, Gower.

8

Fact or fiction? The evidence for the thesis of US relative decline, 1966–1991

John O'Loughlin

How time flies! Within a year of the national acclaim of the victory by the USA over Iraq in the Gulf War in early 1991, a Lou Harris poll reported that 61 per cent of Americans were 'alienated', the highest level recorded in 25 years. This alienation from government has been strongly influenced by deep-seated worry about personal economic prospects, the seeming incapability of the state to handle its twin budget and trade deficits, and the fortunes of the USA in the world economy. The presidential candidates are running on 'America First' platforms; earlier, all the Democratic contenders had issued protectionist position papers and Congress approved trade retaliatory legislation. There is a nearly unanimous belief that Japan and other nations are 'cheating' in trade, with both popular and political support for the idea that Japan is partly responsible for the current economic recession in the USA. In searching for the cause of the prolonged recession, Americans seem more willing than ever to blame political allies with whom the USA has negative trade balances.

One of the remarkable features of the current debate on the problems of the American economy is the interpretation of short-term difficulties in relation to long-term relative decline. Elliott (1991) argues persuasively that Americans, worried about their future prosperity, are making the false comparison with the golden years of the 1950s. Then, USA power peaked after the destruction of other global powers and the post-Depression and post-War spending boom triggered enormous GNP growth. He shows that the more appropriate comparison is with the period between 1900 and 1910, when the USA was literally *'primus inter pares'*.

Since the publication of Paul Kennedy's book (1987) and the responses to its central thesis that the USA was repeating the error of previous global leaders (undermining its own leadership by engaging in 'imperial over-stretch'), the declinist thesis has been widely debated. Evidence of relative decline, for example in trade and industrial output, is strongly countered by evidence of American power, especially its military dominance after the Cold War and its huge economy (Brzezinski, 1991; Elliott, 1991; Friedberg, 1991b; Hormats, 1991; Krauthammer, 1991; Pfaff, 1991). The debate has taken on an ideological edge, with conservatives generally supporting the 'renewalist' counter-thesis (Huntingdon, 1988) while liberals argue for sharp reductions in military spending in order to prepare the USA for the next round of global economic competition (Reich, 1991).

At the centre of the debate on relative decline and future economic growth is the nature and quality of the evidence. While dozens of writers on the topic have marshalled numbers and indicators to support declinist or renewalist positions, to my knowledge there has not yet appeared a thorough examination of the available evidence. Furthermore, it is necessary to place the study of the hypothesis of decline within a broader historical and theoretical framework. This chapter therefore begins with an examination of the thesis of USA relative decline in the context of the theories of hegemonic decline. Both of these main schools of decline, as well as other historical perspectives, anticipated the downward trend in the indicators of American power on the basis of predictable changes in the underlying structures of the world system.

Starting in 1966, I present the evidence for and against the decline thesis, having chosen the indicators on the basis of world-system principles. The choice of starting date is critical; 1966 is useful on many grounds, not least of which is that this date allows a quarter-century of evidence to be sifted and evaluated. There is agreement that the 'artificial' post-War status of the USA had stabilized by the middle 1960s and that the pace of world economic growth (Kondratieff IVA) was beginning to slow (Wallerstein, 1984, 1991). Therefore, the period under examination, 1966–1990, covers the last part of a global boom and about 20 years of a global recession. As world leader the USA was both affected by and affected the nature and direction of the global trajectories. As well as presenting the temporal (year by year) changes in the indicators of relative American power and their consistency, I also examine the spatial dimensions of American fields of influence over time to see if they are stable, expanding or receding. I conclude the chapter with an evaluation of the thesis of American decline and the implications of the findings for world-system theories of hegemony.

US decline in world-systems perspectives

Phases of growth and decline for individual countries are common threads in all long cycle writings (Goldstein, 1988). Where the theorists differ is in the choice of indicators of growth/decline and, significantly, in the timing of the phases. For Wallerstein (1984, 1991), periods of dominance (generally termed hegemony by world-systems theorists) are very rare, occurring for only three brief periods in the history of the capitalist world economy

(Netherlands, 1620–72; United Kingdom, 1815–73; and the USA, 1945–67). Hegemonic powers have an edge simultaneously in the economic (agro–industrial, commercial and financial sectors), military (all have been sea powers) and cultural–ideological arenas (all supported free trade ideology and global 'liberalism').

In contrast to Wallerstein, Modelski (1987a, b), finds that global leadership is more common. Each phase of global power lasts for about 50 years (two generations), from the end of the global war that certifies victory for the new power. By winning the war, the global leader sets the peace and world order terms and ensures its own dominance by monopolizing the function of world order-keeping. After about a half-century, its power status becomes 'delegitimized' by challengers and later 'deconcentrates'. Modelski's measure of leadership is seapower, based on the notion that seapowers have successively been the global leaders; shipping tonnage is therefore a good indicator of commercial and military strength (Modelski and Thompson, 1988). Whereas Wallerstein (1991) dates American decline from the late 1960s (beginning of the Kondratieff IVB downturn), Modelski does not envision US decline for decades into the future because of its military strength and large economy.

One criticism of Modelski's model is that it is no longer appropriate. In a world in which global war would result in annihilation of leader and challengers, global wars would no longer have their causative effect on global leadership position. To use Luttwak's (1991) term, we have moved from a world of 'geo-politics', in which military power was supreme, to 'geo-economics', a world in which economic strength and commercial and financial stature is superseding military strength. A similar theme of the changing nature of world politics is found in Kennedy (1987), Calleo (1987), Nye (1990), Strange (1990a), Mead (1990, 1991), Rizopoulos (1990), Corbridge and Agnew (1991), Friedberg (1991a), Luttwak (1991), Thrift and Leyshon (1991), Reich (1991), Wallerstein (1991) and Agnew (1992). The seminal work on the changing nature of international relations by Keohane and Nye (1989 revised edition) marked the beginning of the 'neo-realist' school, which now dominates the field of international relations. By including non-state actors and addressing the role that economic relations play in the determination of political ties and the strength of states, Keohane and Nye paved the way for the long-overdue incorporation of non-political and non-military affairs into the narrowly realist conceptions of international relations.

The best statement of the new importance of non-military states is Rosecrance's (1986) work on the power of trading states. He argued that since 1945, the old way of achieving victories (seizing territories of opponents by force, achieved through massive military spending and commitments) has been replaced by a new way of obtaining victory, developing sophisticated commercial and financial success overseas by massive investment in domestic industrial and technological bases. If Fukuyama's (1991) vision of the 'Commonmarketization' of the world system is accurate, then success will be measured by positive trading balances, innovative capacity and productive leadership.

Much of the discussion of the relative decline of the USA has featured historical comparisons. Kennedy's (1987) comparisons of Reaganite America to Edwardian Britain have been reviewed by Mjøset (1990: 21–48) and strongly criticized by Nau (1990) and Nye (1990). The critics argue that the comparison is inappropriate because the USA controlled a higher ratio of world resources, was not challenged on the military and economic fronts by a fastgrowing power like Germany, was more democratic and therefore more likely to amend trajectories than Britain, was less likely to drain resources into overseas commitments and, in general, is more capable of renewal than the relatively declining Edwardian state. Renewalists further argue that historical comparisons are invalid because of the changing nature of power over the centuries and because the USA is unmatched in history for the near-global acceptance of its ideology and political and economic values.

Wallerstein (1991), challenging the renewalists, sees 1989 as marking a watershed in the relative power position of the USA. Viewing the Cold War as an exercise in American hegemony over its allies in the face of a perceived Soviet threat while offering the Soviets a 'chasse gardeé' in Eastern Europe, he expects intra-Western core competition to escalate with the disappearance of the threat and the American share of global production and world markets to shrink in proportion to the competition. Wallerstein viewed the Reagan years of high military spending as an attempt to assert by military power what the USA was losing in the economic arena but in the end, 'one can only defer negatives, minimize losses, maneuver to retain some (if less) advantage but one cannot command the waves to halt' (Wallerstein, 1991: 35).

While Modelski and Wallerstein share the view that cycles are endemic in the capitalist world system and in individual country power profiles, Kennedy and his critics prefer to avoid what they see as the 'historical determinism' of temporal cycles. In their view, each world power is unique and had a special set of advantages that propelled it to global status and later a special set of circumstances that undermined its powerful position. The USA is therefore not pre-destined to decline like other great powers of the past but by judicious choice of economic, social and political options, the country can prolong its global leadership (Kennedy, 1987; Chase, 1988; Inoguchi, 1988; Nau, 1990; Nye, 1990; Kuttner, 1991; Reich, 1991). What these commentators fear is that, like van Wolferen's (1991) complaint about Japan, nobody is really in charge in Washington DC and that a deficit of global vision and national priority-making exists at the highest levels of government.

While President Bush's 'New World Order' was the centre of American geo-political discourse in 1990 and especially after the Gulf War, only a few short months later the term had all but vanished from the Washington lexicon. Instead, there is a pre-occupation with the problems of the American economy and the re-casting of American geo-political strategies in the light of the strategic sea changes of the past three years (Rizopoulos, 1990). Most commentators (Chase, 1988; Brzezinski, 1991; Cohen, 1991; Friedberg, 1991a; and Vernon and Kapstein, 1991) agree that the USA cannot continue to commit itself to allies in all places and that difficult choices must be made in determining future 'selective commitments'. For Amin (1991), Cohen (1991), Cooper, Higgott and Nossal (1991), Ishihara (in Ishihara and Prestowitz, 1991) and Rubenstein (1991), the hidden weakness of the American position in the Gulf War is indicated by the fact that American core and Persian Gulf allies paid for most of the war costs under American pressure. This is hardly the action of a uni-lateralist superpower (Hamilton and Clad, 1991; O'Loughlin, 1992). Only the UK could be counted as a follower of the Washington line in the Gulf (Cooper, Higgott and Nossal, 1991), a further re-affirmation, if one was needed, of the 'special relationship' (Agnew, Chapter 7, p. 132–147). Following the common definition of power (getting others to do what they otherwise would not do), the USA exercized its power in the Gulf and the realist belief that only military strength matters in the final analysis was strongly supported in the Gulf War.

For neo-realists, who constitute most observers of the geo-political scene, the USA can regenerate its economy by reappraising spending priorities (the peace dividend), by forcing allies to end 'free-riding' on defence and by rebuilding the social infrastructure neglected in the decades of the Cold War. In this perspective, the crucial relationship for the USA is with Japan. A feeling that a 'Pearl Harbor without bombs' (Toal, 1991) awaits the USA if it does not re-establish its geo-economic and geo-political relationship with Japan is now gaining momentum. Japan is seen as a cheat in international trade because of its supposed closed economy, its huge (but falling) trade surplus with the USA and its penetration of markets, previously-dominated by the USA, in South East Asia and Latin America. What is most galling to the commentators (among them van Wolferen, 1991 and Prestowitz in Ishihara and Prestowitz, 1991) is that Japan seems to have no global vision except to expand its output and markets. But it appears likely that the 'followship' of Japan of the American lead will ebb and that, instead, a reciprocal relationship will solidify. This has already been identified by Funabashi (1991), Isihihara and Prestowitz (1991), Thrift and Leyshon (1991), Corbridge and Agnew (1991), Friedberg (1991b) and Hartland-Thunberg (1991).

The USA takes one-third of Japan's exports; together the USA and Japan account for nearly 40 per cent of world trade. Most significantly, Japanese purchases of American government debt make possible the postponement of the day of reckoning of the nearly $4 trillion American budget deficit, while the USA accounts for over 40 per cent of all Japanese foreign direct investment. Prestowitz (in Ishihara and Prestowitz, 1991) believes that Japan is working to turn the USA into the junior partner of a *Pax Consortis* (Inoguchi, 1988), just as a growing USA moved from a junior to a senior position in the UK–USA relationship around the turn of the century. For Bergsten (1990), Garten (1991), Holbrooke (1991), Mead (1990, 1991) and Pfaff (1991), the USA can redress the economic imbalances in its relationship with Japan, the NICs and other core powers by abandoning its Cold War militarist economy because 'patient investment capital is displacing firepower, the development of civilian products is displacing military innovation and the penetration of markets is displacing military garrisons on foreign soil' (Luttwak, 1991, A15). Despite arguments that Japan has erected disproportionate tariffs on foreign imports, the GATT surveys (General Agreement on Tariffs and Trade, 1990a,b) indicate clearly that the American market is more protectionist than the Japanese one. For free traders, like Bhagwati (1991) and Nishkamen (1991), American actions of retaliation under Section 301 and threats of Congressional trade sanctions against supposedly cheating countries is threatening the whole global free trade system constructed by the USA in the immediate post-War period when it dominated world trade and forced open markets worldwide to American products.

In Wallerstein's world-systems terms, we can interpret American military actions of the past decade, disproportionate military spending (higher than any other core state), and threatening trade postures as the actions of a post-hegemonic state. The USA has lost its productive leadership as high-technology goods are now produced by all industrialized countries. The American trade ratio (exports/GNP), at about 10 per cent, is the lowest of any core state, though American exports of manufactured products rose dramatically after the G–7 Plaza agreement of 1985 to reduce the value of the dollar. American capital investment and savings ratios are also low by comparison with core competitors; it is only in financial services that the USA retains a pivotal global role, though even this position is threatened by the 'Casino capitalism' nature of American enterprise (Strange, 1986). In a view shared with Kennedy (1987: 539–40), Wallerstein (1991) argues that the USA cannot regain through military means what it has lost through the inexorable processes of capitalist shifts in the world system over the past 25 years.

Evaluation measures of the hypothesis of US relative decline are usually of three kinds, military, economic or cultural/ideological. In world-system and long cycle research, all three indicators have been used to test the theoretical notions about the rise and decline of states implicit in these models. However, the Modelski long cycle periodization and identification of global leaders is predicated on the ratio of military strength (especially seapower) of the leader to the challengers (Modelski 1987a; Modelski and Thompson, 1988) while the world systems perspective is very explicit about the processes of economic growth that lead to hegemonic status. For Wallerstein and Modelski, global leaders match economic with military and cultural hegemony but in the flux of global power shifts it is military strength that ultimately determines the success or failure of a leader to prolong its status in the Modelski view; while for Wallerstein the ability of the leader to regenerate its industrial base determines the outcome of the global competition.

The recognition that the arena of world power competition has shifted from purely military to a mixed military–economic one, paralleling the interest in neo-realism, is related to the double challenge to the USA after 1945. The global hegemon was engaged in the great power game with the USSR on the military–political front, while simultaneously slowly losing its economic leadership over its political allies on the production–commercial–

financial front. Post-revisionist views of the Cold War (Cox, 1990; Kaldor, 1990) suggest that the Cold War was mutually beneficial to both super-powers and was arranged by the USA as an exercise partly to keep the core Western allies (and potential economic competitors) in check. In this view, the USA used a set of political structures that were foisted on the defeated Axis powers and Western allies 'to lock economic advantage into place and make it function smoothly' (Wallerstein, 1991: 26). Along with American political–military leadership and economic arrangements came the 'geocul-ture' of American ideology. While Fukuyama (1991) sees this liberal univer-salism as globally unchallenged after the defeat of communism and fascism, Wallerstein (1991) and Taylor (1992) believe that the end of the Cold War marks the end of the unchallenged American leadership and the appearance of hitherto unnoticed anti-systemic ideologies, primarily from the Third World, in a kind of geo-cultural decolonization.

Power measures and evidence of US relative decline

Support for the US decline thesis depends on the type of evidence col-lected. In turn, the choice of evidence is based on what the researcher considers to be the elements of power. Three types of power have been widely discussed, military, economic and cultural–ideological power, simi-lar to Kenneth Boulding's (1989) *Three Faces of Power*, 'the stick, the carrot and the hug'. But power is an elusive concept in world politics, being somewhat of a 'chaotic conception'. Though power is generally agreed to constitute a central concept, Merritt and Zinnes (1989: 26) conclude that 'judging from available research results, no general agreement tells us which variables best indicate power relationships'. But they note a prefer-ence for multiple indicators because:

the nature of our theory of international politics determines how we conceptualize power . . . the attributes of the power concept are directly linked to the arguments made within the theory. The emphasis thus focuses on data applicable to individual theories rather than the search for a universal, all-purpose scale of power relation-ships (Merritt and Zinnes, 1989: 25).

Hanns Maull (1990) has codified the shift from realist to neo-realist views of world order with his distinction between 'hard' and 'soft' power. Working in the Rosecrance (1986) tradition and impressed by the return to world power status of Japan and Germany, the defeated challengers of World War II, he argues that the trading states (called the civilian powers) have succeeded in a world in which economic interdependence reigns. Germany and Japan are seen as 'prototypes of a promising future'. However, both states are viewed with suspicion in the USA because their economies are qualitatively different from other Western economies in size, export capacity, growth, and trade balance. In this new world order, Maull notes that whereas military power is controlled by governments, economic power cannot be as easily manipulated and targeted because of the activities of transnational companies in global markets. (See also Nye, 1990: 15–16; Strange, 1990; Agnew, 1992). Clearly, Japan and Germany do not wish to jeopardize the arrangements that have brought them such economic success but are concerned about the growing demands in the USA for redress of perceived American grievances.

Soft power is the ability to persuade while hard power is the ability to command. If the new post-Cold-War order demands, then the USA will have to change into a different kind of superpower:

(a) acceptance of the necessity of cooperation with others in the pursuit of international objectives;
(b) the concentration on non-military, primarily economic means to secure national goals, with military power left as a residual instrument serving essentially to safeguard other means of international interaction and
(c) a willingness to develop supranational structures to address critical issues of international management (Maull, 1990: 92–93).

Nye (1990) offers the best compendium of decline studies. He starts from the proposition that 'decline is a tricky word because it bundles together two quite different concepts; a decrease in external power and internal deterioration and decay' (Nye, 1990: 14). Clearly distinguishing between hard and soft power as 'carrots' and 'sticks', Nye (1990: 32–3) uses the term 'soft power' to refer to notions of power status that are hard to quantify, such as cultural and ideological power. Here, he shares a Gramscian perspective on power with Russett (1985), Cox (1987), Cafruny (1990: 97–118), Ikenberry and Kupchan (1990a, b), and Rupert (1990: 71–96). The *Pax Americana* was effective because it enshrined the liberal international economic order and the USA was able to obtain a near universal consent on its guiding principles, thereby enshrining the supremacy of the leading state and dominant social classes. While the USA may slip in the quantifiable indicators (GNP, trade shares, military expenditures, Russett (1985), Strange (1987), Huntingdon (1988) and Nau (1990) argue that its preeminence is ensured through the universalism of its 'geo-culture'.

The renewalists are also quick to point out that, contrary to popular belief, the quantifiable indicators do not indicate decline but have been stable since the early 1970s, when the exceptional post-War lead of the USA had diminished. Kennedy (1987: 533) notes that the geographic extent, population and natural resources of the USA suggest a 'natural' share of world wealth and power of 16–18 per cent; it was 40–50 per cent in the post-War period so that the sharp falls in the global ratio are simply indications for the renewalists that the USA is working its way down to its natural share. However, in 1992 the American share of world output is still close to double its 'natural share'.

In addition to the declinists (Kennedy, Mead, Gilpin and Calleo) and the renewalists (Huntingdon, Nau, Nye), a third group of scholars are trying to understand the domestic implications of the global economic challenges facing the USA and to promote governmental policies to cope with them. Olson (1982) attributes slow economic growth to the loss of competitiveness as a result of the actions of special interest groups. Layers of powerful groups (governmental bureaucracies, trade unions and inefficient agricultural and industrial producers) protect their entrenched positions from the winds of economic change. He attributes the slower rates of American and British productivity growth to these entrenched interest groups, comparing the higher rates of growth in other industrial countries starting afresh after World War II. Actually, his comparison is more apt for the NICs. Reich (1991) and Kuttner (1991) worry about the bifurcation of American society into two classes, the educated sector oriented to high-technology industry and services and able to compete successfully in the international economic arena and the growing sector of poorly-educated workers in unskilled jobs, especially in the service sector. They call for policies to rectify the differences between the groups and the result, they believe, would re-establish the USA as a major force in world manufacturing and service exports. Nye (1990) also engages in this exhortatory exercise.

There is very little firm evidence for either the declinist or the renewalist viewpoint. Each author tends to present snippets of information to support the argument, usually one or two indicators at selected time-periods to show decline or stability. Since the power concept is difficult to measure and generally agreed to need more than a few indicators, it seems time to compare the performance of the USA over the past quarter-century on a variety of hard and soft power indicators to evaluate the decline thesis. The rest of this chapter will report the results of that exercise. Though the empirical part of the chapter is not a direct test of the accuracy of either of the world-system models, by determining the weight of evidence for the declinist or renewalist thesis it will provide some evidence for the Wallerstein view that the USA is in irreversible decline or the Modelski view that the USA carries the seeds of its own regeneration to another round of global leadership. Though specifically a comparison of the relative empirical strengths of the declinist or renewalist arguments, it will therefore have important ramifications for the wider historical-structural models of global leadership.

Choice of hard and soft power indicators

In picking the indicators, I chose measures that paralleled the dichotomy between Modelski and Wallerstein in their respective emphases on military and economic power. By the accounts of Gilpin (1987), Kennedy (1987), Maull (1990), and Mead (1990a, b), military power is by definition hard power. Military power indicates the power to command should a foreign policy decision not be accepted by the opposing party. At the time of the war with Iraq in 1990–91, many commentators noted that while the economic sanctions (soft power) may or may not have succeeded in eventually removing Iraq from Kuwait, the demonstration of hard power was immediately effective in achieving American policy goals.

There are two military indicators for hard power, military expenditure and arms sales ratios. Like all the indicators, the measures are relative ones since the decline thesis refers to 'relative', not 'absolute' American decline. Each computes the American share of the world total or compares the value of the American figures over time, from 1966 to the present. (All of the indicators' definitions, measurements and data sources are presented in Appendix, page 175–177.) Other military indicators that are data-accessible (military personnel, numbers of different weapons systems) were evaluated and rejected as not representative of the essence of the concept, the effectiveness of American military power and the relative standing of its armed forces in the world. Military spending by the USA is the most commonly used surrogate for the strength of American forces. Arms sales indicate both the relative success of the USA in the global arms market-place, as well as the political standing of the USA abroad. The purchase of American weapons by high-spending allies is a good indicator that American military alliance is valued. Other hard power indicators are the state of American political relations, in terms of whether the USA is sending or receiving cooperating or conflict acts in its dyadic international relations. Four indicators, derived from the WEIS data set, measure the weighted cooperative and conflict actions sent from and received by the USA in the period from 1966 to 1988.

Hard power is not only military strength, international political relations and arms exports; it is also the domestic economic base. Modelski (1987a, b) notes that the success of global leaders in global wars is in turn based upon the size and productivity of the domestic economy, a feature that his model shares with Wallerstein's (1984). Gross National Product (GNP) is the usual measure of the output of an economy but here the American figure is compared to the other five Great Powers (Japan, West Germany, USSR, UK and France) over time to obtain a relative measure. An indicator of basic American economic strength is the cumulative debt ratio (of GNP) of the USA, an indicator of the long-term governmental expenditure/revenue balance and perhaps a harbinger of future crises (Reich, 1991).

Additions to the economic base could be computed using the GNP growth figures or productivity gains but a more useful measure is the rate of capital formation. Gross capital formation provides the investment basis for further economic growth. Many declinist writings discuss the quality of American life as an adjunct to the consideration of the USA in the world economy but since the trade/GNP ratio is very low (about 10 per cent), it is possible that the external indicators show decline while the domestic economy is prospering. Both international and domestic indicators of hard power are therefore needed (Nye, 1990). A final indicator, median family income, is a generalized indicator of the quality of domestic economic life and measures the extent to which it is improving, stagnating or declining.

Soft power is seen as the ability to persuade and in Maull's (1990) reckoning Japan and Germany are the best exponents of soft power with their powerful, export-driven, economies. Above all else, soft power is measured by performance in the international export markets. The relative competitive trade position of the USA can be indicated in the trend of the terms of trade, the extent to which the volumes of exports are keeping up with the rising costs of imports. A related measure is trade shares and I used both the temporal sequence of the American share of total world exports as well as the spatial expression of the share of imports over time. The former measures the overall performance of American exports; the latter indicates the changing field of American export influence. Another obvious soft power measure is the trade balance in constant dollars. The fourth indicator is the income that the economy derives from services, noting that Wallerstein (1984) sees leadership in financial services as the last stage of hegemonic achievement as well as hegemonic decline. Another indicator, the rate of American net nonfactor income (including services of labour and capital from direct investment abroad, interest, dividends and property, as well as labour income) measures the earnings of American companies and individuals in foreign markets and takes into consideration one of the most important developments of the recent economic history of the USA, the movement offshore of economic interests (Reich, 1991: Kuttner, 1991).

All writers on hegemony and US decline stress the role of innovation. The next wave of global economic growth is expected to be led by the bio-genetics and micro-processing sectors so a good measure of American relative innovation is the share of American patents filed by foreigners. Since the USA is by far the largest market in the world, this ratio indicates the extent to which companies are keeping up with the revolution in manufacturing technology. Two final indicators of soft power are presented. Taken literally, the ability to persuade is most clearly seen in the United Nations General Assembly. There, the USA is one of 160 or so countries of equal voting power but the USA has staked very clear positions on many issues over the years. By looking at the voting distance between the USA and each member state over time, we can estimate the extent to which the USA is isolated or supported in the world body and how the level of persuasion (level of agreement with the USA on the issues that appear in the Assembly) has grown or fallen. Though the final soft power measure, foreign aid spending, can be interpreted as a humanitarian gesture, it should be seen more properly as a foreign policy instrument. It is in that light that the foreign aid bill is presented to Congress each year and the ratio of foreign aid is a useful measure of American influence abroad, working on the reasonable assumption that aid dollars buy influence.

Changes in the indicators of US hard power, 1966–91

The temporal development of the indicators of American hard power over the past quarter-century is shown in Figures 1–5. Each indicator will be discussed individually and the overall hard power trends will be reviewed at the end of this section.

The overall trend of relative American military expenditures is clearly consistent and downward, from about 40 per cent of the world total during the Vietnam War at the beginning of the period to about 22 per cent after the Reagan military spending boom (*see* Figure 8.1). Since 1985 American military spending has dropped in real terms each year and because of domestic spending priorities we can expect this trend to continue. As a proportion of both the federal budget and world expenditures, the American military expenditure share is falling and, as a result, we can

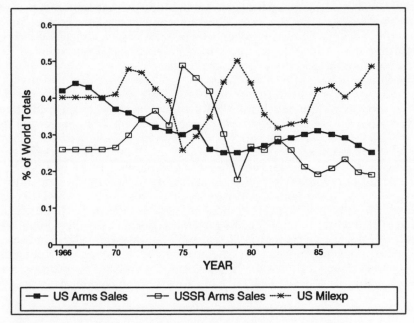

Figure 8.1 American and Soviet ratios of world arms sales and American military expenditures ratio, 1966–89.
Source: SIPRI and Sivard.

expect the power gap between the USA and putative military challengers to lessen. However, with the withdrawal of the former Soviet Union from the global military competition, it is difficult to see whence a serious military challenge to the USA would emanate. What is perhaps most interesting is that the American ratio of world military expenditures is now below its share of world economic output, after exceeding it until the mid-1980s. The military spending ratio is only a gross index: the quality of equipment and troops that it generates is more interesting but harder to measure. The huge imbalance in the quality of the training and material on the Iraqi and American sides in the Gulf War indicates that large American military expenditure is likely to continue to produce an uncontested lead in war preparations over large, poor Third World states, from where the challenge to American global and regional leadership is likely to develop.

The evident rises and falls of the American ratio of arms sales since the 1960s is due to the nature of military sales contracts which tend to extend for a period of years; a major contract (for example, with Saudi Arabia) will produce a sharp increase in the ratio. As expected, the American ratio is in inverse proportion to the (former) Soviet one since the superpowers together have always accounted for over three-quarters of global arms sales (*see* Figure 8.1). Since 1978 the Soviet total has been the greater but in 1991 the USA will far exceed it, partly as a result of the demonstration effects of American weapons in the Iraq War. Future competition in the arms marketplace for the USA will probably come from France, Brazil and Israel, rather than the former Soviet Union. It seems as if this is one export sector where the American lead will be unchallenged.

The international political relations of the USA have fluctuated greatly over the past quarter-century (*see Figure* 8.2) This graph shows the trends of four indexes of how much the USA sent and received cooperation and conflict from the other members of the global system. The general trends are remarkably similar, with cooperation rising quickly and conflict falling during the two détente periods, 1967 to 1980 and 1985 to 1988, in both the weighted acts sent and received. With the exception of 1974, the USA has received more (weighted) conflictual action than (weighted) cooperative ones. Since 1975, the ratio is consistently about two-thirds cooperative to conflict. Conservatives see this development as an indicator of the danger-ous nature of world politics and the precarious position that the USA is in, standing as the global leader in political and cultural terms. Since the index is heavily affected by the state of USA/former USSR relations, the positive value in 1972 simply shows the highpoint of détente and the warming of relations with the (former) Soviet Union was counteracted in the index by

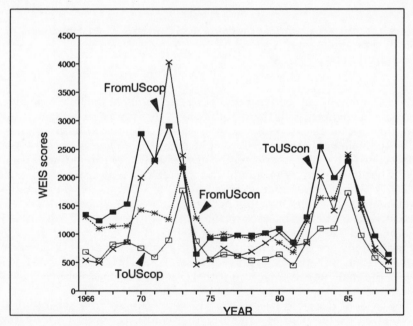

Figure 8.2 International relations of the US, 1966–88.

Source: WEIS.

Notes: From UScop = total weighted cooperation sent by the US; ToUScop = total weighted cooperation received by the US; from UScon = total weighted conflict sent by the US; ToUScon = total weighted conflict received by the US.

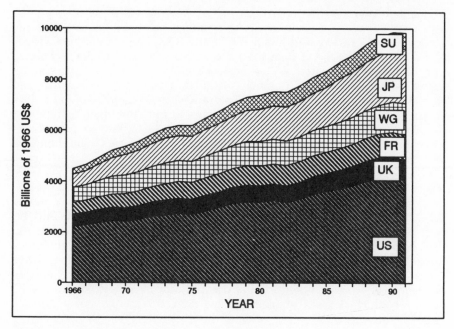

Figure 8.3 Comparative GNP (Gross National Product) growth of the six Great Powers, 1966–91.

Source: Mitchell (1975, 1982), Leisner.

Notes: SU = Soviet Union; JP = Japan; WG = West Germany; FR = France; UK = United Kingdom; US = United States.

the cooling of relations with many Third World states in the Reagan years (O'Loughlin and Grant, 1990).

The detente years are also obvious in the indexes of cooperation and conflict sent from the USA (*see* Figure 8.2). From 1970 to 1973, the ratio was significantly above 1, showing much more cooperation than conflict. Like the actions directed towards the USA, the score has been consistent over the past decade, hovering about 1.0. Interestingly, American actions directed towards the rest of the world community have, in general, been more cooperative than the reciprocal actions sent to the USA. If one expects a global leader to be the recipient and sender of cooperative acts (premised on the belief that power generates respect and fear), then clearly the USA does not reflect that situation. There is no doubt, however, that the USA is by far the most important node in the network of international relations, accounting for about 40 per cent of the foreign policy actions reported in the WEIS data set, which is not unexpected since major American newspapers provide the events used to build the data set.

The American share of the total GNP of the six great powers (the same set considered by Kennedy, 1987) has changed very little over the past quarter-century (*see* Figures 8.3 and 8.4). One way of examining these trends is to note that the rate of growth of American GNP is only slightly less than the average of the six powers and it has been greater than all, except West Germany and Japan (*see* Figure 8.3). These graphs provide a classic case of the use of data by the American relative decline debaters. The declinists stress that a 7 per cent drop over 25 years is profound, following Kennedy's (1987) expression of the importance of even a 1 per cent change in global proportions. The renewalists note that the ratio has been essentially stable for the past 20 years, despite the much ballyhooed shrinking of American output. In terms of size, the American economy is still central in the world system and this central role appears to be changing only very slowly.

When examining the ratio of Great Power GNP, the change for the USA has been from just under 50 per cent to about 43 per cent, with the major drop happening, as noted by Nye (1990) in the years up to 1974 (*see* Figure 8.4). At present rates of GNP growth, it would not be until 25 years into the next century that the Japanese economy would surpass that of the USA. For Modelski (1987a), this temporal lag is further proof that the USA will remain the global leader for another generation. The results of the global competition to increase output are shown in Table 8.1. Since 1979, the USA has lagged its core competitors in industrial output growth in 8 of the 13 years for which data are available. Since 1986, the gap has been consistently negative for the USA. Should these rates of growth continue to

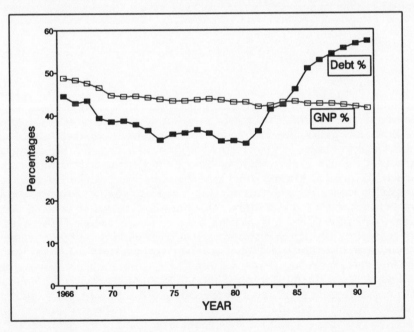

Figure 8.4 US ratio of Great Power GNP and cumulative US debt as ratio of US GNP, 1966–91

Source: Mitchell (1975, 1982), Leisner, Statistical Abstract of the United States.

Table 8.1   United States competitiveness versus
other advanced industrial countries: average annual
percentage change in industrial output.

Year	Other industrial countries average	United States
1979	6.6	4.7
1980	6.7	−3.3
1981	−2.0	0.8
1982	0.6	−3.6
1983	0.7	2.0
1984	6.1	15.6
1985	4.4	0.9
1986	1.6	2.2
1987	5.1	3.8
1988	8.3	7.0
1989	5.9	3.3
1990	3.0	0.4

Source: Statistical Abstract of the United States 1990, p. 850.

remain stable, the outlook for the American share of global economic output is for further, perhaps faster, decreases.

One of most common indicators used by analysts to describe U.S. decline is the debt ratio (*see* Figure 8.4). Since 1979, the ratio of accumulated debt (now over $3.5 trillion) to GNP has climbed from about 35 per cent to almost 60 per cent. With no sign of either tax increases or reductions in government spending, the ratio is expected to continue to climb as yearly federal deficits (now over $300 billion) are added to the cumulative debt. The sharp climb in the debt ratio since 1979 is attributed to the Reagan years of tax cuts and increased military spending, a process not reversed by the Bush Administration. While debt in itself is not always a negative indicator (the debt monies can be used for basic infrastructural investment, for example), it is commonly agreed by both declinists and renewalists that the federal debt is now so large that it poses a long-term threat to the stability of the economy. More immediately, for the nationalistic right, the fact that much of the debt is owned by foreigners, especially Japanese, makes the USA susceptible to pressures from other countries in economic and political terms. Probably no single development had such an immediate impression on the global status as perceived by the domestic voters than the USA moving from the position of the world's largest creditor to world's largest debtor in the decade of the 1980s.

The rate of capital formation in the United States has been quite unstable in the years since 1966 (*see* Figure 8.5). In only 4 of the 24 years has it exceeded the level of 1966 (1973, 1978, 1979, 1984). This index is very susceptible to the domestic economic situation and is cyclical in nature, with capital formation rates falling in recessionary and high inflation years. After years of low capital formation, in a recession for example, the rate will move upward as savers and investors release their accumulated dollars onto the markets. The most consistent development of this index is a downward trend over the past half-decade but because the index is so cyclical this may not be any more than a temporary phase. However, the generally lower rate of the indicator recently does not bode well for the American economy, which needs a major capital infusion to accompany a new industrial policy (Reich, 1991; Kuttner, 1991).

The final hard power indicator, median family income in constant dollars, is the most tangible for the domestic population in the USA (see Figure 8.5). It has been remarkably stable throughout the study period and after a very slow rise in the 1980s, the index is now back to the mid-1960s level. In other words, there has been no change in the average standard of living in the USA over the past generation, which is a remarkable contrast to the previous post-War quarter-century. The notion of each generation having a better quality of life than the previous one is deeply ingrained in civil society and this family income stability hides an even more ominous development, that the poorest quintile had the largest drop in their income status over the past decade while the richest quintile had the largest increase (Elliott, 1991). For the American middle classes, their standard of living is holding stable. In contrast to the USA, the median income is growing in nearly all industrial countries, especially in the countries of peripheral Europe and East Asia. However, when one uses purchasing-power parity ratios, the average standard of living in the USA remains the highest in the world (World Bank, 1990).

The indicators of hard power show that over the past quarter-century there has been some slippage in American status. While the GNP and median family income indices are slightly declining, there have been large fluctuations in the arms sales and capital formation indices that preclude any certainty of a trend. All the indexes of political relations, military expenditures and debt indices show evidence of negative trends. Not one of the eight hard power indicators show a positive development and so the conclusion for these indicators must be, on balance, that the thesis of relative American decline is weakly supported.

Changes in the indicators of US soft power, 1966–91

The American economy has traditionally been more autarkic than that of any other industrialized country (Elliott, 1991) but increasingly, there is a recognition among manufacturers that they will have to be more export-oriented than in the past, to counter the loss of market shares in the USA to foreign, especially East Asian, interests and to maintain profit margins (Reich, 1991). The terms of trade for the USA have dropped consistently since the late 1960s to reach a value that is slightly over half of that of two decades ago (see Figure 8.5). Such a consistent decline in a key indicator, one that anticipates future trade deficits as the price of imports rises relative to the price of exports, is a negative harbinger of future American trade prospects. One of the key reasons for the trend is a consistently high ratio of unprocessed goods among exports, which are relatively of low

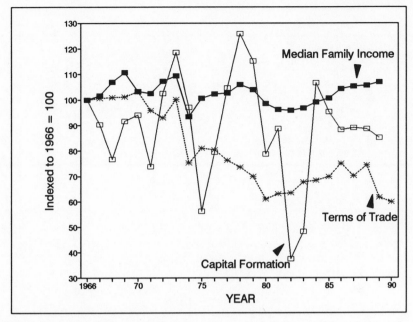

Figure 8.5 US median family income, rate of capital formation and terms of trade, 1966–90, indexed to 1966 = 100

Source: Statistical Abstract of the United States and World Bank.

value, while manufacturing and consumer imports of high value continued to rise.

Though the America economy is by far the largest in the world, in absolute terms, the exports of West Germany are higher (*see* Figure 8.6). While the export-orientated Japanese and German economies have been gaining world export shares since 1966, the American ratio of the world total has fallen, from 16 to 12 per cent, though the trend has not been consistently downward. The level of exports is heavily affected by the exchange rate of the dollar, with noticeable drops in the high dollar years of the early 1980s and a rise after the G–7 agreement to drive down the dollar exchange rate in September 1985. A 4 per cent loss of a rapidly-expanding world market over 25 years is significant, despite the consistent rise of the value of exports. If exports are related to the future prospects of an economy, then the outlook for the economy continues to be bleak.

The world ratio of exports for the USA hides huge country-to-country and region-to-region differences. The changing field of American exports are indicated in Table 8.2. While exports to the Americas and to the countries of the former Eastern Europe have remained remarkably consistent over time, the trends for the ratios for Western Europe/Africa/Middle East and Asia/Australasia have reversed. While the American share of the former region's imports has dropped from 45.4 to 33.9 per cent, it has increased proportionately from 19.2 per cent to 29.7 per cent in Asia. This

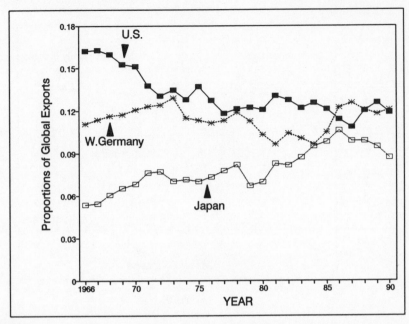

Figure 8.6   US, Japanese and West German exports as ratios of the world total, 1966–90.

Source: IMF.

development is partly a result of the greater integration of the European Community combined with a trend towards the exclusion of imports from outside the bloc, as well as the growing trans-Pacific reciprocal trade that has made this network the most dynamic and fastest-growing in the world (Anderson, 1991).

Table 8.2   Percentage of US Exports to each of the World's Pan-Regions, 1966–1988

Year	Canada/ Latin America	Europe, Africa and Middle East	Soviet Union/ Eastern Europe	Asia and Australasia
Exports				
1966	34.7	45.4	0.7	19.2
1973	32.0	42.0	1.2	24.8
1978	32.1	45.3	2.4	21.2
1983	28.9	44.1	1.4	25.6
1988	35.0	33.9	1.4	29.7

Nierop and de Vos (1988) conclude that the most remarkable features of the post-War trade picture has been the expansion of the Japanese field of dominance, the concomitant shrinkage of the American field and the growing intensity of interaction among the European states. The ratios in

Table 8.2 confirm the general applicability of these findings to the USA. Since 1966, the USA has lost market shares in the countries of the Middle East (except Egypt), in South and East Asia, and in some Latin American countries while increasing market shares only in the rapidly-growing economies of East Asia. The clear connection between the state of political and trade relations for the USA is indicated by the rapidly-changing trade shares in Iran, Egypt, Nicaragua and Ethiopia, consequent upon political changes in these states. By the end of the 1980s, the only world region where American exports were dominant was in Latin America, the Caribbean and Canada but even here, Japanese trade penetration is threatening the previously unchallenged American position (O'Loughlin, 1991). The formalization of the Americas trade network under American leadership through the proposed North American Free Trade Agreement (to include the USA, Canada, Mexico, and perhaps to be extended at a later date to Latin America) can be seen as an attempt to prevent further slippage of the once hegemonic American trade position in this region.

The trade balance is half of the most dramatic and best known picture of the relative decline of the USA. The federal budget deficit is the other half. But a relatively unnoticed feature of the trade balance is that the negative trade balance has been halved since 1987 as a result of the dramatic increase in manufactured exports consequent upon the fall of the value of the dollar (see Figure 8.7). The USA has not had a trade surplus since 1975 but one is possible by the mid-1990s, on present rates of import and export growth. The trade deficit is greatest with Japan and the NICs and has resulted in significant American political pressure on these countries to curb their exports to the USA and to buy more American products. What remains relatively unnoticed is the dramatic drop in the trade deficit with Japan since 1986, the year after the G–7 agreement on the dollar exchange rate. From Figure 8.7, it is also noteworthy that the trade surpluses of Japan and West Germany are falling in tandem with the falling American deficit. Free-marketeers, such as the writers in the *Economist*, view these trends as the classic operation of comparative advantage theory and the importance of exchange rates in the calculus of imports versus exports. As long as the dollar remains undervalued, the trade deficit is expected to shrink and, since the American Administration can effectively manipulate the dollar value (Corbridge and Agnew, 1991), the end result is that the USA can manage its own trade balance to a large extent.

Net incomes from both nonfactor and factor services have experienced an upturn in the past couple of years (see Figure 8.8). These two indices are the brightest elements of the American export picture and they are the basis for the strong American insistence on removal of national barriers to the import of American services in the current Uruguay round of GATT negotiations (Strange, 1990). As noted previously, Wallerstein (1984) sees the financial services sector as the last stage in which a hegemon will gain leadership and the last sector that will be lost so that the USA at the present time still has a considerable comparative advantage in this area. Furthermore, since the financial sector is expected to grow at a faster rate than the manufacturing one, the future for American exports looks better

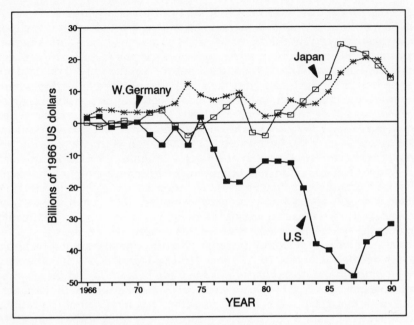

Figure 8.7 Trade balance (exports–imports) of the USA, Japan and West Germany, 1966–%90, in billions of US dollars.
Source: IMF.

than the dismal trade balance figures of the past decade would indicate. However, the future of these sectors is anything but certain and the sharp downturn by over half in the factor income after the late 1970s could easily continue.

Three further indicators of American soft power show evidence of consistent relative decline. The ratio of American patents awarded to foreigners has increased substantially from less than 10 per cent in 1966 to nearly 50 per cent at the present (*see* Figure 8.9). The big jump happened about 1980 and the ratio has only slighted increased over the past five years. It is difficult to say with certainty that the trend in patents is a clear indicator of future manufacturing leadership, though we would expect some connection. By far the largest number of foreign patents are awarded to Japanese companies and individuals and this constitutes further evidence for many observers of the innovation race between the two trans-Pacific economies, presumably resulting in a production lead in the next wave of manufacturing output.

The growing isolation of the USA in the UN General Assembly is immediately obvious in Figure 8.9. The process of isolation has dramatically increased since 1980 so that by the end of the decade, the average distance from all states hovered about +10 (on a scale from 100 to −100). Only a handful of core states have a positive (more agreement than disagreement with the USA) score on the map but since their scores are high (typically about 60–70 for NATO allies), they pull the overall index to a positive score. The UN voting distances constitute a 'very' soft power indicator since the votes carry little weight and instead are an indication of world opinion on controversial issues like a new world economic order, a Palestinian homeland, and neo-colonialism. The USA is the second-most-isolated state in the General Assembly (after Israel) and the Reagan administration tried unsuccessfully to link foreign aid to agreement with the USA in this body (Kegley and Hook, 1991). The uncertainty of the value of this indicator is shown by the fact that close American Third World allies like Zaire, Saudi Arabia, Pakistan and Chile have high negative scores with the USA. Nevertheless, it shows how few states are pre-disposed to support American ideology in a forum that debates the issues with no authority to implement them.

The final soft power indicator shows the decline of foreign aid contributions and the parallel growth of Japanese aid (*see* Figure 8.10), so that by 1989 Japan was the largest foreign aid-giver in the world. Apart from the Japanese increase, the biggest changes have come as a result of the increases in foreign aid by a variety of Organization of Economic Cooperation and Development (OECD) states to compensate for the stagnant American contribution over the past decade. The administrations of the USA have pressured the Japanese to give more aid and to act as a surrogate American aid donor, that is, by giving aid to close allies (Funa-

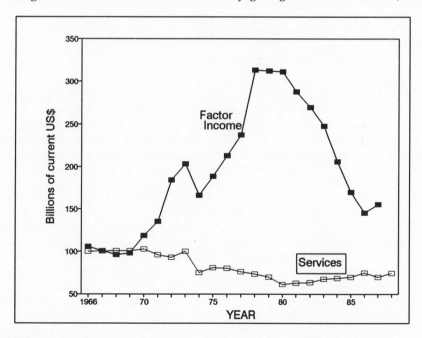

Figure 8.8 Net factor income and service income from abroad for the USA, 1966–88.

Source: World Bank.

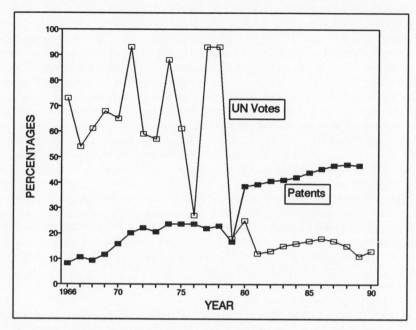

Figure 8.9 Percentage of UN General Assembly members with positive voting record with the USA, 1966–90 and ratio of US patents awarded to foreigners, 1966–90.

Source: UN and Statistical Abstract of the United States.

bashi, 1991). Is a lower foreign aid contribution an unqualified indicator of decline? If we accept the argument that Japan is, in effect, a surrogate donor, then the success of this strategy constitutes further evidence of the hegemony of American geopolitical strategy (Wallerstein, 1991).

Since 1966, all of the soft power indicators show downward trends. The American role in global trade is becoming spatially bifurcated, with a strong element of exports present only in the Americas and in East Asia. Among many commentators, Wallerstein (1991) and Ishihara (in Ishihara and Prestowitz, 1991) have noted the growing ties between the American and Japanese economies and believe that the links between them are so strong that they are now mutually dependent. While Wallerstein (1991) thinks that a trans-Pacific political alliance will ensue from the intimate economic links, others (Hamilton and Clad, 1991; Cooper, Higgott and Nossal, 1991) see a growing difference of opinion between the two largest core economies on matters of global political and economic significance. Whether the end of the Cold War produces a new geopolitical alignment of a trans-Pacific alliance facing a Euro-bloc (Anderson, 1991; Wallerstein, 1984, 1991) or a new global hegemonic struggle (Modelski, 1987a) is difficult to unravel at this time.

Identifying the components of relative US decline, 1966–91

To test the consistency of the 14 indicators of hard and soft power, they were inter-correlated and factor analysed. Two indices, net income from services and UN voting agreement, were not included in the analysis. Because the number of cases is between 23 and 26 depending on the individual index, there is no attempt to extend or interpret the results of these analyses except as a rough approximation of index consistency and similarity of trends. No inferences are made beyond the limited cases under study.

A full range of correlation coefficients is displayed in Table 8.3. Generally, however, with the exception of the capital formation, arms sales and political indicators, the coefficients are positive, which would be expected by the general downward trends for most of the indicators. These three exceptional indicators have shown cyclical developments while the rest are consistently rising or falling over time. The direction and size of the values are consistent and the correlation matrix provides substantial support for the proposition that the choice of indices of the relative decline of the USA was appropriate for their consistency.

A method to determine the underlying components of decline in these indices is to factor analyse the correlation matrix. The resulting factor matrix is shown in Table 8.4. Four factors account for 85 per cent of the variance and the loadings, after varimax rotation, are relatively easy to interpret. The communalities are high, with the exception of arms sales (.53). As might be expected, the indices with the highest communalities are

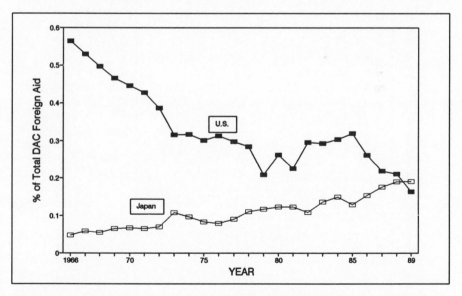

Figure 8.10 Percentages of total DAC foreign aid allocations made by the USA and Japan, 1966–89

Table 8.3 Correlation of 14 indicators of US relative decline, 1966–91

	DAC	GLOTR	INCAB	TERMS	MFINC	CPFOR	PATENT	DEBT	FUSCC	TUSCC	TRBAL	ARMS	GPGNP	MILEXP
DAC	1.0													
GLOTR	.88	1.0												
INCAB	-.72	-.61	1.0											
TERMS	.85	.81	-.85	1.0										
MFINC	.11	.14	-.53	.47	1.0									
CPFOR	.02	-.02	-.09	.21	.43	1.0								
PATENT	-.77	-.77	.51	-.81	-.26	-.28	1.0							
DEBT	-.14	-.20	-.44	-.19	.33	-.04	.47	1.0						
FUSCC	-.05	-.17	-.07	.10	.26	.05	.13	-.02	1.0					
TUSCC	-.27	-.25	.23	-.28	-.31	.10	.13	-.13	-.50	1.0				
TRBAL	.66	.77	-.27	.67	-.02	-.07	-.84	-.68	-.03	-.10	1.0			
ARMS	.13	.09	-.10	.24	-.05	-.14	-.37	-.52	-.02	.16	.53	1.0		
GPGNP	.88	.85	-.62	.78	.16	.27	-.79	-.23	-.17	-.19	.62	.05	1.0	
MILEXP	.94	.87	-.79	.87	.15	-.01	-.67	-.08	-.04	-.23	.58	.06	.87	1.0

Notes: variable definitions – DAC: US ratio of global foreign aid; GLOTR: US ratio of total global trade; INCAB: US gain/loss from foreign income (1966=100); MFINC: Median household income in US (1966=100); CPFOR: capital formation in US (1966=100); PATENT: ratio of US patents granted to foreigners; DEBT: ratio of accumulated debt to US GNP; FUSCC: ratio of cooperative to conflictual acts from the US; TUSCC: ratio of cooperative to conflictual directed at US; TRBAL: US trade balance (1966=100); ARMS: US ratio of world's arms exports; GPGNP: US ratio of Great Power total GNP; and MILEXP: US ratio of world's military expenditures.

Sources: see Appendix 8.1, page 175–177

Table 8.4 Principal components of 14 indicators of US relative decline, 1966–91

Variable	PC 1	PC 2	PC 3	PC 4	Communality
DAC	.96	.11	.05	−.05	.93
GLOTR	.93	.17	−.01	−.73	.90
INCAB	−.81	.31	−.19	−.22	.85
TERMS	.89	.19	.21	.28	.95
MFINC	.22	−.23	.40	.72	.78
CPFOR	.02	.03	−.14	.90	.84
PATENT	−.76	−.50	.05	−.28	.92
DEBT	−.03	−.95	.09	.06	.92
FUSCC	−.15	.08	.87	.12	.81
TUSCC	−.25	.12	−.81	.09	.73
TRBAL	.63	.72	.03	−.08	.93
ARMS	.07	.72	.02	−.02	.53
GPGNP	.90	.15	−.10	.16	.86
MILEXP	.96	.01	.05	−.06	.93
EIGENVALUE	6.54	2.46	1.49	1.37	
% Variance	46.7	17.6	10.7	9.8	
Cum. % Var.	46.7	64.3	75.0	84.8	

Notes: Variable definitions – DAC: US ratio of global foreign aid; GLOTR: US ratio of total global trade; INCAB: US gain/loss from foreign income (1966 = 100): MFINC: Median household income in US (1966 = 100); CPFOR: capital formation in US (1966 = 100); PATENT: ratio of US patents granted to foreigners; DEBT: ratio of accumulated debt to US GNP; FUSCC: ratio of cooperative to conflictual acts from the US; TUSCC: ratio of cooperative to conflictual directed at US; TRBAL: US trade balance (1966 = 100); ARMS: US ratio of world's arms exports; GPGNP: US ratio of Great Power total GNP; and MILEXP: US ratio of world's military expenditures.

Sources: see Appendix 8.1, page 175–177

those with the most temporally consistent trends (foreign aid percentage, global trade ratio, terms of trade, foreigner patent ratio, debt/GNP, global GNP percentage, trade balance, and military expenditure ratio).

The first component, accounting for nearly half of the total variance, can be identified as general decline. It loads highly on foreign aid, global trade, income from abroad (negative), terms of trade, great power GNP ratio, and military spending ratio. All of these indicators, with the exception of the income from abroad index, show a consistent decline over time. This component is important because it shows that the strongest and most consistent element of the power indices is decline over time. Though the percentages may not be large, the trend is well established. The second factor is the growth one, constituting 18 per cent of the variance. It loads highly positively with the trade balance, arms sales, and highly negatively with the debt/GNP ratio. It is not very consistent with the other variables. A third factor is political relations with high loadings for the cooperative/conflictual indices and non-significant loadings on any other index. The final component extracted is based exclusively on the median family income and capital formation indices and could be termed the domestic factor.

The weight of the evidence supports the decline thesis on the basis of the temporal and spatial trends of the indicators selected. While American economic and military presence in the world system is still enormous, there is obvious dip in certain key indicators. While some indicators (military expenditure and global GNP ratios) would be expected to fall 'naturally' as other countries grow, the consistent decline in the temporal trends of the key indicators (debt, trade shares, median income, terms of trade and foreign patents) supports the validity of the decline thesis. Without a major national policy shift, these declines can be expected to continue.

Conclusions

Power, like love, is easier to experience than to define or measure (Nye, 1990: 25). Some readers will undoubtedly take issue with the indicators chosen and press for the inclusion of other indicators, such as measures of cultural power (Russett, 1985), 'behavioral power' (the extent to which a state can influence the actions of other countries in the world system – Ward and House, 1998), military advantage (Nye, 1990), trade policy power (Bhagwati, 1991), high technology and research (Nye, 1990) or political power (Cooper, Higgott and Nossal, 1991). With the exception of the behavioural power index, which interestingly shows a gradual decline in the value for the USA in the 1970s, these conceptions of power cannot be adequately measured. It is interesting that those who argue that US decline has been exaggerated rely to a large extent on the argument that while the statistics suggest decline, the unmeasurable power of the USA in politics and culture ensures its continued hegemonic status (Russett, 1985; Strange, 1990). Except for some indications of supporting data trends, it is difficult to accept their arguments.

Kennedy (1987) gave the decline thesis a theoretical basis in the argument that military spending at the expense of economic investment eventually undermines global power status. Recent work that rigorously tests that hypothesis with historical data for the UK and the USA casts doubt on its validity (Rasler, 1990; Rasler and Thompson, 1991 and Thompson, 1990). In the absence of support for the Kennedy thesis, we return then to world-system explanations. Both Modelski (1987) and Wallerstein (1984,1991), expect the USA as a declining hegemon to face a global challenge from an individual country or combination of challengers. Whereas Wallerstein (1991) thinks that the USA is already in the process of decline, having lost production and commercial leadership while retaining its financial leadership, Modelski (1987b) thinks that the serious challenge will not happen for at least another generation because of the huge American military lead. The evidence from the indicators examined in this chapter offers modest support for Wallerstein in this debate on the future prospects of the USA.

For both world system and long cycle theorists, the world system becomes a dangerous place in the absence of clear, unchallenged leadership. The declining hegemon may be tempted to use its military power to keep economic and other (cultural and political) challengers in line, the so-called 'use it or lose it' option. Amin (1991) interprets the Iraq War of 1991 in this fashion, a view that is similar to that of Cooper, Higgott and Nossal (1991) and Hamilton and Clad (1991). Because the putative challengers are also core capitalist states, it may appear that global conflict is most unlikely as it would prove ruinous to the global capitalist economy. However, it proves instructive to remember that the global wars of this century were fought between powers that shared a similar ideology. Others think that there may be a 'spatial fix' to global capitalist competition, the division of the world into trade blocs, an idea first mooted by the German geopolitikers of the 1920s (O'Loughlin and van der Wusten, 1990; O'Loughlin, 1991, 1992). However, Frankel (1991) finds no evidence that such a trade bloc is emerging in East Asia, though there is strong evidence that one already exists in North America and Western Europe (*Economics Focus*, 1991; Schott, 1991).

The USA should not be seen as the historical inheritor of the hegemonic legacies of the UK, the Netherlands, Spain and Portugal (Mjøset, 1990). It retains two important distinguishing features that separate it from past global hegemons. First, the USA is not *'dirigiste'* (Kennedy, 1987) and unlike past leaders it can adjust to the new global economic realities, should the national consensus judge the American global position to be jeopardized. Second, the USA has controlled a far greater share of the world's resources than previous hegemons and its ability to dictate political, ideological and cultural terms to its allies was profoundly enhanced by this vast lead over all challengers. As noted by Nye (1990), military expenditure ratio (about 5 per cent of GNP) is far higher than any other industrialized country; therefore there are a lot of swords that can be converted into ploughshares. Whether US relative decline is reversible or not will ultimately depend on the political decisions of a country that still seems to be a reluctant believer in the notion of a global community.

Appendix 8.1: Power indicators, definitions and data sources

Hard power

1. MILEXP: US ratio of world military expenditures.
   Source: Sivard and SIPRI.
2. ARMS: US ratio of total world arms sales.
   Source: SIPRI.
3. TUSCC: ratio of weighted cooperative to conflictual actions directed by other countries to to US.
   Source: World Events Interactions Survey (WEIS) data archive.
4. FUSCC: ratio of weighted cooperative to conflictual actions directed by the US to other countries.
   Source: WEIS.
5. GPGNP: ratio of US gross national product (GNP) to the total GNP of

the Six great powers (US, Japan, West Germany, USSR, UK, France).
Source: Mitchell, 1975, 1982 and Leisner.

6. CPFOR: rate of net capital formation indexed to 1966 = 100.
   Source: Statistical Abstract of the US.
7. DEBT: ratio of cumulative national debt to GNP.
   Source: Statistical Abstract of the US.
8. MFINC: median family income in the US indexed to 1966 = 100.
   Source: Statistical Abstract of the US.

Soft power

9. GLOTR: US ratio of total world trade.
   Source: IMF Direction of Trade Statistics.
10. TRBAL: Trade balance (exports-imports) of the US in constant 1966
    dollars.
    Source: IMF.
11. TERMS: relative level of export prices compared to import prices (index
    of average export price divided by average import price) and indexed
    to 1966 = 100.
    Source: World Bank, World Tables.
12. SERV: net factor service income including services of labor and capital;
    covers income from direct investment abroad, interest, dividends and
    property and labor income, in constant 1966 dolars.
    Source: World Tables.
13. INCAB: net nonfactor service income defined as all transport, travel and
    current account income, indexed to 1966 = 100.
    Source: World Tables.
14. PATENT: ratio of US patents granted to non-residents.
    Source: Statistical Abstract of the US.
15. DAC: US ratio of total foreign aid from the OECD countries.
    Source: OECD.
16. UN: voting distance from the US in the UN General Assembly. Only
    votes with less than 90 per cent agreement selected. Votes were scored
    as +1 if agree with US position, 0 if abstained or absent and −1 if
    disagree with US. Weighted distance scores were computed by
    dividing the country total by the number of votes and converted to
    +100 (complete agreement) to −100 (complete disagreement) with 0
    indicating a neutral position.
    Source: author from UN General Assembly voting files in Inter-
    University Consortium for Political and Social Research (ICPSR)
    archive.

Acknowledgements

The research reported in this chapter was supported by a grant from the
US National Science Foundation, from the Political Science and Geography
and Regional Sceince programs under grant number 9002699. The com-
ments of Jan Nijman on an earlier version of this chapter are appreciated.

Thanks are also due to Michael Ward of the Institute of Behavioral Science, University of Colorado for providing the WEIS data and to Sven Holdar for assistance with the data collection

References

Agnew, J.A. (1992), 'The US position in The World Geopolitical Order After the Cold War, *Professional Geographer* **44**, No. 1, 7–10.

Amin, S. (1991), 'The Real Stakes in the Gulf War', *Monthly Review* **43**, No. 3, 14–24.

Anderson, K. (1991), 'Is an Asian-Pacific Trade Bloc Next?' *Journal of World Trade* **25**, No. 1, 27–41.

Bergsten, F. (1990), 'The World Economy After the Cold War', *Foreign Affairs* **69**, No. 3, 96–112.

Bhagwati, J.N. (1991), *The World Trading System at Risk*, Princeton, NJ Princeton University Press.

Boulding, K. (1990), *Three Faces of Power*, Newbury Park, CA, Sage.

Brzezinski, Z. (1991), 'Selective Global Commitment', *Foreign Affairs*, **79**, No. 3, 1–20.

Cafruny, A. (1990), A Gramscian Concept of Declining Hegemony: Stages of US Power and the Evolution of International Economic Relations, in *World leadership and Hegemony*, D Rapkin (ed.), Boulder, CO, Lynne Rienner.

Calleo, D. (1987), *Beyond American Hegemony*, New York, Basic Books.

Chase, J. (1988), 'A New Grand Strategy', *Foreign Policy*, **70**, No. 1, 3–25.

Cohen, S.B. (1991), 'Global Geopolitical Change in the Post Cold War Era', *Annals, Association of American Geographers*, **81**, No. 4, 551–80.

Cooper, A., Higgott, R. and Nossal, K. (1991), 'Bound to follow?: Leadership and Followship in the Gulf Conflict', *Political Science Quarterly*, **106**: 391–44.

Corbridge, S. and Agnew, J.A. (1991), 'The U.S. Trade and Federal Deficits in Global Perspective: An Essay in Geo-political-economy', *Environment and Planning D: Society and Space*, **9**, No. 1, 71–90.

Cox, M. (1990), 'From the Truman Doctrine to the Second Superpower Detente: the Rise and Fall of the Cold War', *Journal of Peace Research*, **27**, No. 1, 25–41.

Economics Focus (1991), 'Shoot-out at Jackson Hole', *Economist*, 31 August: 55.

Elliott, M. (1991), 'America: a Better Yesterday', *Economist* 26 October: 26.

Frankel, J. (1991), 'Is a Yen Bloc Forming in Pacific Asia?' in *Finance and the International Economy 5: Review Prize Essays*, ed. R. O'Brien, New York, Oxford University Press.

Friedberg, A. (1991a), 'The Changing Relationship Between Economics and National Security', *Political Science Quarterly*, **106**, No. 2, 265–76.

Friedberg, A. (1991b), 'The End of Autonomy: the United States After Five Decades', *Daedalus*, **120** (Autumn): 69–90.

Fukuyama, F. (1991), *The End of History and the Last Man*, New York, Free Press.

Funabashi, Y. (1991/92), 'Japan and the New World Order', *Foreign Affairs*, **70**, No. 5, 58–74.

Garten, J. (1991), 'Rethinking Foreign Economic Policy', *Foreign Affairs*, **70**, No. 3, 155–60.

General Agreement on Tariffs and Trade (GATT) (1990a), *Trade Policy Review – Japan* Geneva, GATT.

General Agreement on Tariffs and Trade (GATT) (1990b), *Trade Policy Review – United States*, Geneva, GATT.

Gilpin, R. (1987), *The Political Economy of International Relations*, Princeton NJ, Princeton University Press.

Goldstein, J. (1988), *Long Cycles: Prosperity and War in the Modern Age*, New Haven, CT, Yale University Press.

Hamilton, D. and Clad, J. (1991), 'Germany, Japan and the False Glare of War,' *Washington Quarterly*, **14**: 39–50.

Hartland-Thunberg, P. (1991), 'A Capital-Starved New World Order: Geopolitical Implications of a Global Capital Shortage in the 1990s', *Washington Quarterly*, **14**, No. 4, 21–39.

Holbrooke, R. (1991/92), 'Japan and the US: Ending the Unequal Partnership', *Foreign Affairs*, **70**, No. 5, 41–52.

Hormats, R. (1991), 'The Roots of American Power, *Foreign Affairs*, **70**, No. 2, 132–49.

Huntingdon, S. (1988), 'The US: Decline or Renewal?', *Foreign Affairs*, **67**, No. 1, 76–96.

Ikenberry, G. and Kupchan, C. (1990a), 'Socialization and Economic Power', *International Organization*, **44**: 283–315.

Inoguchi, T. (1988), 'Four Japanese Scenarios for the Future', *International Affairs*, **65**: 15–28.

International Monetary Fund (IMF) yearly *Direction of Trade Statistics*, Washington DC, International Monetary Fund.

Ishihara, S. and Prestowitz, C. (1991), 'America and Japan: Forget Pearl Harbor', *Economist* 30 November: 21–23.

Kaldor, M. (1990), *The Imaginary War: Understanding the East-West Conflict*, Oxford, Basil Blackwell.

Kegley, C. and Hook, S. (1991), 'U.S. Foreign Aid and UN Voting: did Reagan's Linkage Strategy Buy Deference or Defiance?', *International Studies Quarterly*, **35**, No. 3, 295–312.

Kennedy, P. (1987), *The Rise and Fall of the Great Powers: Economic Change and Military Conflict from 1500 to 2000*, New York, Random House.

Keohane, R. and Nye, J. (1989), *Power and Interdependence*, (rev. ed.), Boston, Little Brown.

Krauthammer, C. (1991), 'The Unipolar Movement', *Foreign Affairs*, **70**, No. 1, 23–33.

Kudrle, R. and Bowrow, D. (1990), 'The G-7 After Hegemony: Compatibility, Cooperation and Conflict', in *World leadership and hegemony*, ed. D. Rapkin, Boulder, CO. Lynne Rienner.

Kuttner, R. (1991), *The End of Laissez-faire; National Purpose and the Global Economy After the Cold War*, New York, Knopf.

Leisner, T. (1989), *One hundred Years of Historical Statistics*, New York, Facts on File.

Luttwak, E. (1991), 'America's Setting Sun', *New York Times* 23 September: A15.

Maull, H. (1990), 'Germany and Japan: the New Civilian Powers', *Foreign Affairs*, **69**, No. 5, 91–106.

Mead, W. (1990), 'On the Road to Ruin: Winning the Cold War, Losing the Economic Peace', *Harper's Magazine*, March: 59–64.

Mead, W. (1991), 'The Bush Administration and the New World Order', *World Policy Journal*, **8**: 375–420.

Merritt, R. and Zinnes, D. (1989), 'Alternative Indexes of National power', in *Power in World Politics*, eds., R. Stoll and M. Ward, Boulder, CO., Lynne Rienner.

Mitchell, B. (1975), *European historical statistics, 1750–1970*, New York, Columbia University Press.

Mitchell, B. (1982), *International Historical Statistics: Asia and Africa*, London, The Macmillan Press Ltd.

Mjøset, L. (1990), 'The Turn of Two Centuries: a Comparison of British and U.S.

hegemonies', in *World leadership and hegemony*, ed. D. Rapkin, Boulder, CO, Lynne Rienner.

Modelski, G. (ed.) (1987a), *Exploring Long Cycles*, Boulder, CO, Lynne Rienner.

Modelski, G. (1987b), *Long Cycles in World Politics*, Seattle, WA University of Washington Press.

Modelski, G. and Thompson, W.R. (1988), *Seapower in Global Politics, 1494–1993*, London, The Macmillan Press Ltd.

Nau, H. (1990), *The Myth of America's Decline*, New York Oxford University Press.

Nierop, T. and de Vos, S. (1988), 'Of Shrinking Empires and Changing Roles: World Trade Patterns of the Postwar Period', *Tidjschrift voor Economische en Sociale Geografie*, **25**: 343–64.

Nishkamen, W. (1989), The Bully of World Trade, *Orbis*, **33**: 531–38.

Nye, J. (1990), *Bound to Lead: the Changing Nature of American Power*, New York, Basic Books.

O'Loughlin, J. (1991), 'Conflict, Cooperation and Trade of the United States and Japan with the Countries of the Pacific Rim, 1966–1989', unpublished paper, Boulder, CO, Department of Geography, University of Colorado.

O'Loughlin, J. (1992), 'Ten Scenarios for the "New World Order" ', *Professional Geographer*, **44**, No. 1, 21–28.

O'Loughlin, J. and Grant, R. (1990), 'The Political Geography of Presidential Speeches, 1946–87', *Annals, Association of American Geographers*, **80**, No. 4, 504–30.

O'Loughlin, J. and van der Wusten, H. (1990), The Political Geography of Panregions, *Geographical Review*, **80**, No. 1, 1–20.

Olson, M. (1982), *The Rise and Decline of Nations: Economic Growth, Stagflation and Social Rigidities*, New Haven, CT, Yale University Press.

Pfaff, W. (1991), 'Redefining World Power', *Foreign Affairs*, **70**, No. 1, 34–48.

Rapkin D. (ed.), (1990), *World Leadership and Hegemony*, Boulder, CO, Lynne Rienner.

Rasler, K. (1990), 'Spending Deficits and Welfare Investment Tradeoffs: Cause or Effect of Leadership Decline', in *World leadership and hegemony*, ed. D. Rapkin, Boulder, CO, Lynne Rienner.

Rasler, K. and Thompson, W.R. (1991), 'Relative Decline and the Overconsumption-Underinvestment Hypothesis', *International Studies Quarterly*, **35**, No. 3, 273–94.

Reich, R. (1991), *The Work of Nations: Preparing Ourselves for the 21st Century*, New York, Knopf.

Rizopoulos, N. (ed.) (1990), *Sea-Changes: American Foreign Policy in a World Transformed*, New York, Council on Foreign Relations.

Rosecrance, R. (1986), *The Rise of the Trading State*, New York, Basic Books.

Rubinstein, A.Z. (1991), 'New world order or hollow victory?', *Foreign Affairs*, **70**, No. 4, 53–65.

Rupert, M. (1990), 'Power, Productivity and the State: the Social relations of U.S. Hegemony', in *World leadership and hegemony*, ed. D. Rapkin, Boulder, CO, Lynne Rienner.

Russett, B. (1985), 'The Mysterious Case of Vanishing Hegemony: or, is Mark Twain Really Dead?', *International Organization*, **39**, No. 2, 207–31.

Schott, J. (1991), 'Trading Blocs and the World Economic System', *World Economy*, **14**, No. 1, 1–18

SIPRI (Stockholm International Peace Research Institute), Yearly, *Yearbook*, Stockholm, SIPRI.

Sivard, R. *World military and social expenditures*, Leesburg, VA, WMSE Publications, yearly.

Stoll, R. and Ward, M. (eds) (1989), *Power in World Politics*, Boulder, CO, Lynne Rienner.

Strange, S. (1986), *Casino capitalism*, Oxford, Basil Blackwell.

Strange, S. (1987), 'The Persistent Myth of Lost Hegemony', *International Organization*, **41**, No. 4, 551–74.

Strange S (1990a), 'Finance, Information and Power', *Review of International Studies*, **16**, No. 3, 259–74.

Strange, S. (1990b), *States and Markets*, London, Pinter Publishers.

Taylor, P, (1992), 'Tribulations of Transition', *Professional Geographer*, **44**, No. 1, 10–12.

Thompson, W.R. (1990), 'Long Waves, Technological Innovations and Relative Decline', *International Organization*, **44**: 201–33.

Thrift, N. and Leyshon, A. (1991), *Making Money*, London, Routledge.

Toal, G. (1991), 'Pearl Harbor Without Bombs', Paper presented at the meeting of the International Geographical Union, Commission on the World Political Map, Tallahassee, FL.

United States Department of Commerce (1991), *Statistical Abstract of the United States 1990*, Washington DC, U.S. Department of Commerce.

Van Wolferen, K. (1991), 'An Economic Pearl Harbor', *New York Times*, 2 December,: A15.

Vernon, R. and Kapstein, E.B. (1991), 'National needs, global resources', *Daedalus*, **120**, Autumn, 1–23.

Wallerstein, I. (1984), *The Politics of the World-Economy*, New York, Cambridge University Press.

Wallerstein, I. (1991), *Geopolitics and Geoculture*, New York, Cambridge University Press.

Ward, M. and House, L. (1988), 'A Theory of the Behavioral Power of Nations', *Journal of Conflict Resolution*, **32**, No. 1, 3–36.

World Bank (1990), *World Tables*, Washington, DC, World Bank.

9
Japan as threat:
geo-economic discourses on the USA–Japan relationship in US civil society, 1987–91

Gearóid Ó Tuathail (Gerard Toal)

Economic nationalism is a growing force in American politics.[1] From the beginning of the 1992 presidential campaign the themes and slogans of a new economic patriotism could be discerned (Walker, 1991; *The Economist*, 1991a). Republicans, Democrats and Independents have all sought to articulate variants of an 'America First' rhetoric. Responding to the defeat of his chosen candidate in the Pennsylvania Senate race in late 1991, President Bush first postponed, and then re-cast a planned trip to East Asia in order to appear concerned about domestic economic issues. A presidential visit to Japan, originally scripted as a geopolitical affirmation of American–Japanese partnership in a new world order, was hastily rewritten as a geo-economic mission for 'free and fair' trade. The overriding purpose of his East Asia visit, President Bush declared on his departure in early January 1992, was 'jobs, jobs, jobs.'

The growth of economic nationalism, anti-Japanese rhetoric, and explicit domesticist sentiments in American political culture can be understood as a reaction to the marked transnationalization of the American economy, state and culture in the decade of the 1980s. During this time the American economy became simultaneously more dependent on the world economy and less able to influence its direction. Foreign transnational corporations and world capital flows now play a crucial role in the financial solvency of the American economy (Corbridge and Agnew, 1991). The American state has also become transnationalized with state agencies and governmental elites tied into networks of international organizations and interests (Cox, 1987: 253–65; Gill, 1990: 94). Even quintessential institutions of American culture, such as the Hollywood movie industry, have become trans-nationalized with Sony's purchase of Columbia pictures in 1989 and Matsushita's purchase of the MCA/Universal in 1990.

The new class of transnational managers, global bureaucrats, world leaders, and international intellectuals tied to the daily functioning of the global economy view the articulation of explicit economic nationalism in the USA with some alarm. Their ideological commitments are to 'transnational liberalism,' the economic doctrine of free trade, open markets and capitalist enterprise presided over by a cooperative trilateral alliance between the USA, EC and Japan (Gill, 1990: 20–25). According to its intellectual proponents and defenders, discourses of economic nationalism are 'protectionist,' guilty of 'Japan-bashing' and 'isolationist.' They are potentially dangerous ideologies that can become vehicles for 'demagogic politicians' (Brock, 1989). Yet the production of dissident discourses from transnational liberalism are now a pervasive feature of American political and civil society.

This chapter is a selective investigation into this apparent challenge to transnational liberal orthodoxy within the USA. Rather than examine the current debates among politicians, the chapter concentrates on geo-economic arguments made by public intellectuals in American civil society between 1987 and 1991 on the USA–Japan relationship; in policy journals, popular middle-brow business books, and current affairs magazines produced by well-established publishing houses and media organizations in the USA. Such arguments provide insight into discourses which will shape the political geography of the new world order. Rather than representing Japan in the traditional Cold War manner as a cooperative American ally, they offer a 'revisionist' account of Japan as a new threat to American power and to world order in the 1990s.

This chapter structures its review of geo-economic discourses on the USA–Japan relationship around:

(i)   a brief empirical account of the material changes which have character-ized the USA–Japan economic relationship in the 1980s;
(ii)   a descriptive account of the ideology of revisionism and geo-economics;
(iii) a critical evaluation of the claims made by these discourses.

Because this chapter reviews such a large literature, detailed analysis of specific texts is not possible. The purpose of the chapter is to provide a general overview of an emergent set of discourses whose influence is likely to increase as the USA faces up to inevitable readjustments in its historical global role. It concludes with some observations on the apparent conflict between geo-economics and transnational liberalism in American policy formulation.

Geo-economics, like geopolitics, is a difficult concept to specify abstractly. Luttwak uses the term to describe what he considers to be an emergent dominant force in state action given the demise of Cold War geopolitics. In his definition geo-economics is 'the admixture of the logic of conflict with the methods of commerce.' He arrives at this definition based on abstract, logically deduced, rather than historically observed, assumptions about the nature of states and the international system. States are, he declares, 'inherently inclined to strive for relative advantage against like entities.' The 'bureaucratic urges of role-preservation and role-enhancement' together with the 'instrumentalization of the state by economic interest groups' lead states to act geo-economically. In fact, for Luttwak, states will act geo-economically 'simply because of what they are: spatially-defined entities structured to outdo each other on the world scene' (Luttwak 1990: 19).

Luttwak's account of geo-economics is unsatisfactory for it is tautological and ahistorical. States have a tendency to maximize power and act geo-economically simply because they are states. Yet empirically what constitutes the maximization of power (relative advantage) and geo-economic behaviour is not manifestly obvious.[2] A more appropriate approach is to problematize control of the state and investigate how the state is instrumentalized by certain social classes. This fundamentally involves an investigation into the material conditions, social forces and intellectual discourses that work to produce state action in concrete cases. One cannot define geo-economics abstractly as Luttwak does. Geo-economics must be defined empirically as specific historical discourses about commerce, technology, capital, markets, resources and competitiveness in political and civil society that seek to provide a normative philosophy for state action.

In the case of contemporary American society geo-economic discourses, although variable, usually have a consistent set of common concerns. These can be reduced to a three-part narrative on the USA, Japan, and what needs to be done. In simplified form one has accounts of:

1. The American dilemma: a set of arguments which claim that the nature of power and international relations in the 1980s has fundamentally changed from the geopolitical struggle between states to a geo-economic struggle between states. The American century has come to an end; American sovereignty is being eroded and evidence of decline is incontrovertible. International relations are now characterized by a zero-sum competition between different national capitalisms. Access to markets and the control of finance capital and high technology are held to be the vital stakes in this competition.
2. The Japanese system: a set of self-styled expose accounts of the inner workings of the economic and political system of Japan and its corporations.
3. Policy prescriptions: a set of imperative statements urging the USA to abandon its embedded *laissez faire* ideology and to initiate new measures to improve the conditions of capital accumulation. Policies advocated include moving towards explicit managed trade and attempting, in a variety of different ways, to 'Japanize' the USA (using it positively as a role model and negatively as a call to action) so that it can become more competitive.

Geo-economic discourses reveal both emergent contradictions and continuities in the struggle over articulating a political geography of the new world order. First, such discourses are characterized by traditional territorial forms of reasoning. But traditional territorial descriptions and identifications, such as the 'national economy,' the 'country's industrial base' and 'our corporations' no longer have the same unproblematic territorial identity they once supposedly had. In today's world the nominal nationality of corporations must be contrasted with their actual transnationality (Reich, 1991b). The same can now be said of media organizations, political interest groups and perhaps even government officials. Nevertheless, the use of discourse structured on the basis of unproblematized corporate nationalities, discrete national economies, and the assumed unitary interest of territorial communities is still pervasive in a world economy made up of nominally sovereign states.[3] The divergence between transnational economic realities and territorially defined political discourse needs to be explored by political geographers.

Second, geo-economic discourses are characterized by a style of reasoning which is similar to the classic geopolitical discourses they seek to displace. The metaphors and narratives of war give geo-economic discourses a rhetorical force and urgency that has profound consequences. Contemporary transnational capitalism is transformed into a zero-sum competition between supposedly spatially discrete states. Military language is used to describe economic processes. One has adversarial economics, trade wars, targeting of economic sectors, strategic industries, invasions of markets and a new jingoistic techno-nationalism. The implications of such discourse, in helping write a post-Cold-War world, is a renewed militarization of social and economic life, a re-legitimation of existing forms of bureaucratic authority, a redisciplining of private life in the name of 'competitiveness.' Ironically, this also reinforces the power of transnational corporate capital at the expense of the many social groups left outside the circuits of the transnational economy.

Transnationalization and tension: Nichibei in the 1980s.

In 1970 American imports accounted for 7.3 per cent and exports 8.6 per cent of GNP. By 1988 the figures had risen to 13.1 per cent and 15 per cent of GNP respectively (*The Economist*, 1991b). A large proportion of this huge expansion in trade came in the Pacific where the value of trans-Pacific trade surpassed that of trans-Atlantic trade in the early 1980s (O'Loughlin, Chapter 8, p. 166; Schlossstein, 1989). Both the volume and rate of increase of this regional trade led commentators to speak of a singular 'trans-Pacific economy' (Calder, 1985). Others spoke of a 'nichibei economy,' a huge joint economy between Japan and the USA. The term, a blend of the Japanese characters for Japan (Nihon) and America (Beikoku), seemed appropriate for two economies which today account for nearly 40 per cent of the gross world product.

Geo-economic discourses on the Japanese threat are replete with contentious claims about American–Japanese trade and foreign direct investment in the 1980s. Let us briefly examine the actual empirical record in these areas.

Trade

Between 1980 and 1991 the value of American trade globally rose from $474 billion to $910 billion. After rising significantly in the mid-1980s the global trade deficit has been in sharp decline (*see* Figure 9.1). In 1980 the deficit represented just over 5 per cent of total trade; by 1986 this figure had risen to 24.5 per cent before dropping back to over 7 per cent in 1991, a total of $66.2 billion.

American trade with Japan rose from $51.5 billion in 1980 to $139.6 billion in 1991. During this time the USA ran a persistent trade deficit with Japan which peaked at over 50 per cent of the total value of trade in 1985 and 1986 before declining to 30 per cent in 1990. In 1991 this figure increased once again to 31 per cent, a total of $43.4 billion. Since the overall American global trade deficit was only $66.2 billion the American deficit with Japan accounted for approximately 65.5 per cent of the global trade deficit in 1991 (*see* Figure 9.1). Japan's trade surplus, by contrast, increased sharply from $69.86 billion in 1990 to $113.44 billion in 1991.

In 1985 American exports globally were made up of 25 per cent agricultural and primary products and 75 per cent manufactured products. Exports to Japan in that year comprised $10.3 billion in primary products and $11.9 billion in manufactured products which worked out at a 45 per cent to 55 per cent proportion. By 1990 American primary product exports to Japan had risen to $17.7 billion, while manufactured exports increased to $30.9 billion, a 36 per cent to 64 per cent split (Gold and Nanto, 1991: 30). Broken down into categories of goods, aircraft, spacecraft and their replacement parts were the leading American export category to Japan in 1990 ($3.499 billion) followed by computers ($2.041 billion), logs and lumber ($1.649) and corn ($1.648) (Lohr, 1992).

Identifying and measuring trade statistics such as these on a territorial basis can be misleading. Julius argues that trade measures that exclude the role of foreign-owned firms (FOFs) in the export–import data are 'increasingly partial and misleading as indicators of national competitiveness or fundamental trends in the world economy.' Using data on FOF sales he attempts to develop a measure of ownership-based trade for the USA and Japan (Julius, 1990: 71). This provides a broad measure of the international competitiveness of American and Japanese companies. Using this method of measurement the 1986 US trade balance is transformed from a deficit of $144 billion on a resident basis (net exports) to a surplus of $57 billion on an ownership basis (net foreign sales). Japan's 1983 trade surplus is increased slightly when translated into an ownership basis measure, from net exports of $32 billion to net foreign sales of $42 billion (Julius, 1990: 81–2). Agnew (1993) takes this as further evidence of globalization and fragmentation in the world economy. He also notes that the very notion of 'international' transactions is problematic when perhaps 40 per cent of trade

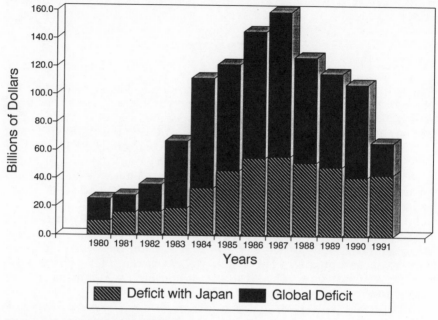

Figure 9.1   US trade deficit 1980–91

Source: US Department of Commerce, *Survey of Current Business*; various issues.

Note; Figures rounded, billions of current dollars.

Automobiles and automobile parts accounted for approximately three quarters of the American–Japanese trade deficit in 1990. The leading import by the USA in that year was motor vehicles ($19.547 billion), followed by computers ($5.924 billion), auto parts ($5.342 billion) and telecommunications equipment ($4.971 billion) (Lohr, 1992).

between countries in actually trade carried on within companies (Reich, 1991b).

Foreign direct investment (FDI).

After an initial drop in the early 1980s global foreign direct investment flows grew strongly in the mid- to late 1980s. From 1983 to 1988 both the USA and Britain (the world's largest direct investors) recorded real increases of over 15 per cent per year. Japan and France, starting from lower levels, recorded increases of more than 30 per cent for the same period (Julius, 1990: 20). In 1985 the net international investment position (portfolio and foreign direct investment) of the USA registered a deficit for the first time in the country's recent history. Total foreign assets in the USA became greater than total assets abroad and have remained so since 1985. However, such an overall figure hides the tremendous rise in the American direct investment position abroad (on historical–cost basis) from the mid-1980s from $211.3 billion in 1984 to $421.5 billion in 1990 (*see* Figure 9.2).

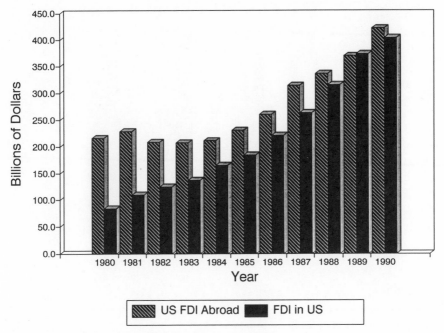

Figure 9.2   US direct investment position 1980–90

Source: US Department of Commerce, *Survey of Current Business*, August 1991: 51, 85.

Note: Figures rounded, billions of dollars, historical–cost basis.

The United Kingdom was the largest foreign direct investor in the USA in the 1980s with assets totalling $108.1 billion in 1990 (*see* Figure 9.3). Japanese FDI surpassed the Netherlands to become the second largest in 1988 and stood at a total of $83.5 billion by 1990 (see Figure 3). Of this, $27.6 billion was in wholesale trade, $15.9 billion in real estate, $6.52 billion in services and $6 billion in banking (*Survey of Current Business*, August 1991).

FDI flows into the United States, however, rose even more dramatically from $83 billion in 1980 to $403.7 billion in 1990. (*See* Figures 9.2 and 9.3).

Interpreting these trade and FDI statistics has been the subject of extensive and ongoing debate within American civil and political society. In a review of studies by Tolchin and Tolchin (1988), Glickman and Woodward (1989), and Graham and Krugman (1989), Kudrle (1989) suggests that most concerns raised about FDI in the USA are either misdirected or exaggerated. He concurs with Graham and Krugman's (1989) conclusion that FDI in general makes a significant positive contribution to the American economy. Kudrle (1991: 420) notes that they fail to stress that the nominal nationality of a firm is becoming an increasingly poor guide to its international employment distribution, trade behaviour, ownership and loyalty. A domestic American firm may export less, import more, and have fewer domestic employees than a foreign-owned firm. Nominally domestic products also may have more foreign content and components than nominally foreign products (Reich, 1991b).[5]

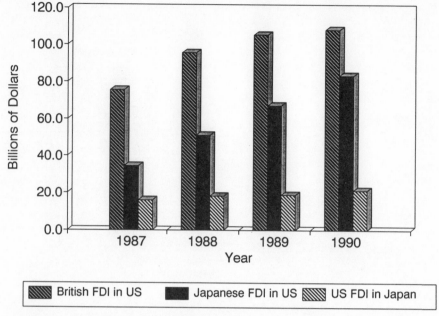

Figure 9.3   Select FDI positions 1987–90

Source: US Department of Commerce, *Survey of Current Business,* August 1991.

Note: Figures rounded, billions of dollars, historical cost basis.

American FDI in Japan in 1990 was concentrated in manufacturing (almost 50 per cent of the total, chiefly in chemicals, machinery and transportation equipment) with $3.8 billion invested in wholesale trade and $2.24 billion in finance (except banking), insurance and real estate (*Survey of Current Business* (1991), August). The most successful American company invested in Japan is IBM Japan which in 1988 ranked fourteenth in the earning league of Japanese companies. Coca-Cola Japan is the next most successful American-owned firm ranking ninety-ninth while Fuji Xerox (50 per cent American-owned) ranked one hundred and fourth (*The Economist,* 1989a). Compared to other advanced capitalist countries the levels of foreign direct investment in Japan are small.

Congressional opposition

The consequences of the increased international competition faced by American industry in the 1980s are well known: deindustrialization in traditional manufacturing regions, renewed foreign direct investment by American transnationals and re-structuring through merger and acqui-sitions (Bluestone and Harrison, 1982). A political consequence was the rise of protectionist sentiment in the US Congress. In 1984 Congressional Democrats sponsored legislation which proposed a 25 per cent tariff sur-charge against Japan and three other nations with large surpluses if the surpluses were not reduced by 1986 (Kuttner 1991: 172). The Reagan administration did its best to fend off such legislation. The passage of the 1988 Omnibus Trade and Competitiveness Act, however, was a partial victory for those concerned about the persistent trade deficits and rising levels of foreign direct investment. The bill included a strengthened section (Super 301) which provided for the naming of unfair trading partners by the USA and the initiation of retaliatory measures against them should bilateral negotiations not remove trade barriers. It also included the Exon–Florio amendment which authorized the president to review foreign direct investment on the grounds of national security. In May of 1989 the Bush administration, under considerable Congressional pressure, was forced to name Japan as an 'unfair trader' along with India and Brazil. Controversy over the co-development of a fighter aircraft (FSX) led to a sustained Congressional debate in 1989 and the first use of the veto by the Bush presidency (Ó Tuathail, 1992). In 1991 the US Congress considered 24 bills to restrict foreign investment in the USA but only a strengthened version of Exon–Florio and a Fair Trade in Financial Services Act are likely to become law. Congressional pressure on USA–Japan relations increased further in December 1991 on the eve of Bush's visit to East Asia. Congressional Democrats, led by Richard Gephardt, introduced legislation that would restrict the import of Japanese cars into the USA if the USA–Japan trade deficit did not shrink to under $5 billion by 1997.

Smoothing USA–Japan Relations

Given the scale of the imbalances in USA–Japan trade and investment it is remarkable that the relationship did not become characterized by even greater friction than was the case in the 1980s. The successful management of the relationship and the tensions it generated in American politics can be explained by a number of critical factors. Firstly, the relationship between President Reagan (1981–9) and Prime Minister Nakasone (1982–7) was a particularly harmonious one. Both men shared a similar geopolitical perspective and were adherents of the ideology of transnational liberalism, agreeing in principle at least on the desirability of free trade internationally (Prestowitz, 1989).

Secondly, specific tensions in the USA–Japan relationship were managed and addressed by sets of bilateral talks. In 1985, in response to the first wave of protectionist sentiment in the US Congress, the USA and Japan established Market-Orientated, Sector-Specific (MOSS) talks. In 1989, in response to the unfair trader citing of Japan both countries established the Structural Impediments Initiative (SII) talks which reached agreements in April and June of 1990. Gold and Nanto (1991: 31) report that between 1985 and 1990 negotiations with Japan resulted in lower import barriers for aluminium, automobiles, automobile parts, leather footwear, medical equipment, satellites, semiconductors, and telecommunications equipment. Over this period American exports to Japan in these categories increased from $1.5 billion to $5.6 billion, a 275 per cent increase.

Thirdly, the Japanese state was extremely deferential to the USA in geopolitical matters throughout the 1980s, from its 1981 decision to exempt the USA from a ban on the export of Japanese defence technology to the 1990–91 payment of $13 billion for the Gulf War. Within the Japanese state, certain agencies like the Ministry of Finance have been particularly skilful in understanding how the USA–Japan relationship should be handled (George, 1991).

Fourthly, transnational corporations (both American and Japanese), foundations sponsored by transnationals (e.g. the Association of International Investment), organizations of internationalist elites (e.g. the Council on Foreign Relations, the Trilateral Commission), and pro-Japan public intellectuals (the 'Chrysanthemum Club') have all actively sought to promote transnational liberalism and co-opt, deflect and mollify anti-Japanese sentiment. Their efforts, however, have enjoyed only qualified success.

Revisionism and geo-economic discourses

Transnational liberal attempts to ensure the smooth management of USA–Japan relations have become increasingly difficult. From the mid-1980s a renewed techno-nationalism and emergent 'revisionist' ideas on the USA–Japan relationship (earlier examples of which can be found in the 1970s within the Nixon administration and Congress) have fiercely challenged traditional transnational approaches to relations with Japan. 'Revisionism' holds that Japan is unlikely to become a consumer-orientated society like the USA. According to its proponents modernization theory implicitly informed American policy towards Japan in the post-World War II period. It assumed that all states progress through particular stages of economic development and eventually became similar to the advanced industrial states of North America and Western Europe. Revisionism, however, holds that such a model in not appropriate for understanding Japan. Chalmers Johnson, a professor of Political Science at University of California, San Diego, argues in that Japan is more properly understood as a 'capitalist developmentalist state.' In nations which were late to industrialize it was the state that led industrialization efforts and played the key role in planning, directing and guiding economic growth. It is the unique role of MITI in postwar Japan that helps explain the 'miracle' of Japanese economic performance since 1945. Capitalist developmentalist states, he argues, work strategically to promote industrial development and secure economic competitiveness for the state's enterprises. They are quite unlike the advanced industrial states of North America and Western Europe (Johnson, 1982).

Johnson, together with James Fallows, the Washington editor for *The Atlantic* magazine, Clyde Prestowitz, a former top trade negotiator on USA–Japan trade with the Reagan administration, and Karl van Wolferen, a Dutch journalist and author, are the intellectual progenitors of this late 1980s 'revisionism.' The group, known as the 'Gang of Four,' approach the question of USA–Japan relations from quite different backgrounds but are united in their view that Japan is a threat to the stability of the world

trading system. In a jointly written article they state that 'the main threat
. . . is the persistently unbalanced economic and industrial relationship
between Japan and the rest of the world, including the continued dis-
placement of industrial sectors and the shift of technological capability
towards Japan' (Fallows *et al*, 1990: 54). It is an operational reality that the
Japanese system is 'more likely to sacrifice the consumer's welfare in
order to strengthen its business.' In Japan individual rights are also likely
to be sacrificed when they clash with what is seen as the whole society's
interests. Japan is less concerned with the removal of racial or sexual
barriers to individual opportunity. The result of these traits, they argue,
is 'a system whose goals and performance may not be accurately described by the Western model of democratic capitalism' (Fallows *et al*,
1990: 55).

The propositions that Japan-is-not-Western and that Japan-is-a-threat
are central to revisionism. However, Johnson, Fallows, Van Wolferen and
Prestowitz are more than revisionists for their interests and agenda extend
beyond Japan or the USA–Japan relationship to interpretations of the
general decline of the USA, and policy prescriptions for reinvigorating
American society and industry. They are the primary organic intellectuals
of geo-economic discourses, discourses whose production and diffusion
depend on a variety of other secondary intellectuals who have plundered,
popularized and propagandized their writings. The composition of this
latter group is largely made up of professional business journalists (Frantz
and Collins, 1989; Holstein, 1990), freelance economic affairs writers
(Burstein, 1988, 1991; Choate, 1990; Tolchin and Tolchin, 1988) and business executives turned authors (Dietrich, 1991; Schlossstein, 1989). In
contrast to the considered analysis found within certain texts by the Gang
of Four the latter writings are often sensationalist and melodramatic.

The substance of geo-economic arguments, both sophisticated and
populist, are considered here using the three-part narrative noted on page
183. Such arguments are far from homogeneous and an attempt has been
made to highlight differences within each section.

The American dilemma.

Geo-economic discourses on the Japanese threat begin from the general
assumption of the relative decline of the USA, a process influentially
described by Paul Kennedy (1987). Like Kennedy, geo-economic discourses explicitly place this decline in the context of the rising power of
Japan. However, the geo-economic narrative on America's dilemma does
not necessarily lead to the liberal solutions proposed by Kennedy and
other 'declinists' (O'Loughlin, Chapter 8). Two different variants of the
argument can be discerned. The first portrays a vulnerable and weakened
USA being outpaced by an omniscient Japan, the second a USA running on
now obsolete notions of security and power. In the first, the erosion of
American sovereignty and power is the predominant theme; in the second,
it is the clash between geopolitical and geo-economic visions of security
within the American state itself.

An example of the first type is Daniel Burstein's (1988) *Yen! Japan's Financial Empire and its Threat to America*. Burstein, like Schlossstein (1989), begins with a dramatic future scenario where Japan places a debt-ridden USA into receivership in the year 2004! (see also Dietrich 1991: 263–6 for a 2015 *Pax Nipponica* future scenario). Japan, for Burstein and other geo-economic intellectuals, is the mirror image of the USA. It 'is strong precisely where we are weak; its economy reverberates with the equal and opposite reactions to our American actions. Thus, while the United States has become the world's leading debtor, Japan has become its leading creditor' (Burstein, 1988: 26). Recalling World War II, Burstein notes that Japan is the only country to have bombed the territory of the USA. Today, he argues, the USA–Japan trade war has for all intents and purposes been won by Japan. Now a financial war is brewing and 'we can see the accelerating pace at which the new Japanese empire is gaining momentum and the American empire is losing ground' (Burstein, 1988: 27).

Burstein's military metaphors and zero-sum reasoning are similar to those described by Servan-Schreiber, the 'invasion of Europe' by American multinationals, 'the first full-scale war to be fought without arms or armour' (1968: xiv). Burstein describes his work as a report 'from the front line of a war that has not yet been declared' (1988: 31). Included are 'expose' chapters on Japanese companies like Nomura Securities, a firm 'twenty times bigger than Merrill Lynch' that has a 'warrior culture' and a president who has a vision of building Nomura's headquarters in the year 2000 on a satellite orbiting the earth. The drive to empire, Burstein (1988: 76) observes, is alive and well in Japan and so are the racist and expansionist attitudes 'necessary to support it.'

In the narratives of Burstein, Dietrich, Fallows, Prestowitz, Schlossstein and others the stockmarket crash of 19 October 1987 (Black Monday) is a critical date in American history.[6] Frantz and Collins (1989: 6) describe it as 'one of those rare days in history when the shift in power from one empire to another can be marked, precisely and indelibly.' Their journalistic account of foreign direct investment in the USA is similar to that of Tolchin and Tolchin (1988) except that their focus is explicitly on Japan. Japanese investment in America, they argue, is different:

No nation holds more leverage over the United States than Japan, which increased its U.S. investments faster than any other foreign country in the 1980s. And no nation is shaped better by its own history and nationalistic necessities than Japan to exercise control over the United States.

For unlike the United States, where corporate plans are measured by the year or the quarter, the Japanese have a centuries-old tradition of thinking twenty or thirty years ahead. This ability enables them to foresee causes and effects of economic policies and manufacturing decisions from a perspective not used by Americans. It allows them to be patient in laying the groundwork for economic domination of the United States (Frantz and Collins, 1989: 11).

The substance of Frantz and Collins' book is a series of racy and sensationalist accounts of how various Japanese interests have 'penetrated' the

American economy.[7] The weakness and susceptibility of American institutions to foreign exploitation is also a theme of Pat Choate. The American system is being used by Japanese and other foreign interests to such an extent that it 'threatens our national sovereignty and our future' (Choate, 1990: xiv). Documenting the influence, lobbying, politicking and propagandizing of Japanese corporations and the Japanese state, Choate develops a picture of an American political system and civil society riddled with 'foreign agents.' The rhetoric of Choate is worth noting for there is a Cold-War-style hysteria underlying his arguments. 'Because of its money politics, Japan has one of the most corrupt political systems in the world (Choate, 1990: 28). Washington too has been corrupted by money and a lack of scruple by former public servants including former Presidents like Jimmy Carter who is pictured in Choate's book jogging with Ryoichi Sasakawa, a Japanese businessman and former Class A war criminal. Choate provides appendices of former federal officials who later represented foreign interests and of Japan's registered foreign agents in America.

The vision of a vulnerable and weakened USA being colonized by an omniscient Japan is not the organizing narrative of Prestowitz but it does become the effective conclusion of his argument. His main theme is how American foreign economic policy making has consistently been subordinated to geopolitical goals and how this needs to change. Drawing on his experience as a Reagan administration trade negotiator, Prestowitz argues that the Japanese government views industrial performance as akin to national security (Prestowitz, 1989: 102; Johnson, 1982: 21) whereas the American government have assumed that the only purpose of the economy is to satisfy consumer needs (1989: 114–15). 'Thus, we respond to the Soviets because defending against a military threat is seen as a legitimate government role, but have difficulty responding to Japan's challenge because the steps required to do so appear to conflict with the requirements of an efficient economy' (1989: 115). Cold War preoccupations and the ideology of *laissez faire* have fatally undermined American industrial and technological leadership. Using the cases of the FSX fighter aircraft and the semiconductor industry, Prestowitz argues that the state has been guided by false and misleading assumptions about Japan. The government and producers must begin to appreciate that 'Japanese society, market, government, and companies do not operate according to the rules and assumptions of Western logic' (1989: 178).

The U.S. state is likened to a 'sleeping giant' whereas Japan's state is run by efficient 'mandarin' bureaucracies according to 'mandarin strategies.' Like other geo-economic intellectuals he uses military metaphors to describe MITI and Japanese industry. MITI is comparable to the US Defense Department (Prestowitz, 1989: 221) and both it and Japanese companies practice long-term 'strategic' planning. 'In lieu of a significant military establishment or policy, industrial policy aimed at achieving "economic security" has become Japan's national security strategy . . . Japan's economic and strategic thinking are integrated' (1989: 284). This integration contrasts sharply with the American state split between 'traders' and 'warriors.' American interests in trade negotiations are hampered not only by a contradiction between the trade policies and security commitments but by poor organization, divided interests, and inexperienced negotiators. The Japanese, by contrast, are professional and highly skilled negotiators.

Prestowitz concludes by evoking the image of Japan's colonization of America. Echoing Kennedy's (1987) arguments about 'imperial overstretch' he remarks that the current USA–Japan relationship is 'surely the first time in history that a territory in the process of being colonized has actually paid for the right to defend the colonizer' (1989: 497). In subsequent articles, opinion editorials, Congressional testimony, and television appearances, Prestowitz has further embellished his arguments and gained for himself a very high public profile. Due to corporate funding from American industry (including Chrysler and Ford Motor Company) he was able to establish the Economic Strategy Institute, a Washington DC, research institution. In January 1992, during Bush's visit to Japan, the Institute released a report on the American auto industry which called for government intervention to stimulate sales and save this 'dying industry.' The report advocated diverting money from military R&D into a low-interest loan for a collective R&D project for the American auto industry. It also advocated a personal income tax deduction for one year to consumers who buy American-made cars, negotiations with the Japanese to encourage American exports to the Japanese market, and requirements that Japanese auto transplants in the USA should increase the amount of American labour and material they use.

The nature of the Japanese system

The arguments of Prestowitz and other geo-economic intellectuals depend on a particular set of scripts about the nature of the Japanese economic and political system. Again two general variants are worth distinguishing. The first portrays Japan as an essentially unified, homogeneous and omniscient actor in international affairs, a Japan Inc. This portrait, sharpened into a caricature by the discursive use of Japan as a foil to America, is derived from Johnson's (1982) notion of Japan as a capitalist developmental state characterized by consensual decision-making practices within its bureaucratic and corporatist structures. The second variant represents Japan as a peculiarly divided actor in world politics with a system which paralyses centralized decision-making and authority. This latter version is closely associated with Karl van Wolferen (1989).

The debate between these two variants of geo-economic analysis on the Japanese system is illustrated by two recent articles in the influential conservative Washington, D.C. journal *The National Interest*. The first article is by Leon Hollerman (1991) who argues that Japan as a 'developmental state' has both central direction and the capacity for coordinated policy change. In the post-War period central direction has been supplied by the Japanese ministerial bureaucracy who have pursued the goal of comprehensive security which has made Japan a 'headquarters nation' in the world economy. Industrial policy is made by the ministerial

bureaucracy, particularly MITI, and economic concentration and carteli-
zation of markets is encouraged so that industrial strategy is efficiently
pursued. Internationally Japanese corporations with the aid and advice
of their government pursue both adversarial trade and adversarial
investment strategies.[8] Japanese investments in Europe, for example, are
part of strategy to recycle surpluses, reduce dependence on the
American market and shift the locus of trade frictions. Hegemony in
global financial markets is another Japanese goal (again the Black
Monday scenario is used). Hollerman concludes that 'Japan is an oligo-
polistic society, conditioned by traditions of centralized feudalism, bureaucracy and imperialism, in which state and business collaborate to
promote the comprehensive security of their country' (1991: 25). Japan's
accommodations to outside pressure are considered to be largely
'cosmetic.'

The second article is by Van Wolferen (1991) and largely concurs with
Hollerman's analysis. He adds, however, that what Japan's 'collusive
oligopoly have wrought is, in the final analysis, out of control' (1991: 27).
The major defect of the Japanese state is its absence of a centre of political
accountability. Van Wolferen (1989) describes the Japanese system as 'trun-
cated pyramid,' a complex of overlapping hierarchies rather than a singular
hierarchy with a recognizable peak. The fact that there is no ultimate
arbitrator between these overlapping hierarchies, composed principally of
a bureaucratic–LDP (Liberal Democratic Party)–business triad, has serious
implications for the international system. In an image signifying both
power and danger Van Wolferen (1991) describes Japan as 'a juggernaut
with no brakes.'

Van Wolferen's analysis, like that of other geo-economic intellectuals,
rests on generalizations about the essentially non-Western nature of
Japanese culture. Rejecting the self-serving 'uniqueness' thesis often used
by power-holders in the Japanese system and Ruth Benedict's (1946)
'cultural singularity' approach van Wolferen seeks to explain Japanese
culture in terms of power. Like Prestowitz, he notes how ethics in Japan
are situational and not governed by general moral rules (Van Wolferen
1989: 10). In the West 'reality' is not often thought of as something that can
be managed or moulded whereas in 'Asian traditions of thought' the idea
of multiple and contradictory truths, or the 'management of reality' is more
readily accepted. Situational ethics and the manipulation of 'reality' are
part of the way power is exercized and legitimated in Japan. Arguing with
Japanese in international exchanges, Van Wolferen notes, can exasperate
'logically reasoning Westerners' (1989: 9).[9]

Van Wolferen's conclusions (1991) about the implications of the nature of
the Japanese system for the world are apocalyptic. Complacency on the
part of the West with a rudderless Japan is dangerous. The editorial
policies of authoritative publications like the *Wall Street Journal* and the
Economist are, he suggests, conceptually blinkered and 'more than irres-
ponsible.'[10] Because they do not address potential crises in the world
economy and the weak nature of civilian power in Japan (the military, he
suggests, are once again in a powerful position) their *laissez faire* ideology

may 'help to bring about the very end that they seek to prevent: the collapse of the world's liberal capitalist order' (Van Wolferen 1991: 35).

Policy prescriptions

The American dilemma and the nature of the Japanese system have prompted geo-economic intellectuals to propose a series of policy prescriptions for the American state. Such proposals can be distinguished ideologically as conservative (e.g. Dietrich, 1991; Schlossstein, 1989) or liberal (e.g. Kuttner, 1991) but are represented by proponents as being beyond traditional ideological categories and party politics. A different but equally problematic distinction is that between positive and negative Japanization proposals. The former view the nature of the Japanese system as a positive model that the USA should try to emulate. Vogel (1979) is an early non-revisionist example. The latter view the Japanese model as inappropriate for the USA. They argue that the Japanese challenge requires a deepened Americanization of the American system which will put 'America's native strengths and traditional values to work to overcome the Asian challenge' (Fallows, 1989c).

Positive Japanization proposals are varied but one can identify five recurrent themes. The first is that the American state needs to abandon its embedded social philosophy of *laissez faire* liberalism and actively guide the process of economic growth through a new MITI-like bureaucracy (e.g. a cabinet level Department of Trade and Industry) and an explicit industrial policy (Burstein, 1988: 303–4; Dietrich, 1991: 257–8; Frantz and Collins, 1989: Ch. 26; Prestowitz, 1989: 511; 1992). Second, the American state needs to structure the economic environment, through fiscal and other means, so that savings are encouraged, the budget deficit eliminated, and overconsumption discouraged. In particular the welfare and retirement systems must be changed. For Prestowitz (1989: 502; 1992: 74) the indexation of social security and government pensions must be revised. Third, the American state should initiate a repeal of existing legislation which hinders collusive relationships between corporations. Specifically, a number of geo-economic intellectuals call for the scrapping of anti-trust legislation (Dietrich, 1991: 231–3; Prestowitz, 1992: 78). Fourth, the state should initiate new legislation to protect its economic and political system from foreign interference. Choate (1989) does not advocate that the American political system should become like that of Japan but his proposals are inspired by what he reads as the Japanese pursuit of their own interest. Similarity Frantz and Collins' call for restrictions on foreign direct investment is influenced by what they see as restrictions operating in Japan (Frantz and Collins, 1989: 93–5). Finally, there should be a re-invigoration of the moral, education and cultural values of American society. For some this involves a revitalization of the family. Schlossstein (1989: 353), for example, is concerned that the USA is 'the most sexually permissive society in the world.' In contrast to the social stability of family life in East Asia, American society suffers from divisive forces which undermine the family which he describes as 'society's fortress.' He recommends tax policies to encourage families to stay together, and corporate policies to provide adequate child care and flexwork procedures for their workforce (Schlossstein, 1989: 469).

Many of the proposals are not strict Japanization proposals for most geo-economic intellectuals recognize that the USA will never be like Japan. Nevertheless it is worth noting the difference between those who would use the Japanese example to inform American policy formulation and those for whom Japanese experiences are particularly inappropriate to American conditions. James Fallows contrasts, in a binary way, the cooperative, disciplined and hierarchically ordered cultures of East Asia with the American 'talent for disorder.' The USA's strength is its individualist, entrepreneurial culture. Ceaseless internal change is good for Americans for it offers them 'the constant prospect of changing their fortunes, their identities, their roles in life' (Fallows, 1989c: 49). Anecdotally illustrating the supposed exceptionalism of the USA ('America is abnormal'), Fallows calls for a renewed faith in traditional values and strengths, individualism, diversity, flexibility and the ability to adapt. 'Our individualism *is* our sense of community' (Fallows, 1989c: 209). The solution to the changed circumstances of the USA, he argues, is to 'reawaken' these values and for leaders to mobilize the 'moral equivalent of nationalism,' a sense of national unity without hatred of others, amongst the American people (1989c: x).

The proposals discussed so far relate to the reorganization of the domestic political and economic environment. Internationally most geo-economic intellectuals advocate that the American state should co-ordinate its defence and economic interests more closely (Prestowitz, 1988: Ch. 11). The USA should not pay for the defence of Japan. Echoing George Kennan, Fallows (1989a) even suggests a policy of 'containing' Japan. Economically, the USA should move towards more 'managed trade' with Japan (Fallows, 1989b). The Gang of Four accept that most trade between the USA and Japan is already managed through quota and other means; and that the USA has long had 'industrial policies' guiding agriculture, aerospace and other defence-related industries (Fallows *et al*, 1990: 55). However, the state must now be more explicit about its interests and drop the charade of free trade (Burstein, 1988: Ch. 12). The active intervention of the state in the process of economic growth should be consensually held philosophy in American political culture and not a 'taboo' issue. The trading policy of the USA should be based on strict reciprocity and designed to assure the survival of strategic industries (Harrison and Prestowitz, 1990: 74). In short, the USA should have a strong instrumentalist state in international affairs.

Evaluating goe-economic discourse

A standard reaction to revisionism in American political and civil society is the charge of 'Japan-bashing.' Its implication of an innate prejudice against Japanese people and culture is one the Gang of Four vehemently reject (Fallows *et al*, 1990). Nevertheless, defenders of transnational liberalism use the term as a means of wrecking the intellectual credibility of geo-economics. In Japan, American revisionism on Japan is provoking a revisionist literature on the USA which holds that the country is in long-term decline (Ito, 1990; Ishihara, 1991).

The relevance of the assumptions of geo-economic discourses, given the realities of transnationalization, is an important intellectual question. The presumptions of discrete national economies, recognizable national industries, and a collective corporate-national interest are all subject to question given the realities of *nichibei* in the 1990s. Reich (1991b) argues that discrete national economies are being displaced by a global web of interactions between and within transnational corporations. Groups of people in one nation are developing closer relations with similar groups in other nations than with their fellow citizens. In sociological terms the community presumed by the territorial nation is being undermined by the 'succession of the successful' within the nation (Reich, 1991a; 1991c). In economic terms recognizable 'national champions' of the past (like General Motors in the USA) have transformed themselves into transnational corporations with only limited loyalty to the nation-state. That the strength of the American economy is synonymous with the profitability and productivity of American corporations is, Reich writes, 'an axiom on the brink of anachronism' (1991b: 135).

The divorce of the new transnational class and transnational corporations from the territorial nation (and its territorial economy) calls into question both the analysis and policy prescriptions of geo-economic discourses. In the new global environment, Reich argues, the standard of living of a nation's people increasingly depends on the skills, capabilities and value added by its citizens to the world economy. The purpose of the state is to maximize these so economic well-being and a high standard of living can be secured for its citizens. The question of whether people work for an 'American' or a 'Japanese' corporation is incidental.

Reich's (1990) position is rejected by Kuttner (1991: 284) who suggests that at some point in the next century corporate ownership may be truly indistinguishable but 'until that day comes U.S. policy needs to make sure that American-based enterprises are around to compete.' According to Kuttner, Reich's views require either Japanese firms to behave just like textbook Western firms or a bureaucratized 'labour mercantilism' under which foreign investment is vetted to make sure it indeed provides high value jobs for the USA. Neither alternative, he believes, is likely.

Criticizing Reich's policy prescriptions does not undermine his arguments about the realities of transnationalization (a process that is easily caricatured because national economies remain enormously significant). Below is a specific evaluation of the geo-economic themes already outlined. In most cases the single most important difficulty with these discourses is their failure to appreciate the changed nature of the world economy. Their story of the demise of the USA and the rise of a threatening Japan should really be a story of the transnationalization of the world economy as a whole in the 1980s, the weak nature of the state in both Japan and the USA, and the threat unregulated transnational corporate capitalism poses to the subaltern classes in both states.

Reading the demise of the USA: foreign conspiracies and imperial overstretch?

In their desire to produce sensationalist copy for a mass audience Burstein (1988), Choate (1989), and Frantz and Collins (1989) come closest to the popular image of 'Japan-bashing.' The style of such books, with their dramatic future scenarios and conspiratorial reasoning, is closer to fictional spy novels or geo-financial thrillers than to serious economic journalism. The 'plot' of a vulnerable and weakened USA being taken over by an omniscient Japan is reminiscent of American public discourse in the early Cold War. In Burstein (1988) no consideration is given to the global debt crisis. Frantz and Collins (1989) do not address the largest FDI in the USA in the 1980s: the British. They also neglect the domestic effects of American FDI in the 1980s (see Glickman and Woodward, 1989: Ch. 6). Finally the Tokyo stockmarket fall of 1991–2, the losses experienced by Japanese investors in the USA and the reverse flow of capital into Japan has exposed the superficiality of their arguments.

Choate (1989) does not offer a perspective on the vast power the state continues to wield in the world economy. As one critic crudely put it:

The businessmen of satellites need to bribe superpowers. The businessmen of superpowers don't need to bribe satellites. They just get their government to tell the satellite what to do. And behind all kinds of face-saving facades, they evertually do it (Auer *et al*, 1991: 100).

Prestowitz's arguments (1989) are of a more serious nature. His argument that the state subordinates economic considerations to geopolitical priorities appears to be substantiated by the historical record and his own experiences. However, Prestowitz's argument (1989) can only address with authority the process of foreign economic policy formulation within the American state. Extending his geopolitics subordinating geo-economics theme to explain, firstly, generalizations about the causes of American decline and, secondly, generalizations about Japan's 'colonization' of the USA are dubious. Like Kennedy's 'imperial overstretch' thesis (1987) or Kuttner's (1991) broadening of this, too much is claimed to be explained by the costs of geopolitical hegemony. While the prominence within the state of a geopolitical management philosophy is important, explanations of the complex re-structuring of the 1980s must go beyond the state to consider the role of global economic and cultural changes, and the responses of American industry and institutions.

Representing the Japanese system: a new orientalism?

Discourses which have represented Japan as an essentially unified, corporatist nation (Japan Inc) with a 'headquarters nation' strategy have tended to underestimate changes in Japan and the actual effects of transnationalization on the country (Calder, 1990; Lincoln, 1988; Schmiegelow and Schmiegelow, 1990). Yoon's (1990) analysis of the shift from export to FDI strategies by Japanese industry notes the resultant increase in unemployment in Japan's traditionally most efficient industries. The perception that labour could now be employed in higher productivity growth industries is not supported by the evidence. Most unemployed people, he notes, were absorbed into lower productivity growth sectors. Furthermore, the negative effect of the hollowing-out of export industries on productivity growth in Japan will be greater than it was in the USA because Japanese development has depended more on a few key export industries. Yoon is sceptical of official Japanese arguments which suggest Japan will develop higher value products and skills. He suggests that the transfer of lower level products abroad leads to the loss of ground for the development of higher level products and breaks intra-industry linkage. The continuing transnationalization of Japanese manufacturing and finance, Yoon concludes, will exacerbate income inequality within Japan rather than improving the domestic standard of living.

Besides underestimating the transnationalization of Japan geoeconomic, discourses have also recently come under attack for their cultural representation of Japan. Jung-en Woo (1991) draws upon Said's (1978) notion of 'Orientalism' to describe what he sees as a 'new Orientalism' in American writings about East Asia. Historically, he argues, Americans have regarded East Asia as a frontier to be conquered, organized and civilized. Today 'Americans see the countries of East Asia as not part of the real world, as free riders on defense issues and predators on economic ones. East Asian countries are said to be sapping the strength of the United States . . .' (Woo, 1991: 453). Taking particular issue with Van Wolferen's analysis of Japan, Woo accuses him of 'harmful stereotyping' and producing a troubling ethnocentric reading of the Japanese system:

When van Wolferen peered into the heart of the Japanese system of political economy, he saw, like Joseph Conrad, a horror staring back at him: not liberal pluralism, but an all encompassing and mysterious 'system' with no exit, one as 'inescapable as the political system of the Soviet Union,' only worse because it was more pervasive and culturally legitimate. To see Japan as enigmatic, impenetrable, not individualistic, and run by a mysterious system, of course, recalls stereotypes that go back to the first Western encounters with the Japanese, ones that have popped in and out of the American consciousness ever since Commodore Matthew Perry's 'black ships' first landed in Japan in 1852 (Woo, 1991: 455).

Woo views the alternative vision of Japan as a 'miracle' or the Pacific Rim as a new capitalist utopia as the other side of this new Orientalism. Both utopians and Asia-bashers have difficulty 'grasping that East Asia is neither a miracle nor a menace, but merely a few tens of millions of people working hard to better their lot, coming along late to the task of industrial development, and trying to make the best of it, with a quite ordinary mixture of good and bad human traits' (Woo, 1991: 456).

Woo's critique of the constructed geographical imagination and cultural ethnocentrism of Western public intellectuals is a valuable one (as is the more cultural analysis of 'techno-Orientalism' by Morley and Robins, 1992). The new orientalism, he suggests, conceals two realities of power in East Asia: (i) that the Pacific is still an American lake; (ii) Japan and its East Asian neighbours still tend to interact with each other through Washington. Like Said (1978), Woo's analysis presumes a subordinated East Asia, a silenced 'true' regional identity that needs to find its voice outside of the frame of the new orientalism. Yet such a view exaggerates the power of American hegemony, totalizes the new orientalism, and holds faith in a mythic regional collective consciousness. Furthermore, Woo never tackles the substance of Van Wolferen's thesis or suggests an alternative possible account of Japan's political and economic system.

Van Wolferen's thesis is flawed in that he has a rather idealized view of how Western statecraft works which is drawn from political theory rather than practical history. His portrait of a weak Japanese state should have been balanced by an intelligent appreciation of the equally weak American state. The essentially non-Western nature of the Japanese system can also be disputed. Schmiegelow and Schmiegelow (1990: 573) observe that there is hardly a component of Japan's performance, both system and behaviour, that cannot be explained by some Western theory or concept. Yet, despite its faults, Van Wolferen's portrait of Japan is a powerfully persuasive one. Brock, a strong critic of revisionism, nevertheless concedes that 'the picture of Japanese society emerging from Japan-bashing accounts is on the whole more realistic than the one painted by the old-line Japan-handlers (Brock, 1989: 32).'

Policy prescriptions for whom?

In evaluating the policy prescriptions offered by geo-economics, intellectuals one must ask who is likely to benefit from such measures. Bluestone and Harrison (1982: 214–20) provide one evaluation of proposals which seek to 'Japanize' the American economy. They question whether there is a consistency between the Japanese system and the USA's basic democratic values. The job-guarantee system in Japan, they note, is confined to only a specific segment of the labour force in Japan. Japan has developed a 'dual economy' where fluctuations in demand are handled through the flexible hiring and dismissing of temporary workers who do not share the benefits of the permanently employed. These benefits are themselves questionable with workers in a dependent relationship with their company for retirement pensions and housing. The Japanese system, they conclude, is 'a two-edged sword. It offers economic prosperity and material progress. But it exacts a price in terms of regimentation, autocracy, and institutionalized inequality' (Bluestone and Harrison, 1982: 220).

Luke's (1990) review of the legacy of Reaganism addresses the broader ideological significance of discourses of 'Japanization.' Japan, he argues, is being refashioned by some as a new geopolitical threat while simultaneously 'images of Japanese life are being imperfectly and incompletely reprocessed in the media by the corporate sector, academics, and some legislators to serve as a positive model for America's future social and economic modernization' (Luke, 1990: 35). To reclaim the American dream from South Korea, Taiwan or Japan, Americans are urged to adopt new practices of social discipline:

As a political strategy, the discourses of Japanization stand for a new national strategy, based upon a corporatist fusion of labour, capital and the state in self-sacrificing cooperative arrangements in competition with aggressive foreign rivals to capture leadership in world export markets, high technology innovation, and efficient capital accumulation. Yet it would come with the same price as the Japanese pay. Ordinary redistributive policies and welfare state services would be reduced even more in the spirit of Reaganite privatization as a key means of rationalizing greater capital accumulation. Some slack might be assumed by corporate paternalism, but most of it, as in the case of Japan, will be off-loaded on to the family or it will simply no longer be performed (Luke, 1990: 37).

Japanization, Luke argues, is a means by which Americans can adjust ideologically to diminished expectations and combat narcissistic consumerism. Obfuscating the actual 'South Africanization' of American society – increasing racial inequality, growing class divisions, and armed enclaves of wealthy privilege tied transnationally to similar centres abroad in the midst of domestic expanses of poverty, urban decay and rural decline – Japanization discourses provide transnational corporations and the government with 'a concrete, albeit politically regressive, model for coping with the transition in America to modern informational production' (Luke, 1990: 38). They fill the vacuum, he maintains, opened by Reaganite attacks on the managerial state with a call for a new kind of 'guided capitalism.'

Luke's analysis tends to attribute an empirically unjustified unity and purpose to Japanization discourses. Particular local variants have undoubtedly been influential in specific instances – in industrial management, in welfare reform, high-tech. collaboration agreements – but the vision of the need for a general Japanization strategy for the USA has made little headway within the Bush administration. Nevertheless, Luke's analysis may be prescient of a post-Bush America. In his 1992 self-financed presidential bid, Texas billionaire Ross Perot articulated a self-sacrificing corporatist strategy for national recovery which he represented as independent, bipartisan and beyond 'politics as usual' (Perot, 1992). Perot's half-hour television 'infomercials' gave voice to many of the arguments codified by geo-economic intellectuals: the threat of ('foreign lobbyists' working in Washington, betrayal by the elites working in the government (Choate), the incompetence of government officials who do not know the difference between potato chips and computer chips (Prestowitz) and the need to re-discipline American society to clean-living productiveness (Schlossstein) (Perot, 1992). Perot's record of management at his former company,

Electronic Data Systems, revealed a proclivity for policies which are auto-
cratic, socially conservative and militarist in their conception of economic
problems (Wills, 1992).

Conclusion: geo-economics versus transnational liberalism?

The emergent prominence of geo-economic discourses in American civil
society in the late 1980s appears to threaten the continued ideological
hegemony of transnational liberalism into the 1990s. With its declinist view
of the American system, its revisionist view of Japan and its neo-
mercantilist view of economic activity the possible ascension to power of
candidates sympathetic to such discourses within the American political
system could precipitate major changes in USA–Japan relations and give a
radically different shape to the political geography of the *fin de siecle* world
order.[11] On the face of it, the differences between geo-economics and
transnational liberalism are obvious. First, geo-economic discourses
tend to subscribe to a zero-sum view of economic competition. Gains
for Japanese industry come at the expense of American industry. Transnational liberalism, by contrast, believes in an expanding global market in
which all competitive industries can participate. Second, geo-economic
discourses seek to re-conceptualize security in economic terms whereas
current American transnational liberal orthodoxy views security as a
military matter to be dealt through trilateral cooperation under the leadership of the USA (as in the Gulf War). Finally, geo-economic discourses
make the case for strong interventionist state policies to guide economic
development whereas American transnational elites supposedly still subscribe to *laissez faire* principles.

The ideological differences between geo-economics and transnational
liberalism may not be as stark as they appear in political rhetoric. First,
both geo-economics and transnational liberalism share the similar goal of
maintaining a transnational, corporate capitalist world order, organized on
collectively agreed principles of reciprocity and competition, and led
by a trilateral alliance of the USA, EC and Japan. Reading geo-economic
discourses as simply the expression of the interests of a 'national' capitalist
fraction within the USA misses the subtle ways in which geo-economic
discourses also serve transnational capital. American auto makers, for
example, simultaneously support think tanks like the Economic Strategy
Institute and call for government action against Japanese trade practices
while engaging in a series of joint marketing and joint production ventures
with the Japanese. Geo-economic discourses are used by USA-based transnational capital to instrumentalize the state, to make it more responsive to
their interests in the new world order. President Bush's January 1992 state
visit to Japan, the first since Reagan's visit in November 1983, is evidence
that this may be occurring. Not only was the visit recast as a trade
negotiation mission but Bush invited with him 21 top corporate executives
(including Lee Iacocca of Chrysler, Robert Sempel of General Motors and
Harold Poling of Ford Motor Company) to make their case publicly alongside him. Among the concessions 'won' by Bush from the Japanese was a

commitment by auto companies to increase their purchases from American auto parts suppliers from $7 billion in 1990 to $18 billion by 1994. Significantly, less than 20 per cent of the parts will actually be imported into Japan but will be sold within the USA to Japanese transplants (*The Economist*, 1992). Whether all the components used by American auto parts manufacturers are actually made in the USA is a question noone has asked.

Second, as one moves from the realm of public discourse into the institutional and structured environment of foreign economic policy formulation, the previously stark differences between both perspectives tends to blur. Variants of geo-economic discourses already shape American trading policy with Japan which is characterized not by free trade but by *ad hoc* protectionism (Mastanduno, 1991). Around 40 per cent of Japan's exports to America enter under a tariff or some other form of protection (*The Economist*, 1989b). According to GATT, the USA has higher tariff levels than Japan (Economic Focus, 1992; O'Loughlin, Chapter 8). After the FSX debate the Bush administration promised to give economic considerations greater weight in evaluating national security (Ó Tuathail, 1992). Japanese actions, from the FDI strategy of the 1980s to the $13 billion Gulf War contribution and concessions to Bush during his visit, are material acknowledgements of the persistent structural power of the USA in the world economy, a structural power that always secured geo-economic rewards for the American state.[12]

The question remains as to what popular ideological form American adjustment to the 1980s will take in the 1990s. Whether geo-economic discourses become a new 'social philosophy,' like Reaganite 'free market' myths in the 1980s, remains to be seen. The most likely outcome, reflecting domestic necessities and transnational realities, will probably be a scion of transnational liberal pragmatism with a geo-economics gloss as the state and its leaders 'muddle through' the 1990s.

Notes

1 In March 1991 an American opinion poll of 1255 adults revealed that 72 per cent of those asked considered the economic threat from Japan a more serious threat to the future of the USA than the Soviet military threat (*Business Week*, 1991a). In 1990 the figures were 58 per cent to 26 per cent (Destler and Nacht, 1990) and 68 per cent to 22 per cent in August 1989 (*Business Week*, 1989). Polls such as these can be misleading. Most USA–Japan attitude surveys also show that substantial majorities in both states express 'friendly feelings' towards each other. American fears about a perceived inability to compete with Japan and Japanese perceptions of America as a declining power, however, are becoming more evident (Weisman, 1991).

2 Mastanduno's (1991) investigation of the USA's response to Japanese industrial policy in 1989 assumes a realist theory of state action in foreign economic policy. His hypothesis, based on Luttwak's (1990) observations, is that as relative economic power declines and external security threats diminish, a hegemonic state is likely to pursue relative gains more forcefully in economic relations with its allies (Mastanduno, 1991; 82). After reviewing three empirical cases he concludes that he has failed to uncover evidence of such behaviour. He does

argue, however, that clear signs of relative gains-seeking behaviour did appear in the American policy process in the late 1980s.

3 The politics of writing identity in the public discourse of political economy is a theme that is not developed here though it is of great importance in explaining the micro-politics of hegemony. How the identities 'American' and 'Japanese' function to exclude other possible identities, norm hegemonic subjects, and legitimate particular grounds of judgement is, to my mind, best studied by examining specifics since one can avoid calling up problematic unities such as 'the popular imagination' or 'the western imagination' (Luke, 1990 and Morley and Robins, 1992, employ such categories. This chapter is inevitably mired in the problems of writing political economy. Its agnosticism to the problems of signification and normalization of a ground for judgement should be viewed (from a post-modern perspective) as a provisional tactical necessity to enable the generation of a useful analytical narrative within political geography.

4 The Japanese also invested heavily in American securities and portfolios during the 1980s. Data for 1991 suggests a reversal of this trend. Whereas approximately $100 billion used to flow out of Japan in the 1980s it is estimated that $30 billion to $40 billion now flows into the country. Not only are Japanese corporations building fewer plants abroad but foreign investors have recently bought heavily into Japanese stocks and bonds (Sterngold, 1992).

5 Reich uses the example of the American auto industry in general (1991: 126–7) and GM's Pontaic Le Mans in particular (1991: 113–114). For debates on the 'Americanization' of Honda see Business Week (1991b).

6 Conservative versions of geo-economic discourse make extensive use of medical metaphors in describing the demise of America. For example Dietrich (1991: 10) suggests that Black Monday was like a heart attack brought on by overconsumption and bad economic habits. 'Our economic failures put us in jeopardy no less than smoking, high cholesterol, excess weight, and lack of exercise cause heart disease.' The rhetoric is more than a sublimation of the preoccupations of white middle-aged business men. For organic conservative intellectuals society is represented as a body and not a social organization made up of competing social groups. A rhetoric of remedy is then enabled which presents class specific policies in general benevolent medical terms. Discourses on fitness and national health become the ideological vehicle for renewed assaults on the welfare state and subaltern classes.

7 The story of the influx of foreign capital into the USA in the 1980s has been covered by the established business and current affairs press in the USA. While none of these are stories explicitly geo-economic they do reproduce the opinions of geo-economic advocates and their representation of the issues. (See, for example, the cover stories of Business Week 1986; Newsweek, 1987; Time 1987). A contributing author to Business Week's stories on Japan, associate editor, William Holstein (1990) argues for a new 'economic patriotism' in the USA as a national strategy of response to Japan. In response to Sony's $3.4 billion deal for Columbia, Newsweek ran a cover story (1990b). (The Pacific edition, which is sold in Japan, used the headline 'Japan Moves Into Hollywood.)' Before Bush's visit to Tokyo in January 1992, Newsweek ran a Van-Wolferen-inspired cover story which asked 'Who's in Charge?' in Japan.

8 Drucker (1989: 129–32) described adversarial trade as associated with the emergence of new non-Western trading countries, particularly the Japanese, into the world economy. Competitive trade is associated with the emergence of the USA and Germany as trading nations in the mid-19th century. It aims to create a customer whereas adversarial trade aims at dominating an industry. Thus trade

becomes a zero-sum conflict between states. Hollerman (1991: 22) describes adversarial investment by discussing how Japanese corporations deliberately create overcapacity (e.g. in automobiles and chemicals) for the sake of the ultimate domination of an industry.

9 Observations such as these rest on orientalist foundations. The racist assumptions of discourses which frame 'Japan' in the West are evident in Michael Crichton's (1992) novel about a Japanese corporation in Los Angeles – remarkable not simply for its stereotypes of 'the Japanese mind' and the 'mask' it wears to disguise its true intentions but for its 'non-fictional' afterword and bibliography on the Japanese threat to America. See the review by Buruma (1992) and Morley and Robins (1992) on the representation of 'Japan' in orientalist discourses, what they call 'techno-Orientalism'. The line between fiction and non-fiction is often blurred in accounts of Japanese investment in the USA.

10 Fallows (1991b) also takes issue with the *Economist* and *Wall Street Journal* editorial view that Japan is becoming more and more market-minded. There is a contradiction, he suggests, between the ideology of the editorial line and the complex reality the news articles try to report. They point out that things in Japan are not quite evolving according to editorial plan.

11 Friedman and Lebard (1991) speculate on this possibility. Because of its provocative title the book gained much more attention than its superficial analysis deserved (see Fallows, 1991a). Friedman and Lebard (1991) argue that war between Japan and the USA is inevitable because after the Cold War the USA badly needs to solve its budget deficit and balance of payments problems. This will force the USA to construct a regional free trade zone in the Americas and to exclude Japan from the American market. An isolated Japan will to be forced to create its own trading bloc and further militarize in order to protect its resource lifelines. The result will be war.

12 From negotiations during Bush's visit to Japan the USA secured a promise of better access to Japanese glass, paper, legal services, computer and auto markets. The SII talks are to be reinvigorated. Clyde Prestowitz criticized the president for overemphasizing the importance of car exports and underplaying new technology (Barber, 1992).

References

Agnew, J. (1993), 'The United States and American Hegemony', in P. Taylor (ed.), *The Political Geography of the Twentieth Century*, London: Belhaven.

Agnew, J. (1993), 'Timeless Space and State-centrism: the Geographical Assumptions of International Relations Theory, in S. Rosow (ed.), *The Global Economy as Political Space*, forthcoming.

Auer, J., Jansen, M., Lincoln, E. and Calder, K. (1991), 'US–Japan Relations: the End of Interdependence?' *SAIS Review*, Winter–Spring: 93–112.

Barber, L. (1992), 'Bush Seeks to Dispel Campaign trail Anxieties', *Financial Times*, 10 January: 14.

Benedict, R. (1946), *The Chrysanthemum and the Sword*, Boston, Houghton Mifflin.

Bluestone, B. and Harrison, B. (1982), *The Deindustrialization of America*, New York, Basic Books.

Brock, D. (1989), 'The Theory and Practice of Japan-bashing', *The National Interest*, **17**, 29–40.

Burstein, D. (1988), *Yen! Japan's New Financial Empire and its Threat to America*, New York, Simon and Schuster.

Buruma, I. (1992), 'It Can't Happen Here', *New York Review of Books*, 23 April, 3–4.

Burstein, D. (1991), *Euroquake*, New York, Simon and Schuster.

Business Week (1986), 'Japan in America', *Business Week*, 14 July: 44–53.

Business Week (1987), 'Japan on Wall Street', *Business Week*, 7 September: 82–90.

Business Week (1988), 'Japan's influence in America', *Business Week*, 11 July: 64–75.

Business Week (1989), 'Rethinking Japan', *Business Week*, 7 August: 44–52.

Business Week (1991a), 'Americans Resent Japan's No-show in the Gulf', 1 April: 28.

Business Week (1991b), 'Honda: Is it an American Car?' 18 November: 38–42.

Calder, K. (1985), 'The Emerging Polítrics of the Trans-Pacific Economy', *World Policy Journal*, **3**, 593–623.

Calder, K. (1988), 'Japanese Foreign Economic Policy Formation: Explaining the Reactive State', *World Politics*, 517–41.

Calder, K. (1990), 'US–Japan Cooperation and the Global Economy of the 1990s', *Washington Quarterly*, **13**: 97–105.

Cerny, P.G. (1989), Political Entropy and American Decline, *Millenium*, **18**: 47–63.

Choate, P. (1990), *Agents of Influence: How Japan's Lobbyists in the United States Manipulate America's Political and Economic System*, New York, Alfred Knopf.

Corbridge, S. and Agnew, J. (1991), 'The US Trade and Budget Deficits in Global Perspective: an Essay in Geopolitical Economy', *Environment and Planning D: Society and Space*, **9**: 71–90.

Cox, R. (1987), *Production, Power and World Order*, Baltimore, Johns Hopkins University Press.

Crichton, M. (1992), *The Rising Sun*, New York, Ballantine Books.

Destler, I. M. and Nacht, M. (1990), 'Beyond Mutual Recrimination: Building a Solid US–Japan Relationship in the 1990s', *International Security*, 15, No. 3: 92–119.

Dietrich, W. (1991), *In the Shadow of the Rising Sun: the Political Roots of America's Decline*, University Park, Penn, Penn State University Press.

Drucker, P. (1989), *The New Realities*, New York, Harper and Row.

Economic Focus (1992), 'Japan's Troublesome Imports', *The Economist*, 11 January: 69.

The Economist (1985), 'Reaching Out. Japan: a Survey', *The Economist*, 7 December: 1–30.

The Economist (1989a), 'Land of Eastern Profit', *The Economist*, 19 August: 52.

The Economist (1989b), 'Trade: Mote and Beam', *The Economist*, 6 May: 22–3.

The Economist (1991a), 'Economic Nationalism: Bashing Foreigners in Iowa', 21 September: 48–52.

The Economist (1991b), 'A Survey of America: the Old Country', 26 October: 1–19.

The Economist (1992), 'Japan's Car Imports: the Big Stick', 11 January: 68, 70.

Fallows, J. (1989a), 'Containing Japan', *The Atlantic Monthly*, May, 40–54.

Fallows, J. (1989b), 'Getting Along with Japan', *The Atlantic Monthly*, December, 53–64.

Fallows, J. (1989c), *More Like Us*, Boston, Houghton Mifflin.

Fallows, J. (1991a), 'Is Japan the Enemy?' *New York Review of Books*, 30 May: 31–7.

Fallows, J. (1991b), 'The Economics of Colonial Cringe', *Manchester Guardian Weekly*, 29 December: 16.

Fallows, J., Johnson, C., Prestowitz, C. and van Wolferen, K. (1990), 'The Gang of Four Defend the Revisionist Line', *US News and World Report*, 7 May, 54–5.

Frantz, D. and Collins, C. (1989), *Selling Out: How We Are Letting Japan Buy Our Land, Our Industries, Our Financial Institutions, and Our Future*, Chicago, Contemporary Books.

Friedman, G. and Lebard, M. (1991), *The Coming War with Japan*, New York; St Martin's Press.

George, A. (1991), 'Japan's America Problem: the Japanese Response to US Pressure', *Washington Quarterly*, 14, No. 3: 5–19.

Gill, S. (1990), *American Hegemony and the Trilateral Commission*, Cambridge, Cambridge University Press.

Glickman, N. and Woodward, D. (1990), *The New Competitors: How Foreign Investors are Changing the US Economy*, New York, Basic Books.

Gold, P. and Nanto, D. (1991), 'US exports to Japan', *Congressional Research Service Review*, October–November: 30–31.

Graham, E. and Krugman, P. (1989), *Foreign direct investment in the United States*, Washington, D.C., Institute for International Economics.

Harrison, S. and Prestowitz, C. (1990), 'Pacific Agenda: Defense or Economics?' *Foreign Policy*, **79**: 56–76.

Hollerman, L. (1991), The Headquarters Nation, *The National Interest*, **25**: 16–25.

Holstein, W. (1990), *The Japanese Power Game: What it Means for America*, New York, Charles Scribner.

Ishihara, S. (1991), *The Japan that Can Say No*, New York, Simon and Schuster.

Ito, K. (1990), 'Trans-Pacific Anger', *Foreign Policy*, **78**: 131–52.

Johnson, C. (1982), *MITI and the Japanese Miracle: the Growth of Industrial Policy, 1925–1975*, Stanford, Stanford University Press.

Julius, D. (1990), *Global Companies and Public Policy: the Growing Challenge of Foreign Direct Investment*, New York, Council on Foreign Relations.

Kennedy, P. (1987), *The Rise and Fall of the Great Powers*, New York, Random House.

Kudrle, R. (1991), 'Good for the Gander? Foreign Direct Investment in the United States', *International Organization*, **45**: 397–423.

Kuttner, R. (1991), *The End of laissez-faire: National Purpose and the Global Economy After the Cold War*, New York, Alfred Knopf.

Leaver, R. (1989), 'Restructuring in the Global Economy: from Pax Americana to Pax Nipponica?' *Alternatives*, **14**: 429–62.

Lincoln, E. (1988), *Japan: Facing Economic Maturity*, Washington, D.C., The Brookings Institute.

Lohr, S. (1992), 'Blaming Japan has its Risks: so does Bush's Visit to Tokyo', *New York Times*, 5 January, 1–2.

Luke, T. (1990), 'The Future of Critical Theory: Political Theories and Political Realities', paper presented at the Conference on The Future of Critical Theory, Elizabethtown College, 23–5 February.

Luttwak, E. (1990), 'From Geopolitics to Geo-economics: Logic of Conflict, Grammar of Commerce, *The National Interest*, **20**: 17–23.

Mastanduno, M. (1991), 'Do Relative Gains Matter? America's Response to Japanese Industrial Policy', *International Security*, **16**: 73–113.

Morley, D. and Robins, K. (1992), Techno-orientalism: Futures, Foreigners and Phobias', *New Formations*, **16**: 136–56.

Newsweek (1987), 'Your Next Boss May Be Japanese', *Newsweek*, 2 February: 42–8.

Newsweek (1990a), 'What Japan Thinks of Us', *Newsweek*, 2 April: 18–24.

Newsweek (1990b), 'Japan Invades Hollywood', *Newsweek*, 9 October: 62–72.

O'Loughlin, J. (1993), 'Fact or Fiction: the Evidence for the Thesis of US Relative Decline, 1966–91, in C. Williams (eds), *The Political Geography of the New World Order*, London, Belhaven. 148–180.

Ó Tuathail, G. (1992), ' "Pearl harbor without bombs": a Critical Geopolitics of the US–Japan FSX Debate', *Environment and Planning*, A, No. 24: 975–94.

Perot, R. (1992), *United We Stand: How We Can Take Back Our Country*, New York, Hyperion.

Prestowitz, C. (1989), *Trading Places: How We Are Giving Our Future to Japan and How to Reclaim It*, New York, Basic Books.

Prestowitz, C. (1991), 'Forget Pearl Harbour', *The Economist*, 30 November: 30, 20, 25.

Prestowitz, C. (1992), 'Beyond *laissez faire*', *Foreign Policy*, **87**: 67–87.

Reich, R. (1990), 'Who Is Us?' *Harvard Business Review*, 68, No. 1: 53–64.

Reich, R. (1991a), 'The Secession of the Successful', *New York Times Magazine*, 20 January: 16–17, 42–5.

Reich, R. (1991b), *The Work of Nations: Preparing Ourselves for 21st Century Capitalism*, New York, Alfred Knopf.

Reich, R. (1991c), 'What is a Nation?' *Political Science Quarterly*, 106, No. 2: 193–209.

Said, E. (1978), *Orientalism*, New York, Random House.

Schlossstein, S. (1989), *The End of the American Century*, New York, Congdon and Weed.

Schmiegelow, H. and Schmiegelow, M. (1990), How Japan Affects the International System, *International Organization*, **44**: 553–88.

Servan-Schreiber, J.J. (1968), *The American Challenge*, London, Hamish Hamilton.

Sterngold, J. (1992), 'Japanese Shifting their Investments Back Towards Home', *New York Times*, 22 March: 1, 12.

Time (1987), 'The Selling of America', *Time*, 14 September: 52–62.

Tolchin, M. and Tolchin, S. (1988), *Buying Into America: How Foreign Money Is Changing the Face of Our Nation*, New York, Times Books.

Van Wolferen, K. (1989), *The Enigma of Japanese Power*, New York, Vintage.

Van Wolferen, K. (1991), 'No Brakes, No Compass', *The National Interest*, **25**, 26–35.

Vogel, E. (1979), *Japan As Number One*, New York, Harper and Row.

Woo, Jung-En (1991), 'East Asia's America Problem', *World Policy Journal*, 8, No. 3: 451–74.

Walker, M. (1991), 'An America That Has Lost Its Way', *Manchester Guardian Weekly*, 29 September: 10.

Weisman, S. (1991), A Deep Split in Attitudes is Developing, *New York Times*, 3 December: 16.

Wills, G. (1992), 'The Rescuer', *New York Review of Books*, 25 June, 28–34.

Yoon, Y-K. (1990), 'The Political Economy of Transition: Japanese Foreign Direct Investments in the 1980s', *World Politics*, **43**: 1–27.

10
Conclusion: unresolved issues

Colin H. Williams

Throughout this volume we have been at pains to capture the dualism and nuances of the new world order. As we mentioned in Chapter 1, uncertainty and ambiguity accompany the triumphalist celebrations of the demise of Soviet control over Eastern Europe, and the re-emergence of the UN as a genuine global actor. The world has changed, but is it better, is it safer? It is certainly no easier to understand or interpret the myriad processes which constitute global reproduction at the end of the superpower era. Humbled by the failure to predict significant global events or to cope with environmental and human catastrophes such as nuclear disasters and persistent mass starvation, scholars have scrabbled around for interpretive theories which rely on chaos or crisis or catastrophe. The optimism of the adolescent social sciences and geography has given way to a caution which Peter Jackson interprets as a 'crisis of confidence affecting western scientific thought at the end of the twentieth century' (1993: 198–214). We used to debate whether humans were masters over their environment or merely stewards (Williams, 1991: 53–75). Now we must ask whether that environment itself can continue to sustain us (Redclift, 1987).

Faced with such stark realities, most of the old articles of faith which legitimized positions of authority in the advanced industrial world are subject to intense scrutiny. We no longer accept that the state is the ideal or desired instrument for all decision-making or policy implementation. We no longer perceive the world in two dimensional Mercator-like terms, even if we persist in describing it in a crude simplistic manner as a North–South divide, or as a core, semi-periphery, and periphery system. We no longer give due credence to the absolutes of religion and morality. All is relative, to be negotiated, constructed and made meaningful by compromised action and lived experience.

From one perspective such challenges to the old order represents chaos and fragmentation. But what lies behind such challenges? Certainly it is an attack on absolute truth and establishment authority. But such attacks have been the norm since the *Aufklärung* movement and have gained pace throughout this century in Europe. Is it not rather a response to the dread logic of democracy and to its handmaiden popular mass education? When we are free to think, we are also free to criticize. The conception of popular democratic criticism is of central importance in the development of the contemporary world. Like all such practices, it has its history, its ideological baggage and policy implications, but above all it has its own power. Part of the power is the extraordinary diversity of interests which are encouraged in an open democracy. There are more free standing interest groups in society than ever before, and their myriad connections form a new geography of communication. The free flow of information and calls to action threaten simultaneously to overwhelm decision-makers and defy long-term strategic planning because events unfold in such an unpredictable manner.

If the new world order is about anything, it is surely about coping with the extraordinary pace and scale of this change a pace which has its own momentum which none can truly control. All we can do is to set up mechanisms which regulate the most beneficial consequences of such change and seek to channel some of the most positive aspects in desired directions. Coping rather than controlling is thus the watchword of the new world order.

There are a number of potentially ambiguous leads in contemporary conceptions of the 'new world order'. One which has preoccupied us here is the question of the relative decline of the USA. Why is it so significant? At one level it has obvious implications for global security politics and international trade. But were the USA not to have such a large debt and severe domestic problems in such basic areas as health, housing and education, we would not be so concerned about a slight decline in its projected power. Domestic difficulties coupled with a reluctance to re-source its role as world policeman will inevitably pressurize the USA into acting in a less confident manner in the short term. Despite presidential rhetoric to the contrary, at the end of the Bush administration the USA had yet to get to grips with the disjuncture between its economic power and geopolitical authority. This disjuncture contributes to a 'new world disorder' in three profound ways. (Ó'Tuathail, 1992). First, American foreign policy 'demonstrated a marked reluctance to recognize the changed geopolitical environment' of the post-Cold-War era. Its 'Cold War institutions, alliance structures and ideological proclivities' remained intact but it had lost its *raison d'être*. No longer able to use the Soviet threat as a means of manipulating its allies, particularly Germany and Japan, the USA is now indebted to these allies to help finance a $348 million budget deficit in 1992 and a gross federal debt approaching $3 million. Yet it continues to maintain its ideological and structural hegemony, formed by Cold War priorities and orientations.

Secondly, Ó Tuathail asserts that there is an imbalance between the economic power of states like Japan and Germany and their diplomatic and military standing. As we saw in Chapter 9, both states are seeking to renegotiate their position within the world system, commensurate with Germany's position as the leading economic force in Europe, and Japan correspondingly so in Asia and beyond. Such a realignment would be the final undoing of the World War II settlement and could herald a new superpower era within advanced capitalism.

Thirdly, the rash of unsolved military, ethnic, ecological and ideological conflicts contributes to global insecurity and to a 'disorderly state' of affairs. The only order discernable to American eyes would be that which saw defence leading to world peace with the 'US as the uniquely chosen guardian' where 'western security would continue to be run by a small white male internationlist elite' (Ó Tuathail, 1992: 449). However, such an analysis would be misguided for, as so many observers have quipped, the Cold War ended 'not because the superpowers finally succeeded in making detente work, but as a result of the collapse of the Soviet superpower' (Nijman, 1992: 694). Revisionist studies suggest that the Soviet Union never really challenged American hegemony, for it was 'the rise of other powers that constrained American superpower' (Nijman, 1992: 694). The Soviet Union, as Smith (1993) has shown, was increasingly preoccupied with its own internal problems towards the end of the Cold War, a better contender than the USA for Kennedy's (1987) 'imperial overstretch' thesis, and unable to reform itself adequately. We should not be surprised therefore at the prevalence of conflict in former socialist lands.

A second ambiguous lead is the assumption that the 'sovereign nation–state' is also facing long-term decline. No one would deny the salience of new regional actors on the world stage or that the construction of closer unions, such as the European Community or NAFTA, permits the establishment of looser federal systems in the north. But such federations will only gain their strength from the constituent 'national' building blocks. No matter how much national separatists, liberals and ecologists may argue to the contrary, the future of the new world order will still be a majoritarian future, sealed within long recognized state units, rather than on the basis of a confederation of functional regions. The power of state nationalism is recharged within each generation and we are unlikely to see a sea change in the direction of devolved regional assemblies, and a federal European Parliament without a virulent rearguard action by dominant state interests. And yet so many of our contemporary problems demonstrate convincingly that the state is incapable of dealing with global issues, particularly in the environmental and humanitarian fields. Interdependence theorists have exposed the weaknesses of the realist position without replacing it as a dominant paradigm in international studies. We recognize that we live in a transitional period from the age of the nation–state to a post-modern but largely uncharted future. The challenge to political geographers, among other scholars, is to interpret this transition without misreading its implications. The state will continue to remain the most powerful unit of political organization, even if its limitations are increasingly exposed from above and below. But our thinking about the state must perforce be influenced more by the global context. A third ambiguous issue is the question of globalization with which we began our considerations. At one level we live in a 'world without borders' in an increasingly unified world system. Yet at another level the confirmation of old borders and the re-imposition of barriers to interaction also characterizes many situations, as we saw in Chapters 2 and 6. Without doubt we are experiencing a process of convergence of locality and globality (Mlinar, 1992: 167). Such convergence encourages a shift of emphasis from the 'space of places' to the 'space of flows' and seeks to capture the dynamism of contemporary reality, as was demonstrated in Philip Cooke's economic analysis of the EC in Chapter 3.

Increased flexibility between actors and structures reflects the diversity of modern society and creates quite staggeringly different life styles within the same places, deepening our awareness of the inequality of life chances in most of the world. But globalization, as Mlinar observes, also implies the increasing inclusiveness of diversity, imposing a higher level of generaliz-ation (1992: 166). Nowhere is this more problematic than in the attempt to define and maintain a certain degree of individual autonomy, either at a personal or a group level. Minorities faced with the demands of accommo-dating to a majoritarian order are particularly sensitive to this issue. If we are to preserve genuine diversity in the new world order, then we have to pay particular attention to the question of individual and minority rights in increasingly multi-cultural societies.

Finally we need to address the manner in which our discipline mirrors the dualism inherent in the world order. After a generation of geographic mutation, spawning new geo-specialisms, we are intensifying the search for integrative theories and methodologies best illustrated by the essays in R.J. Johnston (1993). The simultaneity inherent in the global–local nexus is mirrored in the generalist–specialist debate within geography and social science. The quest for holistic analysis will dominate our thinking in the medium-term as we seek to respond to the challenge of a world in tran-sition. We may echo Dicken's call for 'the breaking down of subdisciplinary barriers within geography' in order to both study and influence the real world (Dicken, 1993: 31–53). We may also welcome the return of geog-raphy to the 'big issues', to the global view (Johnston, 1993: 176; Taylor, 1993: 181–97). But above all we should welcome the fact that geographers are increasingly concerned that their voices should be heard by the informed public. If this volume has anything worth saying, it is surely that the world will not wait for us to catch up with it while we sort out our intellectual priorities and preferences. The new world order is upon us. Part of the geographical tradition has been its evolutionary and pluralistic character (Livingstone, 1992). There is no intention to suggest that this volume is a comprehensive survey of the contemporary world, far from it. It is only a selection of specific European and American issues, set in a global context, but it does reflect some of the central concerns of our discipline in recent times.

The agenda which political geography is currently formulating moves us on from the overconcentration on the core states which have occupied us here. Our next task must surely be to interpret the growing disparities between the developed and developing world which are exacerbated by the tendencies examined in this volume. Chief among these will be the search for peace, health and security in an increasingly competitive world system. In future work we will need to examine how the world system influences the race for earth's resources, and its environmental degradation, the emergence of new shatter zones, the rise of the Islamic world and newly industrializing Third World regional powers, especially China (MacLaughlin, 1993). All of this will require a re-invigorated United Nations framework. Let us leave the last words to that prescient world watcher, Dennis Healey:

A strong Europe, united from Brest to Brest, and from Crete to Kirkenes, could form at least one essential pillar for a New World Order. With luck, Japan might perform a role in the Far East as valuable as Germany in Europe, thus creating another pillar. In the less stable parts of Asia and Africa, however, only the United Nations is likely to offer an acceptable framework for peace and stability. Even so, its present constitution will require drastic revision, particularly if it is to assume a lasting responsibility for security.

The United Nations must be the foundation of any New World Order, if only because some of the major problems of the next century will defy handling on a purely regional basis. The greenhouse effect and other ecological dangers are now global problems. We seem to be moving into an age of mass migrations – into Europe from the east and the south, into the United States from Latin America and Asia. These will cry out for international regulation and control, particularly since the world's population is doubling every fifty years. Above all, there is the need for global arms control and disarmament before the proliferation of new weapons of mass destruction passes the point of no return.

The prime responsibility for supporting policies through which the United Nations may approach these problems will lie with the richer and more powerful regional groups in the northern hemisphere, working with one another as well as with the peoples of the south. Only if the United States and its partners in Europe and the Far East can learn from the mistakes they made in tackling the Gulf crisis may we hope, after all, to see the United Nations create the framework for a New World Order (Healey, 1991: 270).

References

Dicken, P. (1993), 'The Changing Organization of the Global Economy, in R.J. Johnston (ed.), *The Challenge for Geography*, Oxford, Blackwell.

Gellner, E. (1992), *Postmodernism, Reason* and *Religion*, London, Routledge.

Healey, D. (1991), When Shrimps Learn to Whistle, London, Penguin.

Jackson, P. (1993), 'Changing Ourselves: a Geography of Position', in R.J. Johnston (ed.), *The Challenge for Geography*, Oxford, Blackwell

Johnston, R.J. (ed.), (1993), *The Challenge for Geography*, Oxford, Blackwell.

Kennedy, P. (1987) The Rise and Fall of the Great Powers. New York, Random House.

Livingstone, D.N. (1992), *The Geographical Tradition*, Oxford, Blackwell.

MacLaughlin, J. (1993), 'The changing World System: Geocultural Issues', *Journal of Multilingual and Multicultural Development*.

Mlinar, Z. (ed.), 1992, Globalization and Territorial Identities, Aldershot, Avebury.

Nijman, J. (1992), 'The Limits of Superpower: the US and the Soviet Union since World War II', *Annals of the Association of American Geographers*, 82, No. 4: 681–95.

Ó'Tuathail G. (1992), 'The Bush-administration and the "End" of the Cold War: a Critical Geopolitics of US Foreign Policy in 1989', *Geoforum*, 23, No. 4: 437–52.

Redclift, M. (1987), *Sustainable Development: Exploring Contradictions*, London, Methuen.

Smith, G. (1993), 'Ends, Geopolitics, Transitions', in R.J. Johnston (ed.), *The Challenge for Geography*, Oxford, Blackwell.

Taylor, P.J. (ed.), (1992), *The Political Geography of the Twentieth Century*, London, Belhaven.

Taylor, P.J. (1993), 'Full Circle, or New meaning for Global?' in R.J. Johnston (ed.), *The Challenge for Geography*, Oxford, Blackwell.

Williams, C.H. (1991), 'Language Planning and Social Change: Ecological Speculations', in D.F. Marshall (ed.), *Language Planning*, Amsterdam, John Benjamins.

Index